I0829914

Pantomime Terror:
Music and Politics

WHAT PEOPLE ARE SAYING ABOUT

PANTOMIME TERROR

This book starts with the countless provocations that surround us in the ambient war on terror. However, rather than retreating into either loathsome self-pity or indignant self-righteousness, Hutnyk responds with the thumping provocation to think and get real!

Nikos Papastergiadis, University of Melbourne

For two decades, Hutnyk's research on diasporic music and politics has been at the political and scholarly cutting edge. Moving from ADF and Fun-Da-Mental, to MIA and Wagner, his work is always contextualised with relevance and an unstinting anti-racist, anti-imperialist commitment. Here in the not-so-great British tradition of pantomime parody with its Molotov cocktail caricatures of hero(in)es, villains and sidekicks, Hutnyk urges us to look at how horror is accompanied by the ludic, and how the culture industry is reined into the post 9/11 war on terror: 'the pantomime of politics, the theatre of power, the double-plays of deception'. War peculates through every cell and membrane in our numbed bodies, only to be resigned to the waste basket of disposable culture. With its cogent attack on what have become cultural icons, *Pantomime Terror* updates Adorno for this terror-saturated age – masterful in its sweep, engaging in its style and thought-provoking in its analysis.

Raminder Kaur, University of Sussex

Pantomime Terror: Music and Politics

John Hutnyk

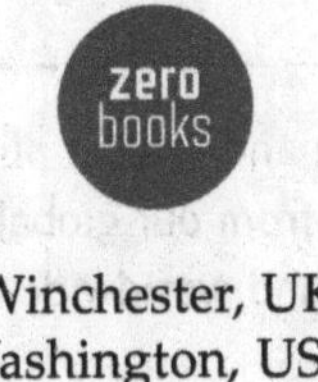

Winchester, UK
Washington, USA

First published by Zero Books, 2014
Zero Books is an imprint of John Hunt Publishing Ltd., Laurel House, Station Approach,
Alresford, Hants, SO24 9JH, UK
office1@jhpbooks.net
www.johnhuntpublishing.com
www.zero-books.net

For distributor details and how to order please visit the 'Ordering' section on our website.

Text copyright: John Hutnyk 2013

ISBN: 978 1 78279 209 3

All rights reserved. Except for brief quotations in critical articles or reviews, no part of this
book may be reproduced in any manner without prior written permission from the publishers.

The rights of John Hutnyk as author have been asserted in accordance with the Copyright,
Designs and Patents Act 1988.

A CIP catalogue record for this book is available from the British Library.

Design: Lee Nash

We operate a distinctive and ethical publishing philosophy in all
areas of our business, from our global network of authors to
production and worldwide distribution.

CONTENTS

Dedicated to lost comrades:
Imogen Bunting, Rosie Wright, Paul Hendrich.

Acknowledgements

This book tunes into music in three acts. I have written on these performers before, and so thank them again for the opportunity to return to their stories. The approach is a continuation of a research project and collective political effort that I joined when I first came to Britain in 1994. This iteration rehearses this work for London and in relation to twenty first-century terrors, as well as returning to a long beloved articulation of divergent interpretations of critical theory, especially the work of Theodor Adorno. In the introduction, there is a first rendition of the theme of *pantomime*, which will resonate throughout, and perhaps perversely, the end of the intro starts in on the end of the video *Cookbook DIY*, examined more fully in the next chapter. I advance this end because the point of this book is to record how peripheral 'messages' are too often ignored. In this sense, the project of 'pantomime terror' *as distraction* will be affirmed. I thank Aki Nawaz and Dave Watts for what is now a long collaboration.

The first chapter proper was presented as my inaugural professorial lecture at Goldsmiths College in 2007, introduced by Geoff Crossick, but also heard in presentations at Jadavpur University (thanks Abhijit Roy and Moinak Biswas), Concordia (Joel McKim), the small triple-a at High Falls (Michael Taussig), the University of Auckland (Cris Shore, Nabeel Zuberi) and the Freie Universität (Erika Fischer-Lichte, Frederik Tygstrup, Helen Carr, Janis Jeffries). The next chapter requires acknowledgement of John Pandit of Asian Dub Foundation and the formative influence of Ash and Sanjay Sharma, themselves linked to a group of (still) young scholars that included Virinder Kalra, Raminder Kaur, Tej Purewal, Meeta Jha and Bobby Sayyid. The traces of a Marxist origin in that group are also acknowledged in the subject matter of the chapter – not that we were urban lumpenproletarians by any means, but we were interlopers in relatively privileged spaces and inclined towards a solidarity that was not accommodated by the established theorists we critiqued. The final chapter has much to say about M.I.A. and Wagner. I leave it to readers to decide if this rendering of pantomime develops the narrative further. I feel it does the work needed to clarify the words on Adorno and Auschwitz offered at the end. A critique of art in the service of politics while under culture industry sway should never go out of style. I have presented this material in Oslo and Copenhagen (thanks Annemette Kirkegaard), Braga (Isabel Ermida), Lisbon (Sónia Pereira, Isabel Gil) and Gothenberg (Aleksander Motturi. Sara Westin, Nathalie Bödtker-Lund).

I have learnt from those mentioned above, but also just as much from those who read this work in draft. Thanks to Sophie Fuggle for looking at everything with love and care. To all those at Goldsmiths who heard this over and over in earlier forms, including the obsessive repetitions about buses, storytelling and Frankfurt School theory. To Lara Choksey, Rachel Rye, Anna Geschwill, Anjana Raghavan, and Joanna Figiel for eradicating stray asides. To Simon Barber for insights into sound and zen, and for tributes to bibles and brandy. Camille Barbagallo, always and forever for being there (but on the wrong side of the river). Also Gayatri Chakravorty Spivak, Tom Bunyard, Carrie Clanton, Hassan Khaled, Alison Hulme, Vivek Bald, Rana Brientjes, Ewa Jasiewicz, Klaus Peter Koepping, Jeff Kinkle, Mary Claire Halvorson, Howard Potter, Biju Mathew, Vijay Prashad, Raul Gschrey, Tariq Mehmood, Theresa Mikuriya, Atticus Che Narain, Michael Dutton, Enis Oktay, Maria-José Pantoja-Peschard, Olivia Swift, Daisy Tam, Karen Tam, Anamik Saha, Tarek Salhany, Polly Phipps-Holland, A. Sivanandan, Bhaskar Mukhopadhyay, Rico Reyes, Seth Ayyaz, Simon McVeigh, Tom Henri, Tara Blake Wilson, Louise Fabian, Ben Rosensweig, Liz Thompson, Angela Mitropoulos, Rebecca Graversen, Adela Santana: thank-you all. Any glitches that remain are mine, though I am happy to blame the two little rebels, Theodor Anthony Apollo Hutnyk and Emile Mouat Blake Hutnyk, for the delay in getting this text to press.

Parts of the introduction appeared in Stephanie Menrath and Alexander Schwinghammer (eds) *What Does a Chameleon Look Like? Topographies of Immersion*, Köln: Herbert von Halem Verlag (2011); parts of the chapter 'DIY Cookbook' appeared in the *Journal of Creative Communications*, 2(1-2):123-141 (2007) and in Ian Peddie (ed) *Popular Music and Human Rights*, Farnham: Ashgate (2011); parts of 'Dub at the Movies', in a very early version was presented as an talk to Howard Potter's project group at the Working Lives Institute, Metropolitan University Dec 12 2005, and parts appeared in much different form in Henrietta Moore and David Held (eds) *Cultural Politics in a Global Age: Uncertainty, Solidarity and Innovation*, London: Oneworld Publications (2008); parts of 'Scheherazade's Sister: M.I.A.' appeared in *Social Identities*, 18(5): 555-572 (2012), under the editorship of Pal Ahluwalia. Substantially rewritten, nevertheless thanks for allowing the reversionings.

John Hutnyk
Goldsmiths University of London
John.Hutnyk@gold.ac.uk

Introduction

The war on terror thrives on pantomime demons. Whatever the actuality of threat or ideological purchase, a repetition compulsion operates a monstrous theatre. Grotesque characters are created and maintained by political opportunism, convenient stereotype and, I have to say it, an uncritical celebrity scholarship. Osama, Saddam, Gaddafi are, indeed, cartoon caricatures, but to a lesser extent, *any* public figure can be misrepresented – a musician or performer for example. Musicians who dare say things that disrupt polite keep-calm, carry-on complacency are targeted. The so-called 'suicide rap' of Aki Nawaz, the Gaddafi opera and street politics of Asian Dub Foundation, the blood-splattered schlock video of Roman Gavras and British Sri Lankan musician Mayathangi Maya Arulpragasam, aka M.I.A., are popular culture works that critique – and are each contextualised within – a white supremacist political drama which pays them back with censure. This *pantomime* offers equal parts reassurance and complicity, with war *over there* and a low-intensity commuter paranoia *here*.

There is a recurrent symbolic or regulatory terror alongside the real horror of war. Not just an imaginary smokescreen or backdrop to actual killing, but part of the production of death. The war is not only a battlefront, or rather, the battlefront is distributed, diversified, intimate, and often up close. Singing the same war-weary songs, our image of conflict has been contained in cinema and television newscast as fantasy horror, while vicious narratives of the everyday masquerade, in ways to be recounted, as less explicit, but nonetheless military, operations in the cultural zone. The dramaturgy of war involves us in a killing field in the war theatre and a theatre of war where we live – the latter also the mundane everyday of business-as-usual injunctions to 'keep on shopping' and 'look after yourself and pay no attention to your unlucky neighbour' as the airport security guards swoop (Mitchell 2011:162). Terror alerts and ethnic profiling, a culture of fear and a national chauvinist resurgence; these are the syncopated facets of a secondary conflict that impacts upon us all, with devastating consequences. Even the most anodyne and superstructural, culture industry, rarefied genre specific, mere entertainment, sonically obscure corners of our lives are recalibrated on a war footing. With this in mind, and focusing upon music television, internet video, streaming news and the pop promo, this book documents some of the ways contemporary war stories play out in the capitals of capital. The operations assembled here amount to a commentary on the ways soft or media power supplements force of arms. NATO plus newspapers, security announcements and ipods, Police checks and advertising.

London Bus.

The red double-decker bus is the iconic symbol of London. So much so that it appears in almost any movie about the city, with access via a step platform at the back, an internal staircase, and red livery. The London bus was reimagined and updated in the twenty first century by Wrightbus when the older Routemasters were deemed too rickety for use. A stylised double-decker was used as a prop in China for the handover of the Olympic flag in 2008, and in 2012 in the London games the bus was the least incongruous of the many props deployed in the opening and closing ceremonies – also featuring a not-so-veiled critique of austerity cuts to the National Health Service, an 'amusing' celebration of the smokestack pollution of industrial Britain – itself now demoted to service sector, finance and entertainment 'industry' – and of course the bus, always the bus. London's buses are iconic, even though perhaps the most noticed one to come along in recent years was a disaster. I refer to the devastating terrorist attack on London on July 7th 2005, in which three tube carriages and a number 30 Dennis Trident 2 bus (#17758) were destroyed, leaving 56 people dead. This tragedy is potently captured in the image of the wrecked bus in Tavistock Square, photographed by US-based photojournalist Mathew Rosenberg. One of his pictures, appearing in most newspapers the next day, showed the bus from a 45% frontal angle with a film advertising placard visible on its side. The placard was for the film *The Descent*, due to be released the next day (2005 dir. Neil Marshall). *The Descent* was a schlock horror-thriller about a group of friends visiting a cave, who become lost and are subsequently killed off one after the other by inhuman monsters. The cave is the least of the coincidences however, as a stunned London read reports and looked at grainy mobile phone video footage from the underground, absorbing the irony that the portion of the film placard left intact on the bus after the explosion clearly displayed the message: 'Outright Terror, Bold and Brilliant – total film'.

As this book will be a sustained critique of culture industry war-mongering, perhaps we should remember Theodor Adorno for his comment on Ernest Newman's exhaustive biography of Richard Wagner: that to follow up the facts of a story so passionately means you may 'ultimately become aware of the dubiousness of the concept of the factual itself' (Adorno 1947/2003:404). Fact: a British South Asian youth, Hasib Mir Hussain, was said to be the bus bomber. This is questioned by some people who must be called conspiracy theorists, even though any 'theorising' here seems somewhat limited. Conspiracy, like stereotyping, does duty for an altogether more pernicious ideological maintenance, contained yet public. Hiding in the light, palimpsest, a strange mysterious appearance form of that which dare not appear except as farce. Paranoid examples would include the bus passenger and witness Daniel Obachike in his book *The Fourth Bomb* (Obachike 2007), or the allegations of Maud'Dib – a *Dune* inspired sci-fi pseudonym for John Hill – in *The 7/7 Ripple Effect* (2007), in which the events of that day are registered as a 'training exercise' used to frame, and kill, innocents to drum up support for the war on terror (also see Rudin 2009). Describing himself as being accused of 'thought-crime', Nick Kollerstrom details incongruities and other disputed interpretations of the July 7 Inquest briefings, and in particular alleges that the Tavistock Square bus was pre-engineered with electric saws to enable the roof of the bus to be destroyed with spectacular, sardine-can like effect (Kollerstrom 2011). Others allege Hussein was a stooge and patsy set up by MI6, and that various training exercises, inside knowledges – and more believably, agency bumbling – led to the tragic events. In 2008, the Inquest was welcomed by 'Graeme' commenting on Andrew McGregor's guest post on Kollerstrom's blog: he wrote, 'The pantomime season began early this year when a brand new stage production, called the "7/7 INQUEST", opened at the Royal Courts of Justice' (McGregor 2010). Amongst the varied and sometimes shrill scenarios, some make the effort to narrate something they fiercely call 'truth', others fuel speculation and uncertainty, usually with the very same 'crusader' attachment to 'the facts'. It is the case that testimony and evidence has been officially sifted and sanctioned, and while some significant evidence remains unavailable – for example CCTV footage from the underground system and the bus, testimony from certain identified passengers on the bus – this book is not about judging the actual and the real. Rather than scrutinising the facts of the case, might the framing be questioned – the parameters of inter-pretation, the whys and wheretofores of speculation and expli-cation, what knowledge or theory is deployed, and by whom. For example, motives: while it is widely accepted that it was indeed Hussain who detonated his bomb some 52 minutes after the three tube explosions, so much of the commentary revolves around asking why there was this delay? We might find this revealing.

The predominant suggestion was that, having planned to also blow up a tube carriage, Hussein had lost his nerve and was fleeing the scene, perhaps accidentally and incompetently setting his bomb off while trying to diffuse it – there were reports of him fiddling with his rucksack, dropping his rucksack, buying a new battery, being generally confused and in panic. Equally, there are reports that do not mention a rucksack, that picture him making phone calls to his alleged co-conspirators for 20 minutes after he would surely have assumed they were dead, and he is only placed on the Tavistock bus by disputed witness identification. Hussein of course cannot be called upon to testify, because, like any 'successful' suicide bomber, he is dead. Suicide is an extreme mode of self-censorship – 'their message will never be heard' (Spivak 2012:386) – so it is not possible to decide if Hussain had intentionally targeted this particular bus with this particular sign on its side. All very convenient both for government intrigue and conspiracy theory alike. Attributions of indecision on Hussein's part were not uncommon among academics. For example, Victor Seidler says the Tavistock Square bus bombing was 'unplanned' (Seidler 2007:10). Was there a plan? Was there a message? What is written on the side of the bus becomes a semantic marker just as much as the explicit and planned message bequeathed to us by Hussain's co-conspirator, Mohammed Sidique Khan in his justificatory videos. Broadcast afterwards, there is no mention of any buses.

The July 7 attack was a troubling episode. It transformed the city, shook its population and ushered in a new anxiety that had ramifications far and wide. Gayatri Chakravorty Spivak, writes on suicides, and suicide bombing – from Bhubaneshwari Bhaduri, in the essay 'Can the Subaltern Speak?' (Spivak 1988), who kills herself to avoid betraying comrades, through to contemporary incidents in Palestine or Kashmir and in the generic 'War on Terror' (Spivak 2004, 2012). For Spivak, suicide is 'an exceptional death', and writing this is itself an 'impossible phrase' (Spivak 2012:386). Perhaps what is to be learnt from such difficult-impossible thought is an obligation upon the scholar of the humanities that would strive to train the imagination so as to take a chance on an understanding that does first rush to judge. Planned or unplanned, a great trouble in this theatre is, I think, that we have been far too quick to decide there is nothing more to be discussed once our most prominent Euro-American scholars have had their say. In this book I want to read explanatory narratives of theory from the likes of Slavoj Žižek, Susan Buck–Morss, Alain Badiou, and others, alongside the sign on the side of the bus. I feel we should read more carefully, slowly, not to confirm any conspiracy, nor because any particular incident in the ten-plus years of the war of terror should be singled out for more special attention, but because much of the commentary on representation since the advent of the terror war has been, somewhat, lacking. A too-fast-and-loose theory of one-to-one representation and ascription of motive and meaning has had deleterious consequences: from the multi-billion arms industry bombing of innocents abroad, to increased racist conflict on the streets and immigration policy fear at home – in between, every manner of pathology and unthinking prejudice to the extent that a common reaction seems to have been to stop thinking at all. Conspiracy theorists and 'regular' theorists have been guilty of this, both.

Alongside the bus, another 'major event' (Jacques Derrida, in Borradori 2003:88) is immediately conjured here. It might by now be a commonplace to acknowledge that the twin towers have been so often represented that it is barely possible to see them today for fug and smoke. 'The date has become a cognitive fetish' suggests W.J.T. Mitchell, a 'fabulous gift' for neoliberal 'Post 911 pundits', who 'declared an end to postmodern irony and scepticism, an end to critical thinking' (Mitchell 2011:162). The images replayed over and over, watched aghast from the street and on all our screens. In a certain sense, and for some critics, the question of representation itself collapsed on that day in September, 2001 – with 'collapse' a favoured inappropriate trope, for example see Jacques Rancière (2010:98). The symbolic order *crashed*, it was even sublime, and everything has already been said about it, if nothing heard. The towers are silent, the lives erased then, and the many more taken since – and the billions in war credits – are also verbosely inarticulate. Both the 'terrorists' and those who were intent on the 'War on Terror'™ had a common interest in a high televisual visibility which had the images say what they wanted them to say. Derrida calls this a 'pervertability' of the image (in Borradori 2003:109). This pervert characterisation is also true of the July 7 bus sign 'Total Film.'

Pantomime.

In his book *Film Fables*, Rancière offers the provocation that documentary fiction 'invents new intrigues with historical documents'. It 'joins and disjoins – in the relationship between story and character, shot and sequence – the powers of the visible, of speech, and of movement' (Rancière 2001/2006:18). Rancière is talking of Chris Marker's film *The Last Bolshevik* (dir. Marker 1992) and Jean-Luc Godard's 'Maoist theatricalisation of Marxism' in the pop age. These fictions, which use historical documents and make pointed reference to political struggles and current events – the collapse of Soviet power in the USSR; the cultural revolution in France – are glossed by Rancière as an indication that it is premature to lament the vacuity of contemporary commercial culture. Mass television is not yet the death of great art, nor are we talking about the impossibility of cinema after Auschwitz. The pop culture screen is not just a 'machine for information and advertisement' (Rancière 2001/2006:19). Rancière has a more nuanced, even Adorno-esque critique – and I do not mean the Adorno as rendered too simply as an elite critic of mass culture, but the Adorno that wrote of the stigmata marks of the two torn halves of bourgeois culture, the ripped promise of freedom, which cannot, perhaps should not, be repaired (Adorno 1977:123).

Rancière writes:

> cinema arrives as if expressly designed to thwart a simple technology of artistic modernity, to counter art's aesthetic autonomy with its old submission to the representative regime. We must not map this process of thwarting onto the opposition between the principles of art and those of popular entertainment subject to the industrialization of leisure and the pleasures of the masses. The art of the aesthetic age abolishes all these borders because it makes art of everything (Rancière 2001/2006:10).

Although there is no explicit reference in this passage to Adorno, nor even to Marx's notion of real subsumption, there are reasons to consider the predicament of the political fable here. We should do this as the problem Adorno brought into Marxism, in however European a way, and consider the possibility that the question of art remains a ground of struggle for representation and politics in the widest sense. Adorno's sentence about the 'secret omnipresence of resistance' (Adorno 1991:67), so often quoted, seems apt yet again here as I try to bring forward the discussion of the soundtrack of war and terror to include not just the art-house staples that reach from Eisenstein's battleship montage through to Marker or Godard's radical Maoism, but also the much more prosaic film art of the pop promo, surveillance video and television documentary. In the high visibility slow-motion moments of the period immediately after Rancière's text was delivered, we can ask if representation self-combusts, or if there is, rather, a secret resistance to be revealed in the strange political silence of the images about which we hear so much? One iteration of this present book is as an attempt to work with and through these sounds and scenes towards something more than the melodrama or melancholy that Rancière diagnoses as innocence become a guilty sacred mission (Rancière 2001/ 2006:186). It is a brilliant scene when he recognises that what he calls the burlesque body – and what in a minute he will call pantomime – provides us with a 'dramaturgic machine' for cutting 'the link between cause and effect, action and reaction'. I will argue, against Rancière perhaps, that the best pop promos do this by throwing 'the elements of the moving image into contradiction' (Rancière 2001/2006:12). Did not Godard already register this in the versioning of Maoist discourse that held what Rancière calls a 'pantomime' verbal power over the little-red-book-waving Parisian students in *La Chinoise*? (Rancière 2003/2007:37; *La Chinoise* dir. Godard 1967). Reaching back into a critical-political musicology so as to reanimate, or resonate, Rancière's critique, I take *pantomime* as both a symptom and consequence of the current conjuncture, in which we see this secret contradiction at work.

Pantomime is what Siegfried Kracauer identified in another field, discussing Offenbach, as a publicly recognised distraction:

> People wished at all costs to be distracted from politics and memories of the year of horror through which they had just passed. Pantomimes took them out of the banal, everyday world in which they lived, plunged them into a world of magic, and effectively prevented them from thinking by bombarding them with lavish spectacle (Kracauer 1937/ 1972:321)

Kracauer was talking here of Offenbach's Paris in the wake of the war with Prussia, the capitulation of the city, the end of the Second Empire, the Commune, and the repression that swiftly followed with the Second Empire reformed. In contemporary times this scenario is instructive, and we should ask sharp questions about why any musical or artistic style gains prominence alongside a certain political conjuncture – think of dada, surrealism or constructivism after the trauma of WWI and the hope of the Bolshevik Revolution. Or think of the decade of Seattle Grunge and YBA artists in London in the last years of the twentieth century, where a heady mix of heroin-fuelled alienation and conceptual posing fits neatly with a political repression that does not exactly found a new Empire, but anticipates one in both neo-liberal and 'alter-globalisation' form. Radical *chic* academic sentiment is its theoretical articulation in both art theory as architectural institution – aka Tate Modern – or in post-communist rapprochement in Michael Hardt and Toni Negri reviewed by Francis Fukuyama in the *New York Times* (Fukuyama 2004). Whatever the fortunes of the theory of *Empire*, I think what is key here is how *pantomime* has become a trope of the media war that fetes despots one minute only to tear them down the next. Demonised figures abound and for a time, sometimes annually, dominate our screens – and always without reference to the ways we *know* these are political distractions. *'He's behind you!'* is the old audience participation call. Ignored. Osama was a nurtured agent of American interests, Saddam a loyal paid friend, Gaddafi flip-flopped from demon to LSE pal to fiend again. The real screaming terror for me is this observed and consciously deferred delinking of cause and effect. And in front of this distraction we are expected, and too often indeed choose, to remain verbosely silent. Head down, shuffling in step, chanting a mantra.

In this book, more detail will be needed on pantomime figures, on the caricatures of this mutation and the blindness of representation, but is it enough at first only to usher the villains onto the stage and note that in his 2008 book *Violence*, Slavoj Žižek called all terrorist attacks and suicide bombings a 'counter violence', a 'blind *passage à l'acte*' and an 'implicit admission of impotence' (Žižek 2008:69)? We will go over this terrain again and again in the chapters to come. Similarly, and earlier, Alain Badiou writing of September 11, 2001, starts his essay on

'Philosophy and the War on Terror' by saying 'It was an enormous murder, lengthily premeditated, and yet silent. No one claimed responsibility' (Badiou 2006:15). Susan Buck-Morss, in her book *Thinking Past Terror*, offers: 'the destruction of September 11 was a mute act. The attackers perished without making demands … They left no note behind … A mute act' (Buck-Morss 2003:23). As we will see, Buck-Morss qualifies this with a question 'Or did they?', yet the choice of an absent verbal – *twice* mute – message is something we should return to, listen closely to, consider again, and not just with our eyes scanning for evidence on the side of the bus, but with our ears and minds as well. The horror is that those on the bus themselves become mute, and those of us who saw it become blind to what the text may say. The very terms used by Žižek, Buck-Morss and Badiou in their widely circulated books, addressing violence and terror, are just these words that confirm distraction – mute, blind, silent, 'act'. I cannot but contrast this register with the perverse refrain of former British Prime Minister Blair in defending British foreign policy in the wake of the London bombings: 'there was no link between … [the] … bombings in London and the Iraq war' (Blair 2005).

Should we pass over the curiosity that Žižek chooses the infirmities of *blindness* and *impotence* to characterise the terrorist suicide bomber, as if the twin towers indicated a doubled scene of masturbation and castration – too much and you lose your sight, or worse. The greater loss is impotence, and with the symbolic castration of the towers, the old masculanist psychoanalytic staples are invoked. In later works this complex will be called a parallax, and still later, in *Less Than Nothing*, the attacks on the towers, the bus and such 'zero-level' protests like the car-burnings in Paris in 2005 and the August 2011 uprisings in London, are mere 'violent outbursts that wanted nothing' in a 'post-ideological society'. The 'problem' is that these protests are 'reactive, not active, impotent rage and despair masked as a display of force, envy masked as triumphant carnival' (Žižek 2012:998). Here Žižek's links between London in August 2011 and the *banlieues* of 2005 *and* the attacks of September 11, 2001, proceed by way of the language of theatre in which the participants are 'masked' like pantomime figures. This makes me think, with Kracauer, that we should diagnose reference to masks, indeed, to double masks, as words of distraction too, because the task of a critical commentary is not just to stop and stare, it is not a matter of listing ever more detail on the symptomatic eventuality which is then pathologised, via fables and pantomime, in order for it to be impotently dismissed.

War Diary.

With due acknowledgement of Gil Scott-Heron, the revolution may not be televised, but a counter-insurgency war of oppression is obsessively screened. Catatonic heads nod not so much in agreement as if to a rhythmic bludgeoning that is ideological through and through. Television news and media reportage trope the stereotypes to shuffle through a kaleidoscope of nationalist images and cycles of pain. While Mitchell points out 'it is never enough to simply point to the error of a metaphor, or the lack of reality of an image', the critique of terror imaginaries must renounce the 'easy victories' of exposing unreality, and instead 'trace the process by which the metaphoric becomes literal' (Mitchell 2011:xviii). This is why I argue that it might be more useful to listen up to images. Open your ears to see (Henriques 2011:99-104). It might be more than a cliche to insist music expresses a widespread opposition to global injustice – war on terror, urban anxiety, destruction and death – while simultaneously acting as a soundtrack for violence (as Goodman 2009 points out). That this can even effect a violence without violence, which registers on screen as background, as soundtrack, while running on unacknowledged it nevertheless affects us to our core. Music as an expressive form of culture can articulate alternate versionings of a world at war, and yet the predicaments in which musicians, and fans, find themselves are rife with contradiction. This book explores the efficacy of music as organising platform while recognising the risks, and the disconnects, in a climate that simultaneously exhibits resignation and fear.

The book runs through a playlist of popular culture performance, from Aki Nawaz and Fun-da-mental being banned as 'suicide rappers'; Asian Dub Foundation screening *La Haine* and *The Battle of Algiers* and performing operatic versions of 'Gaddafi'; Guantánamo interrogators blasting Van Halen and Madonna at the inmates; to M.I.A. stereotype-bashing that gets the stereotypes to sit up again, convoluted. Along the way mediation from lyrical terrorists, false dossiers, missing CCTV, the Eiffel Tower, Freud, the underpants bomber, the Kumars, Dick Wittington, Frank Zappa and Haussmann's Paris. The theorists are Theodor W. Adorno, Gayatri Chakravorty Spivak, and Jacques Derrida, while Michael Ignatieff, Vic Siedler, disgraced British PMs and US Presidents all put in an appearance. We travel from Hunan to Lagos, the Whitehouse Situation Room to Vietnam, rural Bengal to East London, with Naxalites and Nazis, with anti-racists and Assange. Each chapter has a major distraction: an exploration of the publishing history of the Arabian Nights in chapter one, the ethnography of urban crowding in chapter two or the fantasy playgrounds of Wagner's opera in chapter three. Extended asides play out the pantomime argument beyond music and video, but I hope deepening the analysis rather than distorting. The reader will judge, not too quickly I trust.

The book has a South Asian diasporic inflection, but I am no advocate of *desi* identitarianism. I am convinced there are reasons to attend to a Muslim and South Asian orientation to public debate worldwide, but the stakes are higher than any faith-based, subcontinental or diasporic telling. As will become clear, there is a popular, wider, performative and fashion element to all of this

– masks, dress-ups and exotica. But it is not quite enough to simply invoke Walter Benjamin's storyteller in oriental drag to explain how the narratives of Asia seep into an ideological crusade and geo-political power game, too often glossed merely as 'emerging economies' or 'rising India'. As I will explain in detail, I have in mind the overture from Benjamin to the story-teller, in his 1936 essay, where the old hashish-muncher mentions Scheherazade three times. A story itself repetitive. In present times, I fear, orientalism has become counter-insurgency and punitive detention, such that a negative speculative dream version of the Scheherazade tale would have our virtuoso narrator kidnapped, rendered and interned in Guantánamo, as will happen in the first chapter. Kept on her own in a cell except for a daily interrogation when she is brought before her captors who demand she dance a tune. She obliges them with composi-tions that serenade in ever more siren tones, yet which also provoke yet more draconian crackdowns and higher and higher terror alert ratings. The production of this narrative, which might also be known as the Afghan War Diary, must be read as an indictment of us all. War Diary is what this study pretends to be, in its most insecure and paranoid moments, hoping one day to look back and see where the tunes led the way. The copyright of the phrase War Diary is probably Wikileaks, but I get it from the performer M.I.A.'s sometime pseudonymous persona 'Vicki Leekx'. By the end of this book I will argue that such music does not yet organise, but at least signals an almost forlorn and wistful hope, and it is what Adorno meant about poetry after Auschwitz – a crisis point of a dialectic that also undermines critical reflection. The need to cut through this impasse is clear.

I feel any adequate scholarship for a book like this is not a matter of the critiquing of essences or complaints about reduc-tions and omissions as such, but of rounding out the fables, the pantomime and the morality tale, the melodrama and the anecdote, as both ideological tricks and as rhetoric, as forms that themselves are condensations with a perverse intent, and ones which can also be expropriated. The storytelling morality-tale melodrama reduces the world to narrative for sure, but such forms bank on an economy that perhaps makes it all worthwhile, on several sides. It could be transmitted in shorthand: codification saturates all areas, trinketisation abounds – the message is telegraphed and as a cipher and works all the more. It is not that Žižek's or Buck-Morss's moves are irrelevant, but for me, a presentation of grand theoretical or ethical erudition is less urgent than the question of adequacy. What storytelling would be adequate – theoretically, politically – to win with regard to anti-racism, anti-capitalism, anti-war? Interwoven between the tales of modern monsters and contemporary atrocities, villainy and crime, another set of stories. Following the lead of Gayatri Spivak, as well as Gargi Bhattacharyya and Marina Warner, this book risks a gamble that confronts power with intimacy, orientalism against orientation, exoticism operationalised, even doubled in a long uncertain embrace. The political diagnostic is one that risks complicity and involvement with colonial and neo-colonial knowledge regimes – the institutional power of the book, publishing, the university, the archive, the military, the surveillance, the 'homeland', the televisual and monetised matrix. Affective, seductive, even 'informed' – the storyteller in the *1001 Nights* must still time the intervention carefully, mute sometimes, verbose at others. It remains uncertain at what point just one more sentence will do – if it is better to call a tactical halt before the brutal dawn. The episodic engagement of story is also superseded, necessarily. This is the epic outrageous, quixotic, a romantic disposition that flies in the face of those that advocate realism: pundits of despair, annotators of compliance. The radical posture is an odd move too, accusing engaged theorists with obscurantism and non-committal is itself perhaps 'smugly exaggerated ... [and] ... reactionary' (Adorno 1966/1973:35).

In a world of mere appearances, the music promo can think

through all this in a way that accesses a wider audience, even if we are hard pressed to agree the video advert for a pop band product might also have a transformatory import. Perhaps in an unguarded moment we could suggest this – 'bold and beautiful', the bus-borne image – was a little like a twisted kind of Zen, or a postmodern haiku. This reference to haiku is Eisenstein glossed via Rancière (2001/2006:25), with Rancière again doing nothing Adorno had not already denounced – in this case with respect to Benjamin's obsessions with kitsch (see below). But even to comprehend the magic of this haiku, we would need to train endlessly at attending to the silence of a profound contradiction – the bus is terrifying and comic at the same time. Pantomime.

Mediation.

The point of worrying about the theoretical status of music and politics, after Adorno, would be to insist that this is where the illustrative or representational material offers much more than it will explicitly portray. There is *also* a critical theoretical component to assimilate. With regard to literature, Benjamin seems to concede this when, in 1939, in the essay 'On Some Motifs in Baudelaire' he writes:

> A story does not aim to convey an event per se, which is the purpose of information; rather, it embeds the event in the life of the storyteller in order to pass it on as experience to those listening. It thus bears the trace of the storyteller, much the way an earthen vessel bears the trace of the potter's hand (Benjamin 2003:316).

Here Benjamin's tendential agreement is with Adorno. To take the trinket, metaphor, or content at the level of information would be to miss what work the connections and associations of the story, or of the diagnosis, or the theoretical reflection are meant to achieve – at each level these are not exactly the same.

This agreement was thrashed out between Adorno and Benjamin in a now famous exchange of letters. World War Two had not yet begun in earnest, but there is no doubt the anxiety of circumstance pervades all they do – Adorno is writing articles on Jazz under a false name – Hektor Rottweiler (see chapter four). He is in conversation with Benjamin more and more – and the letters were important to Benjamin, who includes a part of an August 5, 1935 Adorno letter in convolute N of the Arcades (Benjamin 1982/1999:466), though with amendments (Moore 2000:157). These letters seem helpful as a way to understand the role of pantomime, or to comprehend the theatrical performance of both politics and scholarship. In 1935 from Adorno we read his 'formulations' on Benjamin's 'dream momentum': that 'alienated things are hollowed out and, as ciphers, they draw in meanings' Benjamin adds to this: 'it should be kept in mind that, in the nineteenth century, the number of "hollowed out" things increases at a rate and scale that was previously unknown' (Benjamin 1982/1999:466). In a letter of November 1938 we see Adorno insisting on a more dialectical rendering of the dream theatre, and arguing the case for a theorised understanding of the players, and insisting on a dialectical theory of mediation.

Adorno is trying to wean Benjamin from his object mania, get him to sort out the Arcades, and get him on a boat to New York. Together, I think they are struggling to invent a theory of trinketisation. Keen to affirm his institutional solidarity with Benjamin, Adorno is careful not to insist on any orthodox version of Marxism, but he also harshly warns his friend against an abdication from Marxist theory:

The impression which your entire study conveys – and not only to me with my Arcades orthodoxy – is that you have here done violence upon yourself. Your solidarity with the Institute, which pleases no-one more than myself, has led you to pay the kind of tributes to Marxism which are appropriate neither to Marxism nor to yourself. Not appropriate to Marxism because the mediation through the entire social process is missing and because of a superstitious tendency to attribute to mere material enumeration a power of illumination which really belongs to theoretical construction ... you have denied yourself your boldest and most fruitful ideas through a kind of pre-censorship in accordance with materialist categories (which by no means correspond to Marxist ones) (Adorno to Benjamin 10 November 1938, Benjamin/ Adorno 1994/1999: 284).

This suggests that Benjamin was merely coquetting with the forms of Marxist theory and not thinking them through – coquetting is Marx's diminutive word in *Capital* for where he used the language and style of Hegel, in an analysis that went beyond Hegel (see the Foreword to Marx 1867/1967). On Adorno's reading – of the draft – Benjamin might be confirmed as 'the [nice, harmless, cute, 'bad'] Marxist that you could take home to meet your mother' (as someone, I forget who, once said). Adorno is teasing and pushing him to be more inventive and rigorous with his connections – all at the same time. And it is connections to which he is attuned, noting:

a close connection between those places where your essay falls behind its own a priori and its relationship to dialectical materialism ... Let me express myself in as simple an Hegelian manner as possible. Unless I am very much mistaken, your dialectic is lacking in one thing: mediation (Adorno to Benjamin 10 November 1938, Benjamin/Adorno 1994/1999:282).

Mediation then would be the theorisation of connections between the 'mere' material observations and fascinations of the Arcades, of the baubles that interest the *flaneur*, of the observations of the analyst, and of the notations of the writer – mediation is the vehicle of analysis. Adorno marks this as a phantasmagorical and mystical error:

> Your 'anthropological' materialism harbours a profoundly romantic element ... The 'mediation' which I miss and find obscured by materialistic-historiographical evocation, is simply the theory which your study has omitted. But the omission of theory affects the empirical material itself (Adorno to Benjamin 10 November 1938, Benjamin/Adorno 1994/1999:283).

At pains not to offend his friend, but also careful to call for something more, Adorno rephrases the same point again and again:

> To express this another way: the theological motif of calling things by their names tends to switch into the wide-eyed presentation of mere facts. If one wanted to put it rather drastically, one could say your study is located at the cross-roads of magic and positivism. This spot is bewitched. Only theory could break this spell – your own resolute and salutarily speculative theory. It is simply the claim of this theory that I bring against you here (Adorno to Benjamin 10 November 1938, Benjamin/Adorno 1994/1999:283).

It might be too easy to score credits here on some biographical outcomes chart, or a research impact assessment for superstar theorists, but Adorno goes on to write *The Dialectic of Enlightenment* with Horkheimer, while Benjamin ends up sitting bleary-eyed far too long in the cafés of Marseilles, and finally does not make it over the mountain. The suitcase he carries is lost and we do not know if these prods in the direction of theory had recast the manuscript. A terrible gap.

The Orange Jumpsuit.

This attention to mediation is at stake in the way we might take up the example of the London Bus or the World Trade Center as spectacle, just as it is the case with the scene of 'pantomime terror' where the musician Aki Nawaz is presented as a 'suicide rapper' in *The Sun* and *The Guardian* newspapers. To make more of these examples than mere 'information' is possibly the task of interpretation, in the ideological narratives of the war on terror as war diary and spin, and also just as much in the strategy of Nawaz's own intervention through the story of *Cookbook DIY* as pop promo intervention. No doubt there are criticalities and complicities in the formats. Consider, to start with the very end of something, the last frames of the video for *Cookbook DIY*: of all the masquerade figures that will appear in that clip, to launch an entire argument we need only note that the figure painting the graffiti quotation from John F Kennedy is wearing orange overalls, thus referencing Guantánamo detention camp. It is of course heavy-handed and didactic in many ways (as detailed below), but perhaps this is why it works. The orange jumpsuit is as recognisably American as the initials JFK. Adorno may not approve of this expediency, but it is a brilliant tactic, quoting a US president as critique of the US Presidency. For the record, the graffiti reads 'If we make peaceful revolution impossible, we make violent revolution inevitable'. This slogan comes from an address by Kennedy at the White House on March 12 1962. It is as if from another time. But since a source for this quote must be offered, here is one that has a certain pointed resonance, and perhaps also illustrates what I earlier had to say about condensation and will later say about repetition. Martin Luther King speaking at New York's Riverside Church on April 4th, 1967 on the topic of the war in Southeast Asia, insists on an end to all bombing and recognition of the Vietnamese National Liberation Front and calls for acts of atonement 'for our sins and errors in Vietnam':

In 1957 a sensitive American official overseas said that it seemed to him that our nation was on the wrong side of a world revolution. During the past ten years we have seen emerge a pattern of suppression which now has justified the presence of US military 'advisors' in Venezuela. This need to maintain social stability for our investments accounts for the counter-revolutionary action of American forces in Guatemala. It tells why American helicopters are being used against guerrillas in Colombia and why American napalm and green beret forces have already been active against rebels in Peru. It is with such activity in mind that the words of the late John F. Kennedy come back to haunt us. Five years ago he said, *'Those who make peaceful revolution impossible will make violent revolution inevitable'*. Increasingly, by choice or by accident, this is the role our nation has taken – the role of those who make peaceful revolution impossible by refusing to give up the privileges and the pleasures that come from the immense profits of overseas investment (King 1967/2007 [my italics]).

Time Magazine called King's speech 'demagogic slander that sounded like a script for Radio Hanoi,' and the *Washington Post* declared that King had 'diminished his usefulness to his cause, his country, his people'; but bringing this forward to contemporary times, and the reference Nawaz makes by way of a simple orange jump suit, is all we need for hypocrisy to be utterly skewered. There is no justification for the torture, the rendition the interrogations – the camps must be closed, the war ended, Scheherazade must be freed.

And isn't that just why the clergyman King should be quoted, because the critical irony gets us hot under the collar here? The provocations of Nawaz or of King are somehow deemed inappropriate and thereby force thought – even though a rapped critique of war is as tangential as a theological critique of the state. We can also see this in what Rancière identifies as problematic with Eisenstein's pantomimes (2001/2006: 27) and also with Bertolt Brecht's identification of the cynical observer with the engaged critic, where the 'lessons of dialectical pedagogy' oscillate with the 'athleticism of the boxing ring or the mockery of the cabaret' (Rancière 2001/2006:30). This is a difficulty with the 'political' haiku that infects the knowing critic with an irony that remains toothless without mobilisation or party organisation. I want to do more with the sign on the side of the London bus. This can happen even as I recognise that Rancière's trans-Atlantic SOS to *Potemkin* from the rail of *The Titanic* does not save us from the contradictions:

> what a century we live in [that we] derive so much pleasure – our Deleuzes in our pockets – from the love affair upon a sinking ship between a young woman in first class and a young man in third (Rancière 2001/2006: 31).

Alerts.

Three security announcements for the pages that follow. I refer to South Asia and 'British Asian' throughout this book – a phrasing which refers, problematically, to the geo-global and conceptual space of diasporic South Asia in its *appearance-form* in London. South Asian itself refers not only and not primarily to the people of those nations of the subcontinent that are normally gathered within the national borders of States that go by the names of Pakistan, India, Nepal, Sri Lanka, Bangladesh, Bhutan and the Maldives. I also have in mind a global Transl-asia (Kaur and Kalra 1996) that ranges far wider than either the subcontinent or my place of work, Britain. It is also problematically a time slot and a satellite frequency in certain ways. There is, in attention to British Asians, a concomitant erasure of other Asias in Britain – the Chinese, Southeast Asians, Japanese and Koreans etc. – and this is a consequence of terminological colonisation that still remains to be undone. In this book I also refer to Asia and Asian as a wide specificity that could include Afghanistan, Pakistan, India, Bangladesh, Nepal, Sri Lanka and the diasporic South Asians discussed as 'Br-Asian' in the volumes Ali, N., Virinder S. Kalra and Salman Sayyid, eds., 2006 *A Postcolonial People: South Asians in Britain*, London: Hurst and Sharma, Sanjay, John Hutnyk and Ash Sharma, eds., 1996 *Dis-Orienting Rhythms: The Politics of the New Asian Dance Music*, London, Zed books. This is not a 'solution' to terminology, as it leaves out many other Asias, East, South-East, Austral- and Middle – a problem best discussed by Spivak in her book *Other Asias* (Spivak 2008).

Similarly, in this book I write quite a lot about *terrorists* and *suicide* bombers and do not feel the need at each turn of the page to point out repetitively that I in no way favour the assassination of innocents, the murder-death-kill we see continually on the news, the carnage of the war, or the culture of fear. You should take it as read that at all times my interest is in a life lived without fear, for equality and justice – such that we have as yet not known – and for a life of peace and co-operation, whatever our differences and their possibilities. In the end I feel there is only a choice between a system in which we are all eventually crushed together, or a greater potential we work in concert to achieve – all of us, everywhere. You can call this abstract but still plausible ideal Full Communism. I want to see it in my time.

Finally, for those who read for structure and coherence, what to say? ... this is a book about pop music overwritten with concerns about politics, overwritten with concerns about theory, itself overwritten with concerns about the politics of theory and the ways both politics and theory become pop. Perfect material for someone with my interests, but how does that sound to you? Dear reader, I was never going to write a conventional fan book about FDM/ADF/MIA, just as much as I wasn't going to write any sort of standard Adorno biography, or some perverse love letter to comrade Žižek and his friends. However, I have tried to make my concerns clear and fair, and in so doing, overwritten with doubt, I do also hope somehow it is all those things, all things to all people. With a little dialectics to get out of any scrapes: pranks, tricks, fooling, contrive, coquette, flirt, dodge, incite, bewitch, plot, conspire, deceive, trump, strategy, tactic, scheme, racket, intrigue, spin, frame, brew, plan, act, stage – the pantomime of politics, the theatre of power, the double-plays of deception. There is something of the gambler and something of elegance in every stratagem of war. Better we know the rules, all the more to ward them off. Red Salute!

2

DIY Cookbook

Visiting the Kumars.

At the end of the last and at the very start of the present century, there emerged a new figure of fun in British media, revealed to also have an ominous underside. Court jesters of culture, the flavour of the month, South Asian comics and comedians became popular and almost ever-present on our screens. For a time, many of us laughed, and many celebrated a coming of age – to be daft like everyone else meant visibility at last. The televised hilarity of *Goodness Gracious Me* and the madcap efforts of Sanjeev Bhaskar on his pseudo chat show *The Kumars at No. 42* were welcome insofar as they promoted manifestations of 'multicultural comedy' as part of a tolerant and inclusive tradition. But this is not – never – the whole story, and I think the popularity of such shows reveals in retrospect some disturbing emergent anxieties. I would argue that the visibility of comic figures did more politically than ever the mischief of the usual court jester as courtier to power achieved. What was signalled, in this chapter, is the working out of a more stark racial contract in the UK, and perhaps the West more generally, where multiculturalism became conformism, and any more difficult engagement, even in the field of culture, was either domesticated or demonised. The humorous and polite on the one hand, pantomime terror on the other, meant the sharp critical edge of postcolonial London, and the heritage of anti-racist, anti-imperialist criticism, was systematically downgraded to a diminutive running joke.

The question of who comes to visit the Kumars, in their acceptable if eccentric domesticity, at Number 42, was a matter of mirth on television. Various celebrities from all walks of life sat with an 'average' – endearingly wacky – South Asian family to talk about their latest cultural product: promoting a film, a play, their new book and so on. As a light entertainment early evening format it was a great success. But such questioning of the neighbours and the to-ings and fro-ings of their associates was then becoming a much sharper confrontation in other parts of Britain, especially in the years after the advent of the War of Terror, the attacks on the World Trade Center in New York and the London tube and bus bombs of 2005. While we weren't looking, while we were watching the Kumars, at the same time the figure of the terrorist in Asian garb became a new manifestation of the old feral scapegoat; the Asian next door made over once again as unwelcome immigrant, never welcome settler. A stereotyped and fear-inducing figure, causing panic and apprehension, scary as in a horror show, made all the more suspect by religious incomprehension, language barriers and ingrained institutionalised xenophobia. A range of studies point out (Wilson 2006, Kundnani 2007, Bhattacharyya 2008) that alongside the harmless visit to the Kumars we also witness special squad investigations and high profile security raids, closures of streets, violent graphic news reportage of incidents recoded as religious conflict or 'jihad'. Emblematic here would be the aftermath of a raid, with police cordoning off areas of quaking middle English suburbia; the nightly news interviewing people living on the same streets of suspects, insisting that 'he kept to himself' or 'they seemed like normal people'; and scenes of the accused being driven off to interrogation and detention under anti-terror legislation. Or average citizens subjected to unprovoked and violent mayhem at the hands of the state, as in Forest Gate, where Mohammed Abdul Kahar was shot in the chest and his brother Abul Koyair kicked and beaten as 250 police stormed their house on June 2nd 2006 (*The Scotsman* 2006) or the Stockwell tube, where Operation Kratos officers shot-to-kill Jean Charles de Menezes on 22nd July 2005, and as planned and prepared for in various terror legislations, police and army procedure manuals, and as called for by right-wing newspapers and talk-back radio shock jocks.

I see the Kumars as the bright side of a sinister kind of theatre that has emerged in Britain in the twenty first century, and I think it can be linked to other seemingly innocent comic aspects of British performance culture, with relevance to similar scenarios throughout the world. This book attempts to unpack the scripts of this tradition.

A Suicide Rapper.

In its June 28, 2006 issue, *The Guardian* newspaper found an absurd headline to put above the slightly modified press release Nation Records put out to promote the new Fun-da-Mental album. The headline, 'G-had and suicide bombers: the rapper who likens Bin Laden to Che Guevara' (Brown and Torres 2006), in effect accused frontman Aki Nawaz of terrorist sympathies, support for Osama bin Laden, un-British sentiments and, devastatingly, punk sensibilities. Despite *The Guardian's* carefully distanced reporting which staged controversy and resistance with Nawaz saying 'he is prepared to face the consequences', this story seemed more likely to belong to the *News of the World* than a left-leaning intellectual broadsheet. *The Sun* duly took up the tale the next day with an inflammatory headline which proclaimed the band's 'Suicide Bomb Rap' had provoked 'fury' and led to calls from MPs for police to arrest Nawaz for 'encouraging terrorism' (Rollings 2006, but see Swedenburg 2009).

Some might have said Aki Nawaz was a past master of provocation as sales gimmick. His initial career outing as the drummer for the Southern Death Cult suggest he learned this mode of work early. His strategy, straight out of the Andrew Loog Oldham/Malcolm McLaren school of promotional work where 'any publicity is good publicity', is still a risky move. Not least because *The Guardian* can turn itself into some sort of sensational tabloid for a day: the headline is particularly inane, but references all the storm-in-a-tea-cup fears that surround those who live in jingoistic crusader paranoid Britain and beyond. As if offering an inventory of the monstrous, the paper zeroes in on how the new Fun-da-Mental album cites bin Laden but manages to tap Che Guevara on the shoulder for good measure. Long ago it became standard for critics to question the commitment with which a pop culture personality might profess political sentiments, and there are endless reams of discussion in the annals of the left concerning the complicity, compromises and commercialism of avowedly leftist 'cultural' interventions. The attempt to simultaneously sell progressive politics and culture industry products without getting some sort of molten plastic rancidity all through your clothes is the sort of thing that is not tested at airport bomb detection facilities, but perhaps should be. Turning into that which you despise is a common media refrain and fans call this 'selling out'. Yet to limit acknowledgement of Nawaz to his role as a rapper rather underplays his diverse activities as impresario of the global juke/sweat box over the past 20 years. As co-founder of Nation Records, Nawaz has been instrumental, pun intended, in bringing a diverse and impressive array of talent to attention: ranging from the diasporic beats of Transglobal Underground, the Drum and Bass of Asian Dub Foundation (discussed in the next chapter), the Hip-hop/Quaito stylings of Prophets of the City, and Qawaali artists such as Aziz Mian and more. With co-conspirator Dave Watts, Fun-da-Mental advance a kind of alternative and left-oriented version of populist world music, as vehicle for a series of targeted provocations against mainstream hypocrisy and racism. Often misunderstood by the music press – there were many who were enamoured at first with their radical stance, but this attitude was soon simplified and resolved itself into sloganeering such as calling them 'the Asian Public Enemy' (see Sharma et al 1996; Hutnyk 2000) and versioning the band, and the Nation label, as a quixotic exotica. No doubt at times Nawaz has played up to this – his persona as rapper 'Propa-Gandhi' clearly marks a knowing ambiguity and many of his comments play on, and yet desta-bilise, conventions of British South Asian identity.

In *The Guardian* piece that broke the story of the suicide rapper, Nawaz is pictured in a post-Propa-Gandhi but still pantomime pose. This could be called a disgruntled chic/sheikh stance if this were not also an awful play on words. The photo the *Guardian* chose to print is particularly revealing of the iconography of terror and fear in present-day Britain. In the print version of this Ladbroke Grove ensemble – the *Guardian Unlimited* web image is slightly cropped – there is an English flag to the right of the picture, alongside a likely looking resident. The bus in the background on the left is behind a young lad with a backpack – this surely refers with pointed significance to the bus bomb anniversary about a week away when this story was printed. I want to read the bus in this ensemble as of crucial significance. All the buttons of contemporary Islamophobia, nationalism and transport system vulnerability, and conspiracy theorising are pushed in this image here – though it is unclear if the photographer Martin Godwin and Nawaz himself contrived to create this scene together, certainly Nawaz in the photograph is both trying to look angry – pantomime villain – and we can tell that inside he is smirking at the absurdity of it all.

And the absurdity of it all is certainly present in the iconic July 7, 2005, Rosenberg photograph that is recalled by means of citation. If the backpack behind Nawaz necessarily evokes the Tavistock Square bus, it does so, intentionally or not, ironically or not, in a way at least deserving of attention. That this has been ignored seems a failure of analysis. Instead of any critical indication of the potency of this scene, neither by the news reporters Mark Brown and Luc Torres, nor by respected commentators, this remains a silent device within the ensemble, associating by visual proximity, Nawaz with the London bombers – a connectivity confirmed and mocked in simultaneity and in the anniversary repetition of the media scare.

Yet, while Nawaz is portrayed as a cartoon-esque suicide rapper in *The Guardian* and *The Sun*, he also uses this notoriety to convey a previously unheard and unwelcome message about the hypocrisy of the so-called 'War on Terror'. The iconography works to open forums previously unavailable for him to raise issues, provoke discussion. Soon he is invited – more than once – onto the BBC news roundtable talkback, his voice heard because he courts 'outrage' with his 'agitational' views. To some degree his provocation does force issues into the open. He is not invited to the Kumars show to promote the album, but instead appears on the BBC 2 *Newsnight* in August 2006 and on *Newsnight Review* in October the same year, and subsequently. Bad publicity enables important interventions on a serious late evening current affairs programme. Possibly a long time coming, but it is in the casting role of villain that the establishment doors were opened to some different ideas – any publicity at all. Several other scenes are worth examining in this process where a former punk drummer with reformed global world music sensibilities coincides with entertainment values and programming requisites to enable political comment with a sharp edge.

1001 Nights.

My view is that we need to work through the moves as they travel from comic outrage to serious debate. For me this means a detour through the theatrical – and for the purposes of this discussion, the comic theatre of British pantomime.

Thinking about pantomime terrors deserves a little historical play. The popular Christmas and summer holiday entertainment form has roots in vaudeville and melodrama and might also be traced back through French mime, Italian Commedia dell'arte, or even to Roman mythology and the flutes of the god Pan (Miller 1978:52-54). A more detailed history of course would have to contend with the long-term relationship of literature to children's entertainment, of the Pied Piper of Hamelin to J.M. Barrie's Peter

Pan, with issues of role reversal, double entendre, drag, slapstick, superstitions – left side of the stage for demons, right side for fairy princesses – and theatre ghosts if not more. The trajectory within the pantomime archive that I find most relevant here is one I will document in the final chapter of this book, but it could start with Scheherazade. I have in mind the stories of *A Thousand And One Nights*, known in Arabic as *Alf Layla wa Layla*, the first 'proper book' I owned as a child. The novelist Hanif Kureishi calls it 'the greatest book of all' in *My Son the Fanatic* (Kureishi 1998:xii). My first copy is illustrated with lavish pictures of Sinbad the Sailor, various alluring princesses on flying horses or magic carpets, Aladdin and his lamp, and of course Ali Baba and the 40 thieves. There is no guarantee that innocent storytelling can protect us from loss, but to hark back to older storytelling forms is perhaps one way to disrupt the walled enclave or 'green zone' that is civil society, polite discussion and public commons, also known as the privileged space of spin. For me, it is easy to see the deployment of fantasy in public – Asian exoticisms – has been going on for some time. Inducted into the *1001 Nights* as a child, exactly as Captain Sir Richard Francis Burton complained that anthropological and ethnological riches might become merely 'a present for little boys' (Burton 1885/ 2003), I still feel betrayed when those stories are not received as wondrous.

That Scheherazade had to tell deviously charming stories to evade death at the hands of the despotic King Shahryar is only the first of the points at which Edward Said-style critiques of orientalism would need to be deployed. Wicked and conniving traders outfoxed by fantastically beautiful maidens told as fairy tales to children, with romance and magic, disguising the violence at the heart of the stories themselves. This does effective ideological duty – 'get 'em while they're young' – and reinforces, as mere story, some pretty unsavoury values. It is 30 years since Said delivered *Orientalism* and though some might have concerns with what has happened in the wake of that text, it certainly alerts us to something important and not yet nearly resolved. In its wake, *Orientalism* released many historical studies (see, for example, Vishvanathan 1989), though despite Said's own work on Palestine, such as *Covering Islam* (1981) and *After the Last Sky* (1986), perhaps not enough followers of Said write of now.

Gargi Bhattacharyya's work *Tales of Dark-skinned Women* (1998) is a text that does engage orientalism with the contemporary, and she works through many of these questions when relating contemporary politics to the tales of Scheherazade. For Bhattacharyya, the 'strange happenings of the Nights' are 'passed off as some kind of accurate depiction' of the East (1998:11). Even if we can agree with her that framing the stories as 'props to the orientalist conspiracy' misses the power of distraction through entertainment, I am not yet sure that the formulation works to undo power in every case: 'The glamour of Scheherazade is her ability to see another story hidden in the despair of the present' (Bhattacharyya 1998:11). Though I share and learn from Bhattacharyya's narration of State crimes against British Asian and British-Caribbean settlers, I suspect more than glamour is required since storytelling is, of course, not analysis, nor redress, even if there is to some extent a back-story of political intrigue and complicity to the *1001 Nights*. Is it not curious that, after 3000 maidens have previously been sacrificed by the Vizier, finally it is his own daughter who is offered up to Shahryar? The sister Dinarzade – more from her in chapter four – as strategist and accomplice, the father executioner expiating sins while eavesdropping outside the chamber door, who writes down the tales if not he – *storyteller-killer, suicide-writer*?

We cannot be sure of the game the Vizier is playing, but then nothing is guaranteed in fantasy. Jacques Lacan also weighs in on this tale, quoting Edgar Allen Poe in 'The Purloined Letter', he reminds us that Scheherazade lives from morning to morning, the repetition of her storytelling the gamble of her survival from day to day (Lacan 1966/2006:29). Her gamble risks telling the wrong story, and in Poe on night 1002 she blunders and must face consequences that are too terrible to tell to kids. My problems with Said and Lacan however have always been that these effects are not just literary and historical, Lacan's comments on the gambler's paranoia should indeed make us wary. The point though is that Scheherazade lives in what seems like an apocalyptic end-times, as recognised by Ruth Ozeki, who mentions her in her novel about the suicide and the kamikaze Haruki Yasutani, and who opposes writing to suicide as the forestalling of death (Ozeki 2013:314). Of course writing is never a guarantee of immortality, since the planet will itself become a fireball, but the exoticist move to read September 11 through the redemption of a kamikaze has a clear strategic purchase.

As Bhattacharyya suggests, there is much documented orientalism closely linked to the *1001 Nights*, and it is necessary only to look at a few sources to see that commentary upon this is itself a culture industry of sorts. The dress-ups, demonisation and fantasy projections track the fortunes of translations, readers, theatre and movie versions and even war on terror propaganda renditions. It is useful however to recognise Bridget Orr's observations that pantomime, and the initial British exposure to stories from the *Nights*, had a political character from the very earliest versions: 'adaptation from the *Nights* was a feature both of pantomime's first great period of success in the 1720s and the decades a half-century later'. These were periods of 'peculiarly intense national and imperial crisis' (Orr 2008:104), during which lines between government and theatre were blurred and, with specific reference to 'the long-running scandal over Bengal misgovernance', pantomime stories from the *Nights* were used 'to dramatize a wide variety of desires and anxieties consonant with the increasingly complex matter of empire' (Orr 2008:110-111). The farce, melodrama and related fictions of the 1700s took parts of the stories, of Sultans, Genii and flying carpets, and adapted them to 'provide more pointed and specific commentary on despotism, slavery, and the wealth of corruption associated with Britain's colonial possessions in the East' (Orr 2008:124).

In the textual versionings, the work had to be more carefully managed, and the initial translations, in twelve volumes, (from 1704-1717) by Antoine Galland, into French, were those of a prominent Arabic scholar and former ambassador's secretary in Constantinople producing a text that had 'an anthropological rather than literary perspective', though this could be disputed since Galland also calls the *Nights* 'art' and 'beautiful in any language' (reported in Dobie 2008:32). Translation into English was at first an anonymous glossing of the Galland, and then selections, like that of Edward Lane (1838-41 – 3 volumes) and John Payne (1882-84 – nine volumes), but the most famed, and perhaps most criticised translator – though sometimes undeservedly – is the aforementioned Burton. His documentation of earlier lesser and expurgated editions in his 'Forward' – Lane, Payne – is sometimes snide, but entertaining (Burton 1885/2001). His language describing other translations is purple: 'limited', 'ruthlessly mutilated with head or feet wanting', 'debased' by 'improvements', 'revised', 'wretchedly edited', 'hideous', a 'melancholy specimen', 'continued with scrupulous castration and ending in ennui and disappointment' and a 'missionary production' (Burton 1885/2007:23). Less beset with petty jealousies, Husein Haddawy reports that the first full printed edition of the *1001 Nights* was published in Calcutta by Fort William College in two volumes (1814 and 1818) edited by Arabic instructor Shaik Ahmad ibn-Mahmud Shirawari. Then there was Breslau's edition between 1824-1838 for the first 8 volumes and the last four volumes in 1842-43. The Bulaq edition, from Cairo in 1835, and the second Calcutta edition edited by William Macnaghten between 1839 and 1842 in four volumes were the versions used by Burton for his translations (1885-86), themselves often reissued and reintroduced, for example recently as *The*

Arabian Nights, introduced by A. S. Byatt (2001). Haddawy, who documents the authenticity, or not, of the old editions, also points out that the Sinbad episodes are a later 'addition' to the Nights of fourteenth century Muhsin Mahdo (Haddawy 1995: xv). Burton is accused of offering a Victorian exoticist version of orientalism, a repressed desire irrupting in outrage and measured titillation from a man who dearly loved to dress up – a strong sense of pantomime, he marches to Mecca famously disguised as a dervish, and offers a lively travel tale along the way (Burton 1853/1964). Curiously, Haddawy means as a criticism what might now seem a compliment: Burton's faulty translation had 'bequeathed to the nation ... no more than a literary Brighton Pavilion' (Haddawy 1995:xxx). This is a strangely florid language – bequeath – since Haddawy is condemning Burton for flamboyance. Nevertheless, the fairy tale diminutive was set in place early.

The greater problem with Burton perhaps is the pattern that this orientalist, but sympathetic language-learning and over-enthusiastic scholar of the east, sets out for emulation. Particularities and specificities of people he meets on his travels are reified into national characteristics and stereotypes in the service of ego, self and national-glorification. That Burton travels to Mecca and learns to speak with others is not nothing, but it is more adventure than scholarship. His fantasy is enacted in travel, but is still fantastic, a narrative of illusions. On reading the stories of the *1001 Nights*, 'as a child' of course, Samuel Taylor Coleridge writes, later, that he 'was haunted by spectres' whenever he was in the dark and that he watched the book with fear. His father 'found out the effect which these books had produced, and burnt them', says Coleridge. It is then that he 'became a dreamer' (Coleridge cited in Fulford 2008: 189). Stories, it seems, have long been a danger, and books have long been burnt. I watch with Coleridge as the sun edges closer to inflame the pages with what incandescent power:

Coleridge, obsessively watching the book in its corner until the sun had struck it, with feelings of 'obscure dread and intense desire', is caught up in a cycle of imaginative reenactment of the Nights. He fears, with Scheherazade and her sister Dinarzade, the despotic power that might at any moment punish those who keep their audiences spellbound with curious tales. But, like the beguiled sultan, who cannot resist hearing first one tale and then another and another, Coleridge too is beguiled by the tales' consumability. Their very strangeness and the fact that he consumes them compulsively render them suspect (Landry 2008:176)

This is not to say the exoticisation of the *Nights* is solely the preserve of the old orientalists. New ones abound, as shown by Makdisi and Nussbaum who write that 'when Uday and Qusay Hussein's palace was laid open to public view after the invasion of Iraq by American and allied troops' it was revealed that the sons had 'apparently decorated their palace with exoticised images of *The Arabian Nights* that seemed to caricature the original Persian, Turkish, and Arabic versions: these images have perhaps the closest affinity to Walt Disney'. While I am not sure of the 'apparent', 'seemed' and 'perhaps' qualifiers here, I don't doubt the strangeness of the scene where a 'Hollywood-inspired mural that offered a grotesque representation of tales' was 'gaped at by incredulous US soldiers' (Makdisi and Nussbaum 2008:17).

There are many versions. Pier Paolo Passolini's *Arabian Nights* (dir. Passolini 1974) is something else altogether, a languid erotic exotic film beautifully staged and shot in multiple locations across the Arab world, plus Nepal, in a time before the present political demonisation. But the *Nights* have always been controversial, and translators and others have often entered into fratricidal debate. For example, the story of Judar in the *Nights* is of interest. Judar is both an asylum seeker and a stranded sailor. His mother, who he always helps, is not the phantom confronted in the cave, he helps his brothers, he feeds the poor. His story extends from night 607 to 624, only to end by his being slain by his brother. Burton inserts two footnotes that are critical amongst the pages dealing with Judar. One denounces the 'biting and carping' critic Andrew Lang, who 'will condescend to notice a misprint in another's book' and yet 'lay himself open to general animadversion by such a rambling farrago of half-digested knowledge as that which composes … [his] … introduction [to Grimm's tales] (Burton 1885/2007(6):230n). The second notable note laments the appearance of books with the newly fashionable title 'New Arabian Nights' which is 'applied without signification' by the likes of Robert Louis Stevenson in a 'pleasant collection of novelettes' (Burton 1885/2007(6):257n). This itself is a poignant complaint, since Burton himself translates a 'new' *Nights* with few of the 'original' stories and his own adaptations, glosses and editorial choices.

Marina Warner offers an excellent commentary on the early cinematic versionings of the *Nights*, including *The Thief of Bagdad* (1924) as parable for children, and the various Sinbads (Warner 2011:379) but today it is through pantomime that infantalised and distorted tales of the *Nights* play an even more sinister role. The politics of distraction works with the *Nights* invented ever anew, and played fast and loose with fact and stereotype under the cover that its fun. The most memorable scenes in Pantomime are the ones of tension. The viewers – children and their parents – watch as the innocent hero is stalked by the dastardly and demonic villain – an evil Genie or Captain Hook perhaps, or an alligator, depending on which side you choose. The children are encouraged to shout out and expose the impending danger, to call out the threat. This theatrical structure lays out a pattern that repeats. The villain that is *'behind you'* in today's real life panto is the sleeper cell living and working amongst us, travelling on the tube, plotting next door, preparing to wreak havoc and destruction unannounced, except for the high rotation security announcements at train stations advising us never leave our luggage untended. A narrative simplified and transparent, yet it works so well that 1001 repetitions cannot yet undo its power. In effect such announcements are part of the terror, strangely absorbed as everyday routine, they are reminders that deflect attention since someone, some bureaucratic policy person somewhere, is clearly saying they are looking after security. Yet 'announcement fatigue' is accompanied by disaster fatigue and empathy numbness since each announcement is a recorded and disembodied voice, emanating from nowhere, stage right – a defence in the abstract, by committee. Alongside this, it was art critic and novelist John Berger who declared the September 11, 2001 attacks in New York to be themselves 'announcements' (Berger 2008:50), and so it is that the logic of 'total film' has us sequestered in a society of more or less planned, more or less ignored routinisation. Similarly spooky allegories might be evoked from the panto stories, Ali Baba is the despot holding the west ransom to the price of a barrel of oil; Sinbad is Osama, with a hidden cave to which only he knows the secret opening code words: 'open sesame' [*The Descent*].

The fears that are promulgated here are of course childish terrors and cliché, but the problem with such stereotyping is their maddening ability to transcend reason and keep on popping back up to scare us. This is not a place for thinking. It is children's theatre, clinging on into the adult world as a petrifyingly anxious residual. So much so that perhaps we might consider the repetition of the historical as seen in Marx's study of Louis Bonaparte in the *Eighteenth Brumaire*: the second time history repeats it returns as high farce. Marx's *Eighteenth Brumaire* is by far the most eloquent articulation of class and ideological politics available – the classic phrases are well known 'they cannot represent themselves, they must be represented' as Bonaparte usurps democracy, the peasants treated as 'potatoes in a sack', and Marx wanting to move on and 'let the dead bury the dead' and so on. The trouble for Marx, perhaps also for Lacan, was the repetition compulsion built into the story. So much so that this suggests to me a Poe-faced, negative speculative dream version of the Scheherazade tale in which her storytelling is calculated to undo the despotic kings of the global crusade: Tony Blair, G.W. Bush, Barack Obama, David Cameron. Each of these despots are stitched into the war story in Afghanistan and Iraq, but she counters them with guile, smuggling in sister Dinarzade to script escapades and hi-jinks that keep them placidly on stage, as if dressed as potatoes in a sack, or as farcical harlequins with clowning and puppets, subject to haranguing monologues that blunt their crimes. They would no doubt think they were particulating in some current affairs interview or campaign stump-speech, but instead they are rendered harmless through improvised diversion and choreographed pacification. All the techniques of mass deception are deployed as weapons to disarm. Despots sit in trance, the storyteller wins. Of course the case is that my dreaming of Scheherazade as political orator for our times is only a conceit – even as I cannot imagine what so many years in detention can do to anyone. A thousand and one terrors assail us all.

Cookbook DIY.

I'm packed up ingredients stacked up my Laptop
Downloaded the military cookbook PDF
Elements everyday chemicals at my reach
Household bleach to extract the potassium
Chlorate Boiling on a hotplate with hate
recipe for disaster plastic bomb blaster
I mix up 5 parts wax to Vaseline
slowly … dissolve in gasoline
add to potassium in a large metal bowl

knead like dough so they bleed real slow
Gasoline evaporates… cool dry place
I'm strapped up cross my chest bomb belt attached
deeply satisfied with the plan I hatched
electrodes connected to a gas cooker lighter
switch in my hand the situation demands
self sacrifice hitting back at vice with a £50 price

I'm 31.. numb …but the hurt is gone
Gonna build a dirty bomb
us this privilege and education
My PHD will free me
Paid off the Ruskies for weapons grade Uranium
Taught myself skills from Pakistan Iran
upgraded its stage two of the plan
Rage… a thermo nuclear density gauge
stolen by the Chechens from a Base in Georgia
I get some cobalt 60 from a food irradiator
so easy to send the infidels to their creator
its takes a dirty mind to build a dirty bomb
The simplicity is numbing genius is dumbing
down the situation to a manageable level
to make the world impossible to live for these devils
a suitcase of semtex a mobile phone trigger
Blow them all to hell for a million dollar figure

I insist I'm a legitimate scientist
paid by the government with your finances
I got a private room in the Whitehouse suite
So I can develop according to presidential Brief
The megaton don Gulf war veteran
The foremost proponent of the neutron bomb
at the centre atomic surrounded on all sides
wrapped in layers of lithium deutaride

> *the bomb detonates causing lithium to fission into helium*
> *tritium neutrons into Fission*
> *The blast causes shockwaves that melt body fat*
> *uniquely though it leaves the buildings intact*
> *I made the 25 megaton daisy cutter*
> *a great blast radius with very little clutter*
> *There's less radiation so you get a cleaner bomb*
> *it's your money people it cost a billion*
> Nawaz/Watts. Nation *All is War* 2006 – Nation Records, with
> permission.

Pantomime Video.

The video is pantomime on film. The first verse, about the homemade bomb, is performed – as is the entire clip – by a dress-up figure before the camera. At the very first appearance this figure appears wearing a white rabbit head. This is strange and already disturbing, but I think references in some oblique way, a kind of cute or innocent image that belongs to the Britain of pet bunnies, or of the world of Lewis Carroll's *Alice in Wonderland*. That this innocent quickly transforms into a lizard figure is commensurate with the fear that works to suggest a constant vigilance – the otherwise unassuming neighbour becomes a threat. The lizard figure becomes a Zebra – again invoking a kind of infant menagerie – before becoming again the rabbit. But looking more closely, the figure here is wearing a St George t-shirt, thereby clearly signifying nationalism at one level, but also citing the popular world cup publicity picture of Wayne Rooney as dragon-slaying hero, saviour to English football fans. This complicates any easy ascription of innocence to the rabbit/zebra/lizard, and – without implicating the English striker – suggests perhaps the homemade bomb is very much a home grown Christian jihad.

In between the verses, disturbing flashes of dolls tied up, ransom images that tamper with our comforts. Children's toys blasted into the political scene. The graffitist in the Guantánamo jumpsuit works on a banner alongside.

In the second verse, the bombmaker is now a 31 year-old PhD graduate disaffected with conventional or domestic means of protest, now gone over to the side of organised resistance. Speaking as if to camera at a press conference, or perhaps as if in a video prepared for an Al Jazeera broadcast, this figure is insistent, aggressive. Dressed at first as a twisted student in graduation robes, kaffiyeh and graduation hat, half way through the verse this figure changes into someone in balaclava and the ammunition belt of a mythic revolutionary figure, possibly reminiscent of Pancho Villa or Rambo. This character, the bandit-terrorist, raises the allegorical volume of threat considerably at the end when spinning a revolver on his finger and transforms into someone in a plain dirty white hooded sweatshirt – 'it takes a dirty mind to build a dirty bomb'. This grubby image surely suggests we are mistaken to locate this threat outside of Europe – in the murky theatres of violence, in the lawless badlands. The point here is to underline the hypocrisy of our geo-political conventions, this image indicative of a failure to appreciate the co-constitution of such badlands with the dubious foreign policy decisions of the imperial powers.

Between verses: images of toy cars, computer games, football paraphernalia and other trinkets from our early adolescent pastimes. The graffiti still not legible.

The final verse clinches the argument about militarism. The 'legitimate scientist' working at his bench in his white lab coat, sponsored by the research funding of the Pentagon, UN flag behind him, developing the most destructive weapons of mass destruction ever know. That half way through the verse this figure transforms into the sinister figure of a Ku Klux Klan member in white hood and smock, then into suited 'Lord of War' wearing a gas mask, presumably only the bureaucrats will survive total war. All this is perhaps heavy-handed, but nevertheless the critical points are not misplaced, the metaphoric substitutions work. The projected indications are sound: the neutron bomb is the violence of racism, of class/bureaucratic inhumanity, the cold clinical cynicism of the (mad) scientist in the employ of even more mad (mutually assured destruction) masters.

By this stage the point is made, finally the full quote is visible from the graffitist. It is a citation from an American president, possibly via the King himself, necessary only to provide a space for reflection while the tune fades. 'If we make peaceful revolution impossible, we make violent revolution inevitable' – JFK.

The RampArts Interlude (notes from a screening).

I insist I'm a legitimate scientist
paid by the government with your finances
– Cookbook DIY

Appalled at the carnage on my television screen, I ventured out. I caught the train to Shadwell in East London and walked to the corner of Rampart and Sly Streets (hmmm, significant street names – *Ramparts* was a 60s magazine of some importance, Sly – well, that's clear enough – at the end of the street there's a great sweet shop…). So, I arrived at the corner to find Aki Nawaz from Fun-da-Mental slumped in a broken office chair beside a dumpster and a pile of crushed cardboard boxes. 'Welcome to my office', he greets me. We sit and chat about the mad media responses to his new album *All is War*; we run through recent events in the horror that is Lebanon; approve the resistance of Hezbollah; and consider the possibility that bruiser John Reid is going gung-ho in his new home secretary job because, like an earlier blind incumbent, he is jockeying for position as a possible future leader of the Labour Party, so acting tough is what he thinks will get him noticed in the press. We talk about how the tabloids make public opinion nowadays and his posturing is mainly a way of scaring people into silence, apathy and into nothing but the joys of shopping. Then a Green Party representative comes over and asks Aki what instrument he plays in the band. I only wish Aki had replied, 'Hi, my name's Pink'.

Then Home Secretary Reid, believe it or not, was a former CPGBer (Communist Party of Great Britain, before liquidation) and perhaps best noticed for calling television presenter Jeremy Paxman a West London Wanker (aka W-L-W) – former Labour Party Deputy PM John Prescott was at the time trying to remain invisible (with two Jaguar cars) and war criminal Bliar was off hiding out in some celebrity Bee Jee holiday resort (aka a Florida terror training camp) after paving the way for the Israeli Defence Force to make pavement out of Southern Beirut. An airport carry-on luggage scare and the arrest of a bunch of teenagers is a great service to the no-hoper piggy-pollies that need the cover, but gung ho is a funny expression; a mix of Bruce Lee and Ho Chi Minh springs to mind, so I best stop using it, because Reid has long ago left the Left behind, and I am told, anyway, that 'gung-ho' as taken up by the US Marines as an abbreviation for any Chinese Communist organisation, so using it to refer to the Labour Party is far too uncanny... I digress (see Mavens 1998) and also contrast the Ron Howard directed film of the same name (*Gung Ho* 1986 dir. Howard) and laugh in dismay. For deep research, check out the expatriate New Zealander Rewi Alley in communist China who, in the late 1930s, 'instigated an industrial co-op movement he termed "gung ho" (work together). Its success led to the phrase entering the global idiom' (*Gung-Ho: Rewi Alley of China*, dir. Geoff Steven 1980, thanks Simon Barber, personal email).

Anyway, politics by tabloid. Aki has himself been noticed in the tabloids quite a bit – *The Sun* branded him a 'suicide rapper' and *The Guardian* had a go – as I have mentioned already. The event at RampArts – an anarchist inspired social centre – is to discuss the controversy, and to host the premiere screening of the video for *Cookbook DIY*. The evening kicks off in somewhat desultory manner with a half hour video on the history of Funda-Mental that presses various key buttons – 'Tribal Revolution', 'Dog Tribe', 'GODEVIL' clips and plenty of send-up footage of a lame Australian TV interviewer who pretty much can't cope with Aki asking if Australian Aboriginals had rights and land back yet – 'what are you doing about it?' 'Nothing.' The point is didactic and heavy handed – it's a music talk back show – but correct.

Slowly the RampArts social centre fills up, and people take their seats to find a gift FDM CD – its not about the sales – and Ken Fero, co-director of *Injustice* – kicks off proceedings by introducing Aki, John Pandit and the guy from the Green Party, noting that two other guest speakers were still on their way. Aki starts speaking about how democracy is a weapon that kills, that there is a silencing that is much to blame, that the leader in Downing Street needs to be put on a donkey and paraded through the city, and that he can't understand why nobody is doing anything. He is really angry. The youth in Britain are angry. There are people being killed in thousands and everyone seems to be going on and on as if there was nothing they could do. They tried to protest against the Gulf War, but were ignored and since then, nothing. Why, he says, aren't people out there burning down town halls and the like? (This last comment almost an aside, but it will become more and more the hot topic of the night). The Green Party representative speaks next, about free speech – frankly, the usual routines – thank-you Shahrar Ali, invited by the organisers *Red Pepper*. Then Natasha Atlas arrives – her music is also released under Aki's Nation Records imprint – and she talks of her Syrian partner, the troubles musicians have getting visas in Europe, her anger and frustration at the war, and she apologises for being emotional. In fact it's the most passionate thing I've heard her say ever, and not at all prima donne-esque. Great. Then the final late speaker walks in, Louise

Christian, human rights lawyer, and she reminds us the event is organised by *Red Pepper*… twice. She speaks in favour of free speech and against the new additions to the terror laws that will criminalise anyone who speaks in favour of – glorifies, encourages – acts of terror. These laws apply even if the alleged glorifier of terror did not inspire anyone to act, even if they were vague about whether they really intended people to go out and – Louise looks over to Aki – even if they say people should go out and blow up buildings. She supposes these laws will not ever be tested, that they are like clause 28 – crime of encouraging homosexuality – or the incitement to racial hatred law, they are a kind of public relations gesture. We should not get paranoid, that at least in this country we can have debates like this – there has been no debate as yet, but restlessness in the audience suggests one might start soon – and debate is something we have to cherish, because – here's the clincher – they don't have it in Turkey, Burma or North Korea.

John Pandit from the band Asian Dub Foundation (ADF) speaks next. Quietly pointing out the need to organise and to do so in new creative ways, to make a new set of alliances. To do the work required to build a movement that is not just protest marches that go from A to B (this will also become a refrain, the issue of how the Stop the War (STW) coalition does all it can to minimise confrontations and have us all hide in Hyde Park provokes considerable agitation). And it is important, he emphasises, not to fall for the self-censorship that means that so many musicians who do have media visibility say nothing.

The first question is from the reporter from the *Daily Star*, Neil Chandler – he told me his column appears in the Sunday edition. I think to myself that I might even buy it as his question was ok and in a short exchange with the reporter from the *Morning Star*, and representative of the STW coalition, Neil seems by far the more credible. But it is the *Daily Star*, so no high hopes eh (and the subsequent article turns out to be the usual tabloid clichés). In any case, in response to questions, the point is made forcefully by Aki that the issue is British foreign policy. A fairly simple persuasive argument he offers runs: we put up with years and years of racism and it did not mean any young people strapped on jackets and bombed the trains; we endured unemployment and it did not mean anyone went out to bomb buildings (well, Baader Meinhof and the like excluded) but the nightly news footage of innocents killed one after the other in their hundreds and no-one wants to discuss it, no-one listens, no debate, no significant movement to defend Muslims; no defence of mosques from attack; no way the STW coalition was going to deliver on its promise that 'if Blair goes to war we will stop the whole country', despite 2 million marching in February 2002… the problem is foreign policy. Change that and its over.

Some audience members were keen to point out that there were ongoing efforts to defeat Blair. Protests against airports and weapons manufacture, dealers, delivery, sabotage, various campaigns. There was some discussion of how music is important as a way of airing issues, that musicians are more than the soundtrack of a movement; that since the 60s Vietnam protests music could be something more than entertainment. But so often it is not. I am of course reminded of Adorno saying that the debate is not yet over about art, and perhaps art still carries the 'secret omnipresence of resistance' (Adorno 1991:67) in its hidden core. But this is not enough in a world of shopping. All this is admirable but it does not get to the question of just what kind of organisation is needed to defeat the imperialist foreign policy. The questions I ask have to do with this: the need for debate and action on all these points; on what sort of organisation is needed; on what sort of action is needed (someone heckles 'but not blowing up buildings'); and on what sort of analysis is needed to support both organisation adequate to succeed, and the actions necessary. This does not get taken up; instead the chair notes there is always resistance, there will always be resistance. Another speaker asks a question about violence, naming Gandhi and the struggle against British colonialism. Aki makes the point that Gandhi was not alone, there was always a range of others involved, from Uddam Singh to Netaji Subhas Chandra Bose. Gandhi, it is insisted, wanted peace, not blowing up buildings – this is becoming the defining phrase, spiralling into architectural defence. Aki exasperated says 'you lot care more about buildings than people' – hands thrown up in the air. Everyone wants a say, a filmmaker is shouting from the back, the guy with the roving mike has gone outside to answer a phone call, with the mike still turned on. Chaos. So the movement shall be organised like this...

Dave Watts from Fun-da-Mental stands up. The discussion has dragged on and his frustration is as clear as that of anyone. He starts by saying he understands why people want to be suicide bombers, he understands the frustration that would make someone want to go out and do it. You can imagine how this rubs up against the Gandhians. Dave says there has to be some understanding of where those who have tried to discuss have now ended up – ready to do violence and blow up buildings [code words]. But then he says he is a man of peace, a lover of peace, but he is angry and we have to fight for peace. The video clip we are about to see is called *Cookbook DIY* and Dave explains it is in three parts, that the person who in frustration because there is no other avenue for discussion, expression, action has made a home bomb for 50 quid, is a small version of the guy who makes a dirty bomb, with materials bought on the black market, but neither are as obscene as the scientist who kisses his wife in the morning – Dave mimes a smooch, playing to the audience – panto – who then goes off to work in a Pentagon lab or some such to make a neutron bomb that kills all the people but leaves the buildings intact. Have a look at the video people... at which point, the screening:

And what is it that *Cookbook DIY* does? This 'suicide rap'

exposes the suicide scientist making the neutron bomb, the daisy cutter, the cluster bombs and all those other armaments that the Lords of War – Blair, Reid, etc. – threaten us with, under their terror laws, their terror regimes, the bombing runs and their surveillance systems. Their free speech that is no speech, their diplomacy and their democracy. Under the veneer of democracy, the bloodied hands of the piggy pollies; under the musical refrains, the resistance; under the cover of the Daily and the Morning Stars, another secret possibility. The global resistance, Zindabad!

All is War.

The promotional provocation that Nawaz offers on the Fun-da-Mental album *All is War* is a dangerous strategy as well, simply because the authorities that have the power to do such things just may well get the wrong end of the night stick and actually think the album is some sort of threat to the Nation. There have been times when Nawaz's friends did think he was destined for Belmarsh Prison on charge of promoting 'terror', especially with regard to the misreadings of the album *Erotic Terrorism*, and of course then with the track 'Cookbook DIY'. Journalists from *The Guardian* only seemed to listen to the first verse before filing their stories, missing entirely the comparative narrative in a major failure of comprehension. Fun-da-Mental have always pushed hard at the complacencies and hypocrisies of our political servility and this is a good thing too – there are those who argue that we *all* need to threaten a rethink of the dubious policies of Bush-Blair Obama-Cameron and the clones, of the terror war they are waging worldwide, of the domestic demonisation of Muslims, of the crushing of civil society. What civil society? That it is too civil is the problem. The stifling numbing dumb dumb dumb of the press is itself mere puppet-show.

There are those in the tourist and airline industries who think that demonisation by way of media propaganda offers 'a win' to 'the terrorists'. That terrorists were 'laughing at us', according to RyanAir chief Michael O'Leary (Kavkazcentre.com 2006), was only one oblique reflection upon the massive disillusionment of the British public with the establishment terror war, also expressed in massive street protests such as the two million who marched against the Iraq invasion in London on 15 February 2003. The laughter of terrorists makes the usual anti-Islamic political editorialising in the media a pro-government pantomime itself. Is this just part of show business – the new replacement for *Top Of The Pops* perhaps? The hit-making music show transformed into an ideological popularity contest with manufactured villains and bland comic book heroes. Of course we can all see that the 'banning' of a music track is only a minor power play in an obscure corner of the culture industry. There are a great many other modes of video violence that might much rather take up the time of the self-appointed guardians or propriety in Britain. Certainly there are examples of video images that might give more cause for concern – racist materials proliferate no doubt, and there will be reason to consider training, recruitment, surveillance, suicide and celebration videos in forensic detail. The pantomime villain is the weapon of hypocrites, a lazy alibi for those who make up dirty excuses for arms traders and NATO invasions. This is not conspiracy theory, but the media playing at demonology – stories to tell children while propping up dictators and despotism in 45 minute bursts of terror. In contrast, Nawaz and the *Cookbook DIY* video is just the sort of threat of which we need to see much more, in the sense that we have to debate, discuss, challenge and change – and absolutely none of this requires any heavy-handed police interventions; or worse. No wonder there are concerns about humour; the laughter that ensues is not easily hushed, it reveals much.

We must acknowledge that a newspaper publicity event for a culture industry music promo is not really 'news', especially while there are more serious debacles to which to attend – the rise of racism, anti-Islamic profiling and the anti-people pogroms of the state machine, saturation bombing, occupations of entire nations, intentional regional destabilisation, war crimes. The gap between music product and international significance surely means it would be a surprise if someone did equate such 'cultural' power with the way the war on terror legislates special rules that permit detention without charge or trial in the USA, the UK, Australia, Malaysia, and so on? In his excellent book *The End of Tolerance: Racism in 21st Century Britain*, Arun Kundnani makes an unanswerable case against the erosion of civil rights and for recognition of the way this impacts particularly on minorities, and by extension on us all:

> Never before has such a vast and rapidly expanding accumulation of state power confronted young Asians, Africans and African-Caribbeans, Muslim and non-Muslim, immigrant and British-born. Under anti-terrorist powers, they face mass stop and search without reasonable grounds of suspicion ... They face new powers of arrest that dramatically extend time held in police custody prior to any charges being brought. They face the threat of raids in the early hours ... They face virtual house arrest without the right to defend themselves in court. They face mass surveillance at places of worship, at train stations and airports. They face the risk of armed police deploying shoot-to-kill tactics. They face prosecution for expressing unacceptable opinions, for protesting, for supporting foreign charities, for being members of political organisations deemed unacceptable to the government. Finally, they face the ultimate sanction of having their citizenship itself stripped away! (Kundnani 2007:167-8).

The news stories referenced obliquely in the above citation would only extend the list if detailed – over-policing and incompetence that leads to the death of civilians like Charles de

Menezes on the Stockwell tube, with no police punished; the Forest Gate shooting of innocent brothers, with ongoing harassment; the persecution of the 'lyrical terrorist' Samina Malik, with drawn out court case to examine her 'crime' of writing rhymes on a scrap of paper while at work at Heathrow; a range of other high profile 'cases' and prosecutions, detentions, deportations... All contributing to a climate of generalised suspicion, such that fellow passengers on the tube are wary, the airport check-in queue is an anxious one, citizens are confronted on the streets, taxi-drivers are beaten, Mosques are attacked – right through to a disproportionate attention to 'community cohesion' and the farce of Government insistence on British values. This escalation can only be described as a polymorphously perverse new mode of racism manifest in bizarre diverse and ubiquitous forms. To oppose all this is an obligation.

The worldwide erosion of civil liberties under the sign of a perverted new anxiety was already anticipated in Fun-da-Mental's ironic album title reference: *Erotic Terrorism*. It is also a species of pantomime argument to think that to mock, minimise and undermine the serious pronouncements of the dominant will undo its power and release us from repression. Thinking of the detention camps in Afghanistan and Iraq, certainly there is some credence to Fun-da-Mental's pre-September 11, 2001, prophecy that 'America Will Go to Hell' – in their anti-war anthem EP release (Fun-da-Mental 1999). The use of the Rap form to express a critique of American and United Nations, NATO or British Military imperialist activities surely indicates also a more nuanced relationship between politics and content than the unidirectionalist historians of hip-hop might warrant. The intervention in lyrics, sound and image is not only a comment on record industry promotional opportunism, but also references the ways commercial imperatives at the same time sanction a certain quietude about the politics of so-called anti-terrorism and the inadequacy of romantic and liberal anti-racism. No mere hybrid multiculti cross-ethnic particularity, Fun-da-Mental's call is to fight against the seductive terrorisms of complicity and conformity, the manipulation of market and law, the destruction of culture and civilisation in pursuit of oil.

What kind of change in the apparatus of the culture industry would be required to orient attention away from the industrial military entertainment complex? What would displace the ways people in the music press and mainstream academic community consistently deploy categories that are far removed from the actualities articulated in the Fun-da-Mental discussion? The critics appear deaf to ideas. In panto it is tradition for the audience to have to yell loudly: *'He's behind you!'* This could be the moment of critique, indicating another way of telling, but more often it is the classic staged scenario, and so I think what is needed is a more incisive and aggressive denunciation of the performance of well-intended hypocrites.

Back to the Kumars.

In pantomime one actor can play many roles, often telling their story through rhyme, song, dance and humour, not necessarily with particularly high literary or artistic pretensions, men in drag, bawdy women, double entendre, burlesque, knowing morals and audience involvement:

> From the very beginning the pantomime was acutely aware of the world around it ... no other form of entertainment has ever devoted itself so wholeheartedly to holding up to the public, for its approbation, censure, or mere amusement, the events, manners, whims and fancies, fads, crazes and absurdities of the time (Frow 1985:136)

This could describe Sanjeev Bhaskar's comedy, but a return to the heady innocent days of visiting 'The Kumars at No. 42' is not possible (BBC Comedy 2005). In the present era, such comedy is no longer so easy. Fun-da-Mental however still keep alive incisive critical expression through their oblique angles on world music in a time of war – it is this versus the clash of civilisations rhetoric that animates press interest today. Recall that pantomime, like comedy, sometimes can still speak truth to power, and thereby reveal its hypocritical co-ordinates, but quite often it is only holiday period entertainment.

Though, I am still not so sure. I used to think the counter-establishment charge of renegade pantomime made a lot more sense than the antics of those in power, but now I have to recognise that it is just as much the case that pantomime has changed, that it has become The News, and the stakes are much higher – and that entertainment must provoke thought and talk, or we die. Theatrical media presentation is not the only operational consideration since the war on terror, but as anxious commuters sit reading free digest tabloids about sports, celebrities and royalty on the tube, there are reasons to see the pantomime metaphor as productive. Stage left we hear the security announcement that reminds you of your bags, a hirsute gentlemen sitting opposite is treated with suspicion, the taxation system groans under a war economy that slides inexorably into the longest crisis, anniversaries come and go hardly questioned, Bradley Wiggins wins the Tour de France. Mediation here is the pantomime theatre write large, as Kracauer already noted for the Paris on the 1870s, 'lavish spectacle' (Kracauer 1937/1972:321) was a welcome distraction. Cue, the Olympic Games 2012, but even beyond the spectacle the necessary distraction sits uncomfortably upon a wider scene. Everyday life is staged, and the stage directions are visible even as they must be ignored. This is the brutality of an alienated self-terrorisation. They know it, but they do it anyway – awareness without escape, violence without violence.

In piercing complacency, Fun-da-Mental and Aki Nawaz took pantomime a step further, and managed to raise issues where others did less. This does not mean that other pantomime events have been displaced. But with *Cookbook DIY* the hypocrisy of ideological spin is creatively punctured. We are not dealing with a war between the West and Islam or something like the good v evil simplified cowboy scenario, but rather the contrast is between bombing campaigns of massive destructive power, devastation of societies – Afghanistan, Iraq, Gaza, Libya, Syria, militarism, the arms trade, detention, rendition, deportation, border controls, assassinations, and death *versus* a critical thinking that would oppose all this, and offer an alternative to this rotten and corrupt, deadly system peopled by uncaring privileged monstrosities. This is where Spivak is most interesting – for her mediation would be something like knowledge, reason, responsibility as material to be conjured with, interrupted in a persistent effort of the teacher through critique to rearrange, without coercion, ordained and pre-coded desires. Not just to fill up on knowledge and information but to further transnational literacy and an ethics of the other. On terror: the ethical interrupts the epistemological. There is a point at which the construction of the other as object of knowledge must be challenged: 'the ethical interrupts [law, reason] imperfectly, to listen to the other as if it were a self' (Spivak 2004:83).

The task suggested here – as accessed by Nawaz, even as recoded 'native informant' – is to accept complicity in a way that makes possible an identification, 'alive to visible injustice' (Spivak 2004:89) as well as 'not to endorse suicide bombing but to be on the way to its end' (Spivak 2004:93). The question is one of whether scholarly commentary achieves such steps, or is rather more concerned with some sort of judicious, but ultimately agnostic, balance. Hardt and Negri for example, play out the script:

> The suicide bomber is the dark opposite, the gory doppel-gänger of the safe bodyless soldier ... both ... deny the body at risk that traditionally defines combat, the one guaranteeing

its life and the other its death. We in no way mean to praise the
horrible practice of suicide bombing or justify it, as some do,
by casting it as the ultimate weapon against a system of total
control (Hardt and Negri 2004:45).

Is there in *Cookbook DIY* a message we can hear without an
automatic move towards punishment and vilification as per
readings like this and that of *The Guardian*? Here the ethical and
archival task that might be learnt from Spivak is that we should
read the text all the way through with a desire to learn what
Nawaz is saying. The track is a commentary on the hypocrisy of
war, and perhaps offers a chance 'to learn to learn' as well what
is in the mind, and what is the desire, or motivation, of the
suicide bomber, but more importantly also to ask about the
motivations and desires of the Pentagon war machine and its
complicit 'legitimate scientists' (Fun-da-mental 2006). Is it too
academic to identify the verses in the video as the process of
scholarly 'compare and contrast' essay-mongering, where the
terrors of suicide are run alongside State violence?

There are the beginnings of a cultural studies theorisation that
would attempt a more nuanced understanding of suicide
bombing in relation to State terror. Talal Asad's book *On Suicide
Bombing* is exemplary (2007), as is the aforementioned work of
Bhattacharyya who points out that there is a 'slim' emergent literature on how we might understand torture – not only why people
might be able to commit such outrages, or the techniques – the
manuals, the photos – but also what she calls the 'theatrics' of
how we might receive such news of pain (Bhattacharyya
2008:129). Other texts deserve a more critical appraisal. The
aforementioned Seidler offers a necessary but possibly too
obvious insistence that what is needed is:

to question the wisdom of the 'war on terror' that suggests a
military solution is possible without grasping the complex

historical, cultural and psychological sources that can help explain what draws ... young men [and women] into jihadist movements so as to engage with the injustices they see as justification for the destructive actions they sometimes take (Seidler 2007: xviii).

In the light of Research Council proposals that were heavily criticised for turning scholarship into politically partisan profiling – proposing to fund studies of how and why young Muslim men are radicalised – the politicisation of Islam becomes more or less overt cultural cleansing. Is it not possible to hear the call and recognise the 'connections' and sense of responsibility articulated in tube bomber Mohammed Sidique Khan's video message that declares 'until we feel security you will be our target. Until you stop the bombing, gassing, imprisonment and torture ... we will not stop this fight' (in Seidler 2007:8). The 'idea that to seek to understand how British-born and educated young men could turn to terror is to impart some legitimacy to terrorist acts' (Seidler 2007:18) is indeed a foreclosure of the breadth of scholarship, and rather committed learning, needed.

Spivak calls for an effort at transnational literacy that attempts – first without judgement – to comprehend and understand suicide bombing as more than a mute and blind event. 'Transnational *literacy* is not "knowledge"' (Spivak 2008:97). Admirable as it may be in terms of correcting the cannon, filling in the gaps by reading Islamic scholars does not necessarily ensure an adequate response to the current global crisis. It is necessary to tamper with the epistemological script. What defies comprehension is what must most be addressed – how can so many democratic, liberal, civilised people, stand by and watch mass murder, indiscriminate bombing, occupations, imperial plunder, and atrocity as televised entertainment without a deep anxiety? The trouble is that a focus on suicide bombing – or the suicide rapper – as a problem of Muslim youth, as a consequence of faulty child care, as something to be handled with 'better education' or 'community cohesion', means ignoring a much needed analysis of how such prejudice is established universally as a part of popular racism.

Spivak talks of a patient effort to rearrange desires. Part of this might be to consider how our desires, and fears, are performed in pantomime mediations. A lexicon consulting, slow and considered undoing/unlearning of privilege, rearranging of habits of knowing in favour of a rampant intelligence and effervescent creativity that would not presume itself the model for humanity, would participate in the multiversity of literacy and plot a way. I am not yet sure that it is impossible nor pointless to try to unmute the suicide bomber, but to do so even in humorous clothes – dressed as pantomime – necessarily accepts and obeys, just as suicide does, the internalised political order that itself does the muting. This is the structure of suicide that is impossible. The muteness of bombers precludes full vocalisation and opens the event to ventriloquy. This is not accidental – the terror is that meaning is unmoored, toppled, undermined, and a scramble to rebuild a shattered certainty exposes that very power that was certain. Spivak suggests we consider the death drive (Spivak 2012:239) and so perhaps the ways aphony releases many echoes and reverberations so that the certitude of narcissistic world trade centre phallocentrocacy can be capped.

Is it wrong to think that the surge of academic commentary on 9-11 and 7/7 itself should be read as a wider message – an enduring, even infinitely interpreted and interpretable event – more than 'less than nothing' (Žižek 2012)? Could this ever excuse a failure to think through the links of the war to the economic crisis? Not to do so is a severe myopia, even while it is continually discussed – and while it is not necessary for every author to relate the story of where they were on the day, from who they heard of the atrocities, in which bar they watched the images, the impulse means something. The subsequent meditations on multiculturalism, cultural isolation, cultural mix, concerns about surveillance and assertions of 'complexity' are all also a message to be read – but as Les Back laments, we have yet to find a way of describing the daily struggle of how to live together (Back 2007:149) without it becoming 'Total Film'.

> In New York, the absence of the twin towers has prompted a constant re-enactment of their twin forms in the city landscape and in the architectural imagining of how to rebuild Ground Zero (Sturken 2007:29).

It is a part of the necessary effort that we take time to read the context of reading. For example, when there is a newspaper report on the terror war we might first ask how the tone seems to channel common-sense and the mundane – as if reading were informed by two parts terror fatigue, one part conspiracy theory and three parts dull acceptance of the creeping constraint of austerity and curtailed civil liberties. Can we read the repetition of 'suicide rap' sensation stories as a clearing operation to filter out the noise of irony or coincidence that might have distracted from the required emotive response that the picture of the bombed-out bus was chosen to provide? The side-on shot would interfere with the choreography.

> Fear of the enemy next door has become a key weapon in statecraft, placating the populism of the tabloid press and garnering political support and public opinion (Back 2007:143)

This is the 'he's behind you' pantomime banality of the news. And indeed we are all potential terrorists now, not citizens but suspects. This is the position of MI5 as gleaned from the classified 'Briefing Note' reported by *The Guardian* that came from the Behavioural Science Unit, funded to the tune of at least

45 million pounds under the British Government 'Prevent' strategy (*Guardian* August 20 2008). The language of the report is glossed by the *Guardian* editorial (we get to read very little of the report itself) to suggest a certain kind of torture of both grammar and concept:

> the majority of radical terrorists are British nationals, not foreigners, and most of those who are foreign are here legally. They are also ethnically diverse (as the UK Muslim population is), including individuals from many ethnic backgrounds, including Caucasians (Guardian 2008)

The newspaper quotes from the report, which circulated amongst the security services in June 2008, read similarly: 'terrorists ... are a diverse collection of individuals, fitting no single demographic profile, nor do they all follow a typical pathway to violent extremism' and 'The majority are British nationals and the remainder, with few exceptions, are here legally' (Guardian 2008).

I am not suggesting that there are no 'terrorists' but that the timing of the report, the wider context of both anniversary of the London bombings and proximity to two legal cases underway at the time (July 21 2005 failed bombers trial and the Munshi trial) – plus the then immanent de Menezes inquest make it important that we do not miss the complexities of media timetabling. There is an anniversary algorithm to the management of the terror war, every July, every September, not unrelated to the dynamics of a beleaguered national polity in an anxious world. A last gasp strategic offensive in the face of the rise of Asian powers, the management of a polarising division posits diaspora as exoticism on the one side and a dangerous multicultural terror on the other. That this must be routinised as surveillance for all is a bi-product of anxiety. Geopolitics on a global scale is one context, the geopolitical scaled down to domestic disorganisation is another.

So, we must ask what spin the civilisation-mongers offer as

cover for their death march? The spectacle of Mr and Mrs G. W. Bush placing a wreath in a wading pool at the base of former WTC on the evening before the fifth anniversary of September 11 2001 was quite bizarre. This was not cross dressing, but crocodile tears – and more images of Bush looking edgy only make it more important to listen to the late Gore Vidal and his concern with the 'the destruction of the [US] Republic' as inaugurated after 2001 in the guise of Homeland Security; Guantánamo; Rendition; endorsement of torture etc. Vidal quips that the term 'Homeland Security' is reminiscent of the Third Reich – 'Der Homeland' was not a phrasing he had heard from an American before 'it was forced on us' by the Government. This was on BBC radio (11 Sept 2006) – Vidal self-styled as 'spokesman for Carthage on Roman radio', defender of 'the Constitution' against the oil and gas tyranny, and against the collusive 'dreadful media'. We have not just lost some buildings, far worse is that we lost the Republic.

This would not be the argument made by Aki Nawaz, but the echoes of concerns with buildings, silencing, freedom and rights recur. I am amazed that the most critical voices that break through the tabloid haze of justifications for war are those of novelists and musicians. Representative politics seems to have avoided such forthright discussion. In the video for *Cookbook DIY*, pantomime characters make the argument in each of the *three* verses. The first entails a cross-of-St-George-wearing youth constructing a strap-on bomb from a recipe downloaded from the internet. That he is dressed as a rabbit and as a lizard in parts of the verse is Fun-da-Mental playing on childlike toys and fears; the second verse references the radical scholar and the figure of the armed guerrilla as the character relates a more cynical employment as a mercenary making a 'dirty bomb' with fission materials bought on the black market in Chechnya or some such; the third pantomime figure is the respectable scientist. Here, the scientist in a lab coat morphs improbably-critically into a member of the Ku Klux Klan and then a suited businessman, building a neutron bomb that destroys people 'but leaves the buildings intact'. This outrageous pantomime allows Nawaz to point out the hypocrisy of an Empire with no clothes. The co-ordinated class response to the inversion of Empire – 'we are here because you were there' – is then articulated in a heavy-handed management of immigration law, police procedure, cultural exoticism and policy privilege – token community-ism. Minor conflicts on the ground are escalated so the new hierarchies can be worked out, with denigration of cultural specificity in favour of an obsolete national mourning. The terrors we are offered every night on the news are pantomime terrors as well, a performance melodrama, operatically grandiose. The scale they require – weapons of mass destruction; Saddam's show trial, the hunt for and execution of Osama – is exaggerated in a way that welcomes oblique internalisation. Here the absurdity of *The Guardian*, and parliamentary, mock scandal over the first verse is easily skewered by watching the next few minutes of the clip, verses two and three. What is more difficult to understand is why in general it is deemed more important to investigate how British youth might be radicalised than the surely more pressing issue of why billions of taxpayers' money can be allocated to a futile war, to the development of huge weapons arsenals, to a global surveillance system and the entire military-industrial-entertainment apparatus. It is not self-evident why we comply, why juvenile delinquency and pranks are more inflammatory than the new crusade. Is it only in pantomime video that these criticisms can be aired? The figures in each of the verses are patently absurd, yet all the more effective as incitements. Alongside this, the political legacy of anti-racist anti-imperialism is in danger of being lost in favour of an abstracted mediation that moves rapidly from politics to art and humour. The contemplation of conceptual, reified, fetishised trinkets is at its worst when art criticism presents itself as critical politics itself.

Perhaps Vidal's Republic was also always a pantomime scene

in the US anyway. But we might also understand the discombob-ulation of the Presidential bloopers – G.W. Bush's varied faux pas or Barack Obama's stalled yes-we-can-hope – as deflection of an otherwise unbearable present. If it were not so serious you would have to laugh; you have to laugh because it is so serious. Pantomime lets you off the hook – a venerably old form, it repeats as nonsense and doggerel that which is also a piece of mischief with brutal effects. Simple contrasts of good and bad, cold climates over hot, white skin over brown, profit over need – the battle is not one between a civilisation that would close down democracy in order to save it and a desperation become hostility through persecution. Rather, each polarised position is a myth-making by those who could not face the gradients of interpre-tation and nuance. The myths told as if to children infantilise ourselves – dressed up as instructional, educational, doctrinal knowledges, we evade confrontation with the blunt truth that the 'better angels of our nature' have been sleeping. Benjamin's historical storyteller remains silent, replaced by a ventriloquist perjury, peddler of lies, merchant of death, arms trader.

The pantomime performance of presidents and prime ministers make me think also of Alain Badiou, in *Infinite Thought* (2005), pointing out the non-equivalence of terror directed at a couple of buildings by a non-State entity – 'the terrorists' – and the retribution that is visited on all of our lives by the State Terror directed by US Forces; aimed first at peasants, villagers and the dispossessed everywhere, but then also directed at those in the 'we' through security legislation and so on. Critical support rendered where appropriate: Badiou's essay on terror in that book is a fine critical academic discussion no doubt. Yet more needs to be done to challenge the way the war on terror has become the name for a framework that adopts horrendous sabotage as an opportunity to mount a decades long counter-attack on the emergent anti-capitalism and anti-imperialist movement in the South. What was a site-specific atrocity became a headline-grabbing permanent state of global counter-insurgency. There are reasons to stress this wider perspective, even as the terror extends to covert activity by secret service agencies; includes surveillance operations across the globe; a plethora of dark underworld gadgetry; removes all vestige of civil liberties at 'home'; and prepares us for perpetual war 'over there'. Having seen-off the Soviet threat by way of an escalating nuclear production race, war fascism and the Marshall Plan, and having seen off the initial waves anti-colonial resistance, and victory in Vietnam, with comprador alliance and development aid, the almost forgotten history of the previous century is superseded by a two-pronged approach of arms sales and bombing patterns – with bombs for democracy to forestall any international Muslim alliance, or 'International' (Žižek 2004a:18), from Kosovo to the Philippines. This triumph of militarism is the logical consequence of – on the face it, depite the sexually potent metaphor, he has a point– the *impotence* of anti-war demonstrations, even when two million march it is also only a kind of pantomime performance. Comments on impotence here can also be read as compensation and displacement for the Left's own abject failure, despite much posturing, to organise a winning opposition to capital at a time when things are ripe and there are genuine uprisings all over, brutally put down by the police, NATO or co-opted by Islamist elements because nothing else was on offer as resistance. The diagnosis here should be treated reflexively, though it is more than symptomatic that Žižek himself can never confess to being mute. Having read our critical theory, onwards we marched to Hyde Park to hide – *'He's behind you'* – we sat down tired to rest when we should have sat on Blair, and not moved till he resigned.

This does not mean I want to bring back the days when pantomime was just a cute summer seaside entertainment and music was just an excuse for dancing. I wish it were possible to laugh this away, but it is not. The point would be to remember theatre as a metaphor for thought or, if Badiou is to be acknowledged as a source for this thought, with dance as restraint, theatre as acting, and as ideas (Badiou 1998/2005:72). What pantomime in its fun-filled public performance form has as a political compliment is the tragic demonisations of an insecure and infantilised politics. Doppelgängers of a pampered megalomaniac will not scan. This can be taken forward with Adorno and Spivak into a conscious working at the double-bind in the performance. Scheherazade's story, like Don Quixote or Odysseus chained to the mast to hear the sirens call – these are allegorical and traps for thinking at the same time. As art, story-telling can only be step one of a politics, although it is perhaps still what we need to rethink and disrupt the usual categories. As provoked by Fun-da-Mental, music and politics can, I believe, destabilise otherwise dangerous certainties: and that can only be better than the unthinking with which we are often now forced to abide. With a wry smile, I have started to listen once again.

3

Dub at the Movies

What a strange pleasure it is to dress up. To have fantasy Peter Pan and pirate adventures, to play at the ritual and extravagance of grown-up pageantry, to unpack the box of mother and father's old fashions and swan about in splendid disguise. Costume and kit, scarves, hats and belts, wide lapel shirts and bell-bottom trousers – accessories beyond the necessary and everyday that encourage whimsy and nonsense. The capers and hi-jinks, escapades and caricatured exaggerations of youth are all well and fine. But now we must have done with juvenilia and put away those things, no longer adolescent or childlike or fools. The time of government and politics and matters of state are upon us. And this turns out to be the greatest stage of all. Pomp and ceremony, flamboyant performance and a greater self-deception than was ever ventured in any sandpit or fairground. I do not mean to demote by analogy or have you acknowledge that issues of importance are metaphorically 'like' a carousel of repetition or a masked ball of intrigue – but I do think matters of state are infantilised, that the tricks of the media circus are just that, tricks, and that clowns rule in Whitehall. Yet the circus is nothing if it does not move. And at many levels the performative expression of adult life has descended into a high-velocity circuit of tendential repetition, and we know this, even as we set it aside as appearance, and all the world is staged and Capital is in slump.

I will turn to art to analyse this, and within art I turn to film music, because perhaps it is the least likely place, perhaps the best – show-tunes! – to sound out the politics of performance. To start with the aestheticisation of politics as the site of a necessary procedure of transparency – it is Ranciére on Adorno who again shows us how to see the 'autonomy' of art as 'a twofold heteronomy' that allows us 'to denounce the capitalist division of work and the embellishments of commodities' (Ranciére 2004/2009:41). The mechanical and inhuman of the autonomous work's 'beautiful technical arrangement' recalls 'the capitalist separation of work and enjoyment' (Ranciére 2004/2009:41). At the very moment that art 'takes up a combat against culture' it institutes a frontline 'of works against cultural products, of things against images, of images against signs and of signs against simulacra' (Ranciére 2004/2009:43). Here the danger is that this 'politics' of art becomes mere testimony to the other, and is not supplemented by anything political at all. Adorno more than Ranciére will lament the failure to achieve a political redress that would make the autonomy of art worth its cause:

> revolutionary art movements ... did not bestow the promised happiness of adventure. Instead, the process that was unleashed consumed the categories in the name for that which it was undertaken ... freedom in art, always limited to a particular, comes into contradiction with the perennial unfreedom of the whole. In it the place of art became uncertain. The autonomy it achieved, after having freed itself from the cultic function and its images, was nourished by the idea of humanity. As society became ever less a human one, this autonomy was shattered ... Yet art's autonomy remains irrevocable. All efforts to restore art by giving it a social function – of which art is itself uncertain and by which it expresses its own uncertainty – are doomed (Adorno 1970/1997:1).

If this can be read as a lament that any revolutionary emancipation in art remains unmatched by a similar social development, it is still the case that Adorno holds that, though it is 'uncertain whether art is still possible' (Adorno 1970/1997:1), an art that is 'perceived strictly aesthetically is art aesthetically misperceived' (Adorno 1970/1997:6). The aestheticisation of politics might be a different matter, and though art might somewhere have kept a distance from slavish attachment to parliament, the insistence from Ranciére that the events of September 11 did not inaugurate any 'rupture in the symbolic order' but rather was a further moment of the 'eclipse of an identity that is inclusive of alterity' (Ranciére 2010:104) seems plausible. Ranciére notes that when the towers fell the then American president did not behave as if he had watched too many Westerns, since the sheriff usually puts his authority on the line to rescue the accused from the lynch mob and deliver them to justice. He instead insisted on 'infinite justice' and in Congress on September 21, 2001 when he gave his 'they hate us because we have the freedom of opinion that we so please' speech the very plausibility of this line would have required at least some of the Congress 'refrain from rising up and applauding in unison' (Ranciére 2010:100). Against consensus then, the autonomy of parliament and the *dissensus* of art as alienated appearance-form of the political struggle we ought to have, but do not.

Adorno also loved Westerns, and Clarence the cross-eyed lion from the wildlife show *Daktari* (Müller-Doohm 2003/2005:467), but this is more interesting when he notes that art – almost alone – refuses to fully dissolve into a rampant commercialism. There are those that think reification and recuperation are complete, but there are others who can discern that something still survives of conflict. I wonder if storytelling can still be redeemed, retooled for a politics of multiplicity in the face of reaction. For example, Adorno notes that even cultural oblivion does not destroy 'The great epics' which in their own age were 'intermingled with historical and geographical reportage' (Adorno 1970/1997:6). He comments explicitly on the *1001 Nights*, as we will see in the next chapter, but here it might be plausible to intentionally misperceive and tamper with aesthetic autonomy in order to retrieve the political element that demands of art the question it set itself when it claimed autonomy and then, impotently, became autonomous. Can there still be an art that questions? 'Only dilletantes reduce everything in art to the unconscious, repeating clichés' (Adorno 1970/1997:9). Contra the malicious pointing at artists as 'tolerated' and 'integrated as a neurotic in a society sworn to the division of labour' (Adorno 1970/1977:9), a recognition that distortion and fantasy in art also indicates a desire for a better world, where muted revolutionary aspirations must be matched by a movement for change. To the extent art points in this direction, the dark cannot be clarified by meaning (Adorno 1970/1997:27), but interpreted as a down-payment 'on empirical research yet to be done' (Adorno 1970/1997:32). Perhaps it is worth exploring Adorno's comment that there 'are historical moments in which forces of production emancipated in art represent a real emancipation that is impeded by the relations of production' (Adorno 1970/1997:33). It is the gamble of this chapter that some epic arts, in particular those involved with sonic interpretations of the screen – music and video – offer a scene on which to work out this emancipation.

Thus, to illustrate what Ranciére might relegate as testimony to the Other in the 'beautiful technical arrangement' (Ranciére 2004/2009:41) that recalls the capitalist separation of work and pleasure, witness a sequence in Gillo Pontecorvo's film *The Battle of Algiers* – scenario Franco Solinas, music by Ennio Morricone, winner of the Golden Lion at Venice in 1966. When the women prepare themselves as if for a party, listening to music, they are about to infiltrate the French quarter and bomb a café, travel agent and market. This is not just a game of cultural dress-ups. There is a plan here, and so good reason to reconsider this scene (discussed further as a coda to this chapter). The scenario is tense, the risks profound, the meaning significant, the transgression a shock – and the fallout continues. It will be my argument in this chapter that these, and other similar, cinema and televisional forms are part of a wider performative and aesthetic politics. Music and theatre are the forum of revolt when established and credited political representatives are too much enamoured by rhetoric and their own comforts to attend to matters that matter. With the industrial scenography of film music as organisational frame in mind, the chapter takes Badiou and Žižek to task for loose comments on 'the riots' – both in Paris and in London – and evaluates Derrida's somewhat Adorno-esque – if that is a word – methodological effort to appreciate the lumpen and the street as inscription. I hope a critique of this by way of Marx, Mao, Spivak and an angular view of New York and Lagos will not seem too out of place.

Representing *La Haine*.

'Music is a weapon of mass destruction' say Asian Dub Foundation, and the reference to the spurious excuses given to justify the launch of the Iraq war resonates here under the sign of terror. The soundtrack of the earlier Gulf War (1991) was already established with heavy metal flyovers on the road to Basra. The 'Turkey Shoot' against retreating Iraqi military and civilian convoys was accompanied by a Van Halen song in one video compilation of the subsequent carnage, released months later. Images from that highway are clear evidence of a war crime, and though they were charged, US forces were not brought before the International War Crimes Tribunal (see the documentary 'Highway of Death' 2007). Perpetual war as melodrama screened in the theatre-courts of civil society proliferates similar scenes over and over presented in similar terms, with AC/DC's 'Highway to hell' played across images of troops arriving in Iraq in 2002 ('Highway to Hell' 2006), and the bombing of Baghdad, tanks, unspent ordinance and manifold death displayed in a remix version of the same song by Marilyn Manson ('Iraq – Highway to Hell' 2006). The George 'Dub-ya' Bush crusade even came with a musical element in the Doonsbury cartoon strip where Humvee patrol squads selected combat ready track mixes for their Government-issue Ipods. As one returned soldier wrote: 'some guys listen to death metal before missions, some listen to melodic pop during fire fights – whatever it takes to get you through', as noted on the Doonsbury Iraq and Afghanistan veterans support pages (Slate 2008). Unsurprisingly, the DJ in the Doonsbury strip takes shrapnel to the head and is returned Stateside wounded and mute. A comic strip pointedly does not carry an audio track and neither can a mediated version of war, lest complacency be disturbed. Some years ago it was sensationally reported that Iraqi detainees in shipping containers were subjected to Metallica's 'Enter Sandman' at high volume (BBC News May 20th 2003) and Guantánamo Detention Camp interrogators made use of music mix tapes blasted at detainees on a rotation that would make Madonna proud if it were MTV. A range of 'acoustic weapons' have been developed by the American Technology Corporation and such weaponry have been part of the US arsenal since the mid-1990s (Cusick 2006:10, Goodman 2009). No doubt music as a weapon of mass distraction also extends to the soundtrack of the screen image of war at home, and in this regard, Asian Dub Foundation's sonic creativity is able to insert a sharp message to catch our attention as we watch. them play music over old films as a way to re-educate and inspire youth, bringing Drum and Bass to the cinema hall and finding new audiences for images and ideas too often overlooked.

The scenes I want to remix in this chapter are also ones where video projection and sound sync/mix technology are made to come and go in curious leaps and loops. Once upon a time the screen image required accompaniment by a live performer at a piano, today, such a throw back to the old black and white days of immediately present live sound is rare, even nostalgic. With ADF's forays into theatre, a calculated and curious staging renews our appreciation of the artifice of sync, although the old piano is now new electric and the 'live' now requires mixing desks, digital precision, planned sequencing and programmed synthesisers. ADF's line-up includes John Pandit, a speaker at the RampArts discussion in the previous chapter. The band's performances over film offer another kind of screening of terror, and another kind of performance theatre. ADF have had considerable success filling cinema halls with new audiences for old films. An impressive revival of a past format, thinking about how this technology is used can perhaps help our understanding of the pursuit of innovative modes of political activism and give a perspective on commentary sorely needed.

ADF screen movies with intent. Their practice is grounded in Community Music youth organising, working with young people and adults from 13 years up to 'provide music making opportunities for people of all backgrounds' (Community Music 2011). They have tinkered with the very format of the band, formed a youth wing, and education wing, collaborated with the English National Opera on an excellent, if critically received, soundtrack for Gaddafi in 2006. On Gaddafi, Steve 'Chandrasonic' Savale of ADF said he wanted to know what was behind the archetype: 'the demon – the Osama bin Laden of his time' (Denselow 2006). Internationally acclaimed, ADF have presented their work at the Royal Festival Hall in London among other prestigious venues. As part of a diversified creative output, for many years now they have used the 1995 Mathieu Kassowitz film *La Haine* as a vehicle for a cinema-music experiment, where the story of three youths caught up in unrest – which itself occurs largely off screen – in the Parisian *banlieue*, is presented with a *live* ADF soundtrack. Kassowitz's most famous film has a particular relevance given that it has come to be taken as anticipating events in the Paris suburbs ten years after, in November 2005, as discussed by several theorists, for example Badiou (2011/2012) and, as already mentioned, in Žižek, especially with his *Violence*, but also in subsequent texts (Žižek 2008, 2012:998).

What is noticeable in commentaries by big-name theorists is a consistent refrain that seems to be on auto-pilot, reiterating a negative assessment. I do not think this is merely a result of spotlight productivity demands – the pressure to say something every time a microphone passes within range, I want instead to link this negativity with the Paris riots and the question of the 'message' content of Kassowitz's film, as a way to tease out an analysis. Unsurprisingly, this will not be the first time the link has been made, or the first suggestion that commentators have misunderstood the youth, the band or the film (Higbee 2006:122). There are many ways in which the search for a message in so-called 'street violence' parallels speculative divination in film criticism, with equally wayward results. However, I do not want to focus only upon representation and the repetition 'in the real' of the events 'in the film' as such, except insofar as this coincidence has governed the framing work of cultural critics, like Žižek, and in the next section of this chapter, the work of Jacques Derrida in *Rogues* (2003/2005). Derrida's comments also predate the 2005 riots and yet they anticipate certain assumptions and anxieties in quite surprising ways. In the first instance however, I am more interested here in the volatile scene of the reworked screening of a French film replayed in Britain, a film which itself is very much alert to the politics of representation. Reanimated by ADF, there is also much to say on the reverberation of screens, the imbrications of the screen and the street – and there will also be much to say about the screen, the street, and of youth with regard to theory – such that when shown in the UK, the film is meant to evoke parallels and differences in terms of race, suburban alienation, and the politics of the imagination, especially with regard to thinking about meaning and terror.

Where is the terror? *La Haine* begins with a Molotov cocktail, set across the background of a shot of the planet as seen from space. The incendiary device is falling, and spinning as it falls, towards the earth as pictured from afar. A voice recounts a story of someone who fell from a tall building, and as he passed each floor on the way down, he said aloud: '*jusqu'ici tout va bien*' (*So far, so good, so far, so good*). Ash and Sanjay Sharma have written perceptively on this film, suggesting that this 'anxious repetition of assurance' might be dubbed 'the inner voice of liberal democracy' (Sharma and Sharma 2000:103). The Sharma brothers link this reassurance to the critical scene of the journalists visiting the suburbs only to be confronted as intruders by the youth, chased with their television cameras back to the safer boulevards. The scene is explosive, the journalists do not get their story, they flee to their car, the youth shout that their home is no theme park, and the critique of journalism is grounded in ways easy enough for every viewer to grasp.

Perhaps not every viewer. It is time to specify in more detail the ways where an outer-urban anti-racism and anti-imperialism, with music – it is easy to say that music plays a crucial role in *La Haine* – might work towards a militancy in the heart of capitalism that remains inaccessible to the grand old men of theory. Neglected mobilisations may offer more in terms of global justice and reparations than the unexamined culturalisms, nationalisms and exoticisms of authorised textbook third-worldist 'resistance' or the revolutionary defeatism of a self-appointed fifth column within the elite theory, art, publishing camp. I have in mind explicitly patronising dismissals of the suburban. In *The Rebirth of History*, Badiou examines an old trope: the 'blind destruction and pillaging of the very place the rioters live in' (Badiou 2011/2012:24) and he explains that a riot is, in the first instance, 'a tumultuous assembly of the young, virtually always in response to a misdemeanour, actual or alleged, by a despotic state' (Badiou 2011/2012:23). The first word to underline here is 'blind' and on the same page Badiou refers to 'sheep-like' assemblies of people, insisting this repeats over the centuries, and indeed works by way of 'contagion' and imitation:

we observe a phenomenon dubbed contagion: *an immediate riot spreads not by displacement, but by imitation. And this imitation occurs in sites that are similar, even largely identical, to the initial focal point. Youth on a housing estate in Saint-Ouen are going to do the same thing as those on an estate in Aulnay-sous-Bois. The popular districts of London are all going to be affected by the collective fever* (Badiou 2011/2012:24 his italics).

I am sure Badiou knows Paris well, but for the moment I will leave aside the question of how well he knows what occurred in London in August 2011, and whether a Police killing can ever be seen as a misdemeanour. For now I want to note again the affliction metaphors – a fever, a contagion and blindness. However hedged these terms may be with contexts and the effort to name vast sweeps of history – the 'communist hypothesis' from Plato to Badiou – the argument of this book will be that characterisations of youth motivation in this way are problematic, and deeply racist. Why is it, for example, important to focus upon youth motivation rather than the consequences of State retaliation? We will have cause to consider some historic examples below, contra Badiou, in support of the United Family and Friends Campaign for an End to Deaths in Custody. To insist on reading campaign materials alongside, and even against, the pronouncements of important current theorists is to risk what Nirmal Puwar identifies as a renegade break with the 'chummy relations' of polite scholarship in the academy (Puwar 2004:138-9). But where Badiou sets out his codec for riots immediate and historical, it is again by way of an affliction, where:

amid the destruction of hated symbols, the profitable pillaging, the sheer pleasure in smashing what exists, the joyous whiff of gunpowder and guerrilla warfare against the cops (Badiou 2011/2012:26)

Even if the reader can tell Badiou finds this exciting, it is still the case that 'a riot cannot purify itself … [and in the riot] … one cannot really see clearly' (Badiou 2011/2012:26). Blind again. This sounds like grumbling – *so far so good*. It should be pointed out that Badiou is trying to set out a typology of riots that will then lead to the 'Historical Riot' which itself produces extensions, it offers a long-term temporality that extends an immediate riot into a pre-political event that endures (Badiou 2011/2012:35). Politely, I reject this starting point, this pathologising at the origins, that we hear in the recurrent language of medicine and diagnosis.

Žižek-degree-zero.

Badiou, as usual, is not alone in his repetitions. Noting that the Paris *banlieue* protests involved mass burning of cars – scenes of vehicles ablaze, overplayed with interviews with various authorities – and claiming these were direct protests at the then interior minister Sarkozy calling the protesters *racaille* (scum), Žižek then calls this an 'outburst with no pretence to vision' (Žižek 2008:63), and a 'zero-level' protest against the reaction to their protests. In an ironic tone, perhaps smartly self-critical, perhaps not, this 'zero-degree' phrasing would be adopted by Žižek over and over, for example also later in *Less Than Nothing* (2012, with slight changes, marked below). Never a thought that was not published, twice, Žižek says there was an 'irony in watching the sociologists, intellectuals and commentators trying to understand and help' (Žižek 2008:64). He warns against the 'hermeneutic temptation' to find meaning or a 'message hidden in the outbursts' (Žižek 2008:65). Any message of the protests is erased and reduced to Sarkozy-bashing, well-deserved I am sure, but condensed, impotent, frustrated. And yet, our commentator himself only offers snap-phrased recycled interpretations, as he turns again to the theme of the absence of meaning that he earlier attributed to the 'event' of the WTC destruction. He says of the

French riots, 'the fact that there was *no* programme behind the burning Paris suburbs is thus itself a fact to be interpreted' (Žižek 2008:64). That this might be described as a 'blind acting out' seems itself ironic and also possibly blind, even when Žižek may be correct to mock the sociological 'search for deeper meaning' (Žižek 2008:65), especially if these searches are undertaken from the comfort of the television viewing room or the boulevard café. But this most favoured passage, which is cut and pasted almost unchanged into *Less Than Nothing*, Žižek himself spends two further pages explaining that the youth wanted to be recognised as French, and locates these events in a particular way as different to terrorist attacks with religious 'Meaning' (Žižek 2012:998). Here I expand the parameters of the quotation already used earlier in this book:

The Paris riots need to be situated in a series they form with another type of violence that the liberal majority perceives as a threat to our way of life: direct ['direct' removed in the Žižek 2012:998 version] terrorist attacks and suicide bombings. In both instances, violence and counter-violence are caught up in a deadly vicious cycle, each generating the very forces it tries to combat. In both cases we are dealing with blind *passages à l'acte*, where violence is an implicit admission of impotence. The difference is that, in contrast to the Paris outbursts ['or British riots' – added in Žižek 2012:998] which were a zero-level protest, a violent outburst which wanted nothing, terrorist attacks are carried out on behalf of that *absolute* meaning provided by religion (Žižek 2008:69).

We cannot be sure Žižek has fully understood Paris, or London, either here, nor should we be detained by his assertion that religion is the *absolute* designation of terrorism – consider the three verses of Fund-da-Mental's 'Cookbook DIY' again. It is the ascription of 'nothing' as the meaning of the Paris-London or religion-motivated riots that raises problems with commentary. The *Less Than Nothing* version capitalises the word 'Meaning' (2012:998) in the updated quote, suggesting that some more assertive – not nothing – ideological underpinning threatens, even as it is left vague as 'blind', 'without vision', undemanding and 'mute'.

Žižek had already made significant claims for meaninglessness and pathology in relation to the September 11, 2001 attacks on New York. His commentary recalls that of Buck-Morss on the spectacular where she suggests that the 'staging of violence as a global spectacle separates September 11 from previous acts of terror' as she also dwells upon the absence of message – 'They left no note behind … *Or did they*?' (Buck-Morss 2003:23-4 my italics). More uncompromising and perhaps mischievous, Žižek in *Welcome to the Desert of the Real*, presents the event in his own peculiarly Lacanian perspective on 'perversion':

> The spectacular explosion of the WTC towers was not simply a symbolic act (in the sense of an act whose aim is to 'deliver a message'): it was primarily an explosion of lethal *jouissance*, a perverse act of making oneself the instrument of the big Other's *jouissance* (Žižek 2002:141)

At least in *Welcome to the Desert of the Real* he does argue something along the lines of the intent of 'Cookbook DIY' when he accepts that there is 'much more ethical insanity in a military strategist planning and executing large scale bombing operations than in an individual blowing himself up in the process of attacking the enemy' (Žižek 2002:141-2). However, he makes himself somewhat obscure when he says of September 11 that 'the ultimate aim of the attacks was not some hidden or obvious ideological agenda but – precisely in the Hegelian sense of the term – to (re)introduce the dimension of absolute negativity into our daily lives' (Žižek 2002:142). What is most disturbing in Žižek's sexualised refrain of *impotence* and *l'acte* is that the various events to which he attaches this sobriquet become interchangeable. An erasure of the specificity of spontaneous uprisings, insufficiently subject to the organising gaze of the organiser who does not organise – waiting as he is, with Badiou, for the event.

This seems to me to be a deeply conservative negativity – even if I am conscious that the 'Total Film' message on the side of the 7/7 bus has, even if not intentional, an ambiguity and uncanny charge. Something like Rumsfeld's unknown unknowns is at play here as well, and I note Frank Furedi's report of Osama bin Laden's radio broadcast of March 1997:

> The hearts of Muslims are filled with hatred towards the United States of America and the American president has a heart that knows no words. A heart that kills hundreds of children definitely, knows no words. Our people in the Arabian Peninsula will send him messages with no words because he does not know any words (in Furedi 2007:78-79)

Is there a message nevertheless? In *La Haine*, when three youths, Vinz, Saïd and Hubert are stranded in the centre of the city, without access to the metro to get them home, they see reports from the 'riots' on a public multi-screen, and learn of the death of one of their comrades. The significance of this death is less often mentioned in other commentaries on the film, though it should be recalled how often a death at the hands of the police is reported as an antecedent for urban uprisings. Let's repeat: it is never just a misdemeanour. Film commentary is not the same as journalism of course, so while I would note this disjunct as also another moment of 'message' disconnection, the focus of film studies on images should also be no surprise. Tellingly, the opening Molotov cocktail does not play a bigger role in the film, though this is a Parisian icon, and the off-screen deployment of Molotov can be assumed as *La Haine*'s back-story. The name Molotov – from the Russian *molot*, 'hammer' – and the importance of this preferred weapon in the historical confrontation of the street, should not be forgotten: first of all used by the Finns, borrowing the technique from Spain, but adding the name from the Commissar. Later, Paris 1968 makes the cocktail a potent symbol of rebellious youth. Fast forward: the Molotov is out of fashion in the Paris of a new century as apparently the 2005 disturbances were not much noticed by Parisians for the first few days because they have become so used to thinking that burning cars are a normal part of *banlieue* life. The 2012 Adorno Prize winner, Judith Butler, commented in 2009 that the 2005 demonstrations in France 'took aim at property, not persons' (Butler 2009:115) and:

> were widely interpreted as the violent and a-relational acts of young men whose family structures were lacking firm paternal authority ... [and so it was argued] the state must therefore act as a compensatory parent ... develop[ing] a host of reasons for regulating family and school life in the banlieue (Butler 2009:116)

This routine of bad parenting and interventionist state will not seem unfamiliar. The grotesque aspect is that even if these were adequate explanations, the standard middle-class rejoinder to the ways the state 'responds to such insurgency through consolidating and augmenting its power in relation to biopolitics and kinship arrangements' (Butler 2009:116) is generally unremarked. Less than nothing is the meaning as the chattering classes go about their business, quaffing their aperitifs with elegant ease, concerned only if it is their car that gets destroyed – as in Hanif Kureshi's hilarious much earlier critique of Sammie's car being overturned during the riots in *Sammie and Rosie Get Laid* (1987 dir.

Frears). Of course upwardly mobile Sammie, or a bourgeois academic sipping café-crème in a bistro on the boulevard in Paris is an easy image to lampoon. Yet the mention of boulevards should alert us to something of wider importance. This is a two-way street and we should not forget the injunction from Adorno that warmongers applaud melodies and the very people that profess an easy appreciation of the arts are also those who burn books and destroy synagogues. In a letter to Benjamin, Adorno describes how his own father was beaten, jailed and his offices wrecked in the pogroms (Adorno to Benjamin Feb 1, 1939, Benjamin-Adorno 1999:298). Today public libraries are closed down in a mercenary austerity drive while mosques are firebombed and English Defence League graffiti defends drone attacks on Muslim lands – a new drawn-out Kristallnacht. Molotov be damned.

Derrida Writes the Way.

Also in receipt of an Adorno Prize, but back in 2001, Derrida meditates in his acceptance talk on a suggestion from Adorno that linked dreams with violence. If we were to pay attention to repetition we might start with a certain worry that 'you have to start by worrying if you want to do a little thinking'. This suggests, for Derrida, the impossible possibility of another thinking, that he has tried to paint in the courses he taught, 'getting out of breath over it… rushing about', a philosophy that might draw some 'ethical, juridical and political consequences' (Derrida 2001/2005:168).

Ethical, juridical and political consequences demand close consideration. There is a sense in which ADF have also made these links, especially in terms of ethical practice and commitment to training younger generations via ADFED – Asian Dub Foundation Education Programme. The director Kassowitz, with his 'so far, so good' refrain, suggests the same path. If we could carefully listen for what is involved, and if we might worry this through, over the presentation of violence and terror on screen, there might be clarity in the repetition. Someone is sending a message, so it would be good to consider the literal iteration of that 'anxious repetition' (Sharma and Sharma 2000:103) in the film-literate protagonists, the flickering multi-screen television news, the cinema as music hall, and in the theoretical text. If the always already were understood as a code for theoretical display, then this would quickly be identified as a matter of asking the same questions of ADF as of Derrida. Specifically the staging of *La Haine* with a new soundtrack might suggest restaging theory and so we have to ask how Derrida constructs his texts. Attention to the protocols of scholarly writing also echoes the suppression of hierarchy and order that should be undone in live performance of the classics.

In *Rogues*, as elsewhere, repetition as iteration is big for Derrida. His comments on dreams and violence are not uncharacteristically linked to writing and the road. It should not be overlooked that the cars that burn in Paris burn at night, as in some dream or nightmare in the dark unconscious that underpins the racist State. This thought can be linked to a wider, longer, more oft-trod path of Derrida's thinking – to do with inscription and presence. The burning cars are certainly unusual and perhaps even weird versions of what Derrida might have called writing in the expanded sense. Is there any mileage in Derrida's notion of inscription, as a way to make sense of the uprising? Certainly the car – and carriage-way – has marked Paris and since Haussmann, we know this is an issue of urban planning and political expediency, as it is perhaps in a different way for the suburbs. Any such inscription is also an erasure. The underlying imperatives of locking in the wage labour system also entailed urban planning road works that would split communities of association. Haussmann is himself like a barricade, against the barricades. In this context I might regret linking writing to rioting. The standard mediation is procedural, methodological, applied: the commonplace 'explanation' is to blame Hip-hop and gang culture. The conventional research questions engage with those involved, but only with meticulous attention to detail, and themes picked up from the press, where meaning is ascribed from afar. The facts! The well-funded studies released after August 2011 in London also suffer from a self-congratulatory micro-attention focussed upon interviews with 'participants' willing to speculate on constructs such as gangs, faulty parenting and urban alienation. The effect of specificity is to perpetrate a distraction from multiple causes or contradictory explanations and any prospect of making things otherwise (see Henri and Hutnyk 2013). Expectations are confirmed and reinforced, and the chance of any other 'reading' is foreclosed.

This kind of terror has to be combated seriously – the link with writing and rioting maybe does have a danger of not being serious. I mean it to be, but then it is also stepping onto the dangerous terrain of Derridada: I mean, 'mileage'.

On October 27th, Bouna and Zied died of electrical burns when they fled from the police. Riots broke out in Clichy-sous-Bois and other housing estates across France. This is the first time since May 1968 that there has been urban violence of this magnitude; it is also the first time that young people from the neighbourhoods have risen up together, realising that they share a common fate. This fate can be summed up as having no future but unemployment, low-income housing, daily humiliation and police racism, a ghetto culture that makes us outcasts, but which on a certain level is also a source of pride, because it's ours (Sketchy Thoughts 2005).

So what to make, also from afar, of the so-called 'French Intifada'? Does the work of Derrida offer us a way to understand the events of Paris in November of 2005? Is the burning of cars a kind of writing – a form of inscription that speaks? Or maybe the question should be one that asks why it was always silenced already in advance, a stalled Intifada, muted by Žižek and blind for Badiou? There were many who scoffed at the very idea of calling the youth actions anything of the kind – intifada, rebellion, protest – and perhaps rightly so. But rather than a matter of finding a catchy name for a volume of rapid-fire essays, this is also possibly the place for a discussion of thinking and its resistances. And in so doing, a chance to rethink those worrying dreams of violence in *La Haine*. Without wanting to claim a privileged or a distanced position as alibi, the question is not only one of speaking to the youth, or not, but being able to comprehend and communicate in the coded languages of street wariness, survival, and creativity. The privilege of 'access' is counter-indicated in the film, especially in the case of the reporters, but also elsewhere, and the trip into central Paris and the bourgeois art gallery private view is indicative of a gap. Kassowitz's film negotiates that gap, in ways that are also inaccessible to our theorists, including Derrida *avant la lettre*. So, with this in mind, I have been keen to interrupt discussions of Derrida in France with scenes from the film that erupt, in order to multiply the performative options available to a reading that should serve, if I have my brief correctly, as an illustration of an alternative method and application. This may be to twist the ADF project to my own ends, but with Derrida as guide – and traffic cop – I want to meditate on the way – on the path, the road, the – you will have guessed what it is by now – the boulevard, and even the Boulevard Périphérique, the ring road which surrounds central Paris and marks that line, crossed in *La Haine* between the inside and outside of respectable French society.

Interrupting music with scenes from a movie brings the screen into the composition. I am keen to do this because the way we look at the city on screen is key. The altered soundtrack to the filmed city opens up a dissonance that might be a possible site of the 'empirical research' often called for by Adorno (1970/1997:32).

This is not the convention of sociological journalistic interview technique, but a more sound sociology. An ethnography with ears. What might these studies look like if not also actual interventions of cinema, oblique movies and multiplying soundtracks? My gamble today is that a sonic orientation counters the ' repressive egalitarianism' that Adorno saw as 'an essential component of a fascist way of thinking' (Adorno 1971:56). The egalitarian theorist sitting sipping latte in the coffee shop of the art gallery really has a god complex, viewing as if from on high. Instead see the city as a place that draws everyday attention in particularly grounded ways. Ask how we look on the street, what our attention is drawn towards, who and how we look at, listen for, interpret which scenes, sounds, screens and faces, with which degree of focus and concentration, through which organ. The look up at the burning buildings, the look along the street, gawping, gaping, wide-eyed at the mangled bus, listening to sirens, standing watching-staring, from the hastily erected barrier, at the shocked and dazed victims, on screen at the news reports, images, interviews, commentary and graphics, at the press the next and following days, at each other on the train. ADF want you to attend to images and stories and lives, and music is played across the screen to wake you.

So let me draw your attention once more, as I will, over and over, to film sound. This discussion is about a score where, although there are those who wish to ignore the fact and say the youth are silent, in every way they are not some kind of voiceless blind uninformed 'object'. 15 year old Bouna Trouré and 17 year old Zyed Benna were killed – electrocuted after being chased by police – and there are many examples of the agency of the youth that should not be ignored. Sarkozy calls them scum, but the youth had – as Žižek notes – a response, and an organised one at that. Deaths in police custody are cited, but never charged in law, in so many other cases it is hard to credit. In *La Haine* it is the death of the youth who is the friend of Vinz, Saïd and Herbert that is tragically like so many other deaths at the hands of the Police: Mark Duggan in Tottenham, London, August 2011, or Smiley Culture in March 2011, or Charles de Menezes in 2005, or... Stafford Scott begins some of this for Tottenham in 2013 – Cynthia Jarrett, Joy Gardner, Roger Sylvester (Scott 2013) and Ken Fero and Tariq Mehmood documented further cases in the feature film *Injustice* (2001, see Bunting 2006). I am loathe to simply collect and list these depressing statistics ... Liz Fekete documents cases in relation to protests in Nørrebro in Copenhagen, which the world read as 'in reaction to cartoons of the Prophet Mohammed', but the youth wrote an 'open letter to the press', entitled 'The Truth Behind the Disturbances'. Largely ignored, this letter stated:

> the immediate cause of the riots was the police mishandling of an elderly man who was beaten with truncheons. But among long-term grievances cited was the police's stop-and-search policies, including routine humiliation through strip searches on the streets (Fekete 2009:208)

Examples could be piled on examples, and while Fekete might suggest that the protests of the youth are 'raw, local and as yet undirected' (2009:208) the targets are chosen and there is a message pretty clear. Scott raises legitimate demands about the quality of justice. Police violence is no misdemeanour. Deaths in Custody inquest now!

The Eiffel Tower.

There is a tower scene in *La Haine* which shows a far greater literacy – sense of French history, film history, sense of place, perhaps even a Parisian intellectual belonging – on the part of the protagonists in the film. The three friends are in the centre of Paris and linger awhile on a hilltop with a splendid view of the iconic Eiffel Tower, built for the 1889 World's Fair. In the film there are knowing references to intertextuality, for example the already mentioned scene where youths chase away the reporters and also where Saïd changes a billboard ad from *vous* to *nous* to detourn 'the world belongs to you' into 'the world belongs to us'. Another scene that presents a critical cinematic reference occurs when 'one of the three tries to "switch off" the Eiffel Tower by clicking his fingers – like [Leos] Carax's *Mauvais Sang* [dir. Carax 1985] and [Eric] Rochant's *Un monde sans pitié* [*World Without Pity*] [dir. Rochant 1989] – but here it steadfastly remains alight' (Haughton 2007, see also Higbee 2006:77). Alice Chapman points out that this is 'the only landmark we see' in the entire film' and when the attempt is made to turn it off' another of the youths wisecracks that such tricks 'only work in the movies' (Chapman 2007). Of course, just seconds after they leave, the tower does power down for the night. Having featured in a great many films over the years, the structure is susceptible to attack as other towers are – it was destroyed in the 1953 version of *The War of the Worlds* (dir. Byron Haskin); it was accidentally blown up at the end of *The Great Race* (dir. Blake Edwards 1965); and melted by Martians, again, in *Mars Attacks!* (dir. Tim Burton 1996). Subjected to many other calamities, it is equivalent, if perhaps more flamboyant, to the double set of towers in New York – and equally symbolic of capital.

The point about the Tower scene in *La Haine* however is not just to show the youth, or the director, as film literate, but to locate the youth relative to the intellectual and cultural milieu of French life itself, for which both the touristic tower – Emile called it the Awful Tower – and the youth of the *banlieues* are effectively excluded by the representative comments of people like Sarkozy. Use of the offensive and racist comment *racaille* threatens all citizens and the ideology of inclusive 'fraternity' that the imaginary of the French nation often proclaims – witness the national reconciliation of the world cup football success in 1998, and conversely, the recriminations after the inglorious exit from the South African tournament in 2010. Damned if you do and damned if you don't Nicolas Anelka? His reported comments to his manager at the time 'Go and get fucked you son of a whore' (Mortimer 2010) did not have the panache of Zinadine Zidane head-butting Marco Matarazzi, for saying something similar, in the 2006 final. *So far so good*. The curious thing is the repetition of the theme of exclusion-inclusion in the tower scene of *La Haine* is itself played out again just seven years after the world cup – the streets on fire, the youth still silenced. The difference we might necessarily note in England that a sporting event can sometimes douse the flames, whereas Zidane near starts a riot and becomes a national hero.

Zidane probably knew what he was doing. Anelka I am not so sure – but the point is that there is a cultural value deployed here that tampers with the usual platitudes of inside and outside in French society. Who is making the case for youth today if not themselves? It is possible now to get emails and read blogs written by *banlieue* youth, both in commentary on the events and in tribute to Bouna and Zied at the time. Certainly also critical of Sarkozy, though perhaps a burning vehicle is a more media savvy statement. Mike Davis has written extensively on the car as 'people's airforce' – himself keeping more to the car-bomb and its history than the Molotov ignited models of Paris in 2005, but in his work the voices of those who drive are also less audible (Davis 2006a). For a sociologist allegedly attuned to street culture, this comes as a surprise, since it is possible to read a wide range of comments from the youth involved, some of these voices also critical of the male participants in the burnings. This was itself debated, even if heard always-already in a kind of code that fixes a series of prejudices about youth, suburbs, the street. And also where the youth street scene itself is a remote pedagogy where the lumpen are schooled in struggles as well as cinema and community history – evident in the rooftop sequences in *La Haine* where Vinz and Saïd are chastised, but cared for, by elder brothers, uncles and cousins. Mediation of the family anyone? The media literacy here, as well as the urban pedagogy and extended family/parenting discourse, entails a criticality wholly unavailable in the set curriculum of the ministry-dictated schools or the theoretical elaborations of the major publishing houses. Inevitable perhaps while the academy remains a privileged reserve – a kind of 'green zone' – in the same way that cinema literacy is preserved for issues of *Screen* or *Cahiers du Cinéma*, not attributed to youth on a night out in the city. It is a forlorn regret that such cultural capital built upon long histories of anti-racist and anti-imperialist struggle, in France as well as England, is kept alive only obliquely in Hip-hop, Rap and Grime. And even then, Kassowitz's Eiffel Tower routine is a slapstick gag of sorts, fully articulated with the culture industry, even if also cool, and just what questioning the constitution of an art 'object' might be about. For sure the press misrepresent the many meanings of the burning cars, but then, to generalise the point of this chapter, so does any writing about rioting that does not worry at the question of the co-constitution of outlook and object, prejudice and theme.

Ruffians, Rabble, Rogues and Repetition.

I wil not be suggesting that all youth are lumpenproletariat, or that ADF, or Fun-da-Mental or M.I.A., for that matter, have privileged access to expressions that resonate with youth more than theory. There is a disjunct to be noticed however, and the question of scale and location marks the terrain. When Derrida meditates and conjugates on the word *Voyou* and links it to the way, and to the road, and waywardness, the transliteration escalates from the street to matters of state too quickly. I read this as an accusatory tone and as *Voyous* translates as rogues, or better, as louts, by any reckoning this is at least close in meaning to Sarkozy's *racaille*. With this in mind, Derrida's reflection could be extended to consider the street and street culture without too wild an associative license, a loose etymology, and perhaps to try to meditate-conjugate something similar with Hip-hop or Drum and Bass played over images of Paris. In particular, a special break-dance mode of movement, Derrida raps.

> Boulevard (French) Boulevard; and Bulwark. From the Old Dutch word, 'bolwerk', a type of fortification: a 'Bulwark'. The word changed in French from, 'boullewerc' to 'bollewerc' to 'boulever' and, ultimately, to 'boulevard'. The French word boulevard originally referred to the flat summit of a rampart (the etymology of the word distantly parallels that of bulwark). Many Parisian boulevards replaced old city walls. Boule in French is ball... (Etymology by Daisy Tam)

Before going down that road, let me interrupt, however, to carefully read the text provided to pave the way. This is Derrida lecturing in the European summer of 2002, thinking of burning cars and revolt – it is no doubt easy in France to imagine this scene since the '68 generation had this romantic image burned upon the retinas of their ambitious gaze...

> The word voyou has an essential relation with the *voie*, the way, with the urban roadways [*voire*], the roadways of the city or the *polis*, and thus with the street [*rue*], the waywardness [*dévoiement*] of the voyou consisting in making ill use of the street, in corrupting the street or loitering in the streets, in 'roaming the streets', as we say in a strangely transitive formulation. This transitivity is in fact never far away from the one that leads to 'walking the streets'... Today the voyou sometimes roams the roadways [*voies*] and highways [*voiries*] in a car [*voiture*], that is, when he or she is not stealing it or setting it on fire' [stealing or setting it on fire! – those rogues, note they are soon to be linked to greater rogues, in a strangely transitive formula] ... Voyous might also, on an

international scale, and this gets us right into the problematic of rogue states, be involved in drug trafficking, in parasiting, or actually subverting, as terrorists in training, the pathways [voies] of normal communication, whether of airplanes, the telephone, email or the Web (Derrida 2005:65).

I want to remark on this list. The transitive next next next that escalates. It moves from the small metaphor to the hyperbolic of global connectivity. Even way back in his 1967 book *Of Grammatology* there was a call for co-constitutive contemplation of the road and writing: 'one should meditate upon all of the following together: writing as the possibility of the road and of difference, the history of writing and the history of the road, of the rupture, of the *via rupta*, of the path that is broken, beaten, *fracta*, of the space of reversibility and of repetition' (Derrida 1967/1974:107). There is no reverse gear here however – famously, the word Tony Blair used to not back out of Iraq, himself channelling the now rusting Iron Lady Thatcher, who was not for turning.

But that was Derrida being prescient. Back to the future. It is another list that I want to get on to read, also taken from *Rogues* - Page 66 for Derrida's discussion of the thugs, gangsters and shysters that constitute the rabble of the French suburbs. But before reading that, I want to signal that I am going to go further back soon, and – it will come as no surprise – to another author writing of Paris some 150 years earlier. One who speaks more in terms of the lumpen – for now, however, I just want to keep close to this word, lumpen, and to remember the lumps. Derrida does mention a number of earlier commentaries on this milieu – Nerval, even Benjamin, but not Marx immediately – though of course he is well aware of that bearded presence in the wings. In *Rogues* Mai 68 is being replayed, here in 2002, as farce.

So that when he merely describes the milieu that is the street, it is with affection and affectation:

Voyoucracy is a corrupt and corrupting power of the street, an illegal and outlaw power that brings together into a voyoucratic regime, and thus into an organised and more or less clandestine form, into a virtual state, all those who represent a principle of disorder ... a threat against public order ... This milieu, this environment, this world unto itself, gathers into a network all the people of the crime world or underworld, all the singular voyous. All individuals of questionable morals and dubious character whom decent, law-abiding people would like to combat and exclude under a series of more or less synonymous names: big man, bad boy, player ... rascal ... good-for-nothing, ruffian, villain, crook, thug, gangster, shyster ... scoundrel, miscreant, hoodlum, hooligan ... one would also say today *banger* [*loulou*], *gangbanger* [*loubard*], sometimes even outside the inner city, in the suburbs, the suburban punk [*loubard des banlieues*] (Derrida 2005:66).

At the end of this list of names, our present stars of the show – the hip-hoppers, still without vocal presence... On Page 67 Derrida does not even forget to include women amongst the rogues, insofar as streetwalkers and liberated feminists may also be found in this zone – some obvious exclusions apply.

Whatever the case, I am not convinced that Derrida is unequivocal in his support for the rogues, even as he wants to appropriate a bit of their street cred. He declares, to a high profile conference attended by high profile philosophers, that he himself would be 'a bit voyou, a bit roguish' if he did not begin by thanking those who gathered to hear him speak – he would be, but he is not – and of course by drawing attention to this he both claims and defers a certain roguishness.

The issue of Derrida's chummy approval *or not* of these elements, these rogues, will become more salient...

Musical Interlude.

But first another list. Music in the film is not incidental, though Vincendeau suggests there is 'surprisingly little' of it (Vincendeau 2005:56). Possibly for this reason it was with *La Haine* that ADF first played a soundtrack live screening event, but in any case the music was already a key part of the 'original'. 'Burnin and Lootin' by Bob Marley; 'That Loving Feeling' performed by Isaac Hayes; 'More Bounce to the Ounce performed by Zapp and Roger; tracks by Expression Direkt and Cut Killer; a sample of Edith Piaf singing 'Je ne Regrette Rien'; Etan Massuri; Cameo Song; 'Tak Hedat' performed by Tak Fari Nas; 'Outstanding' by The Gap Band; 'Lafou Lakari' by Mabiala and Lonningisa; 'The Beat Goes On' performed by Ripple; 'Nsangu Nsangu' by Klay M; perhaps incongruously Schubert's 'Ave Maria'; 'Hard Core' by Solo, and several tracks from The Beastie Boys.

Music and rhythm govern the film and its reception even when the Hip-hop is not explicitly 'there'. Hence *so far so good*, it is the landing that matters, sure. But the rhythm of repetition threads the scenes together, punctuates the urban topography and frames as well the critique that is challenged by the rioting and its consequences. What those consequences are is left open at the end. Indeed, as *La Haine* explicitly renders the *banlieue* as the site of violence it does this without it being the obvious plot except at the very start. *La Haine*'s sensation is that it enacts the sensational at the beginning, only or even in order to offer a greater disruption in the rest of the film where the uprising is off screen, but present. This sets up a doubled perspective. The silent brooding is effective (Sharma and Sharma 2000:107), the film can be seen as the 'aftermath' of the riots, or as a commentary on the constant and everyday conditions that are their context.

Similarly, Hip-hop is a music form that can be read in conflicting ways – of course sometimes as a threat to middle-class sensibilities 'such that several critics "heard" a lot of hip hop in the film' (Vincendeau 2005:56). Although Rap is 'far from dominant' (Vincendeau 2005:57), the boys own adventure and urban toughs atmospherics confirm conservative readings. The absence of women in the film is striking, but as the Sharmas argue, the pathologising of the suburbs is an old sociological, anthropological and Hollywood standard, where inner urban tradition demands alienation and decay, disaffection and lawlessness, reinforcing the racism, even as *La Haine* challenges these easy moves (Sharma and Sharma 17-3 2000:103). Thus, Kassovitz's soft-touch use of Hip-hop is one that is never transmuted into mere burning and looting. Certainly a dysfunctional mythos fuels marketing of 'gangsta' content to disaffected and dispossessed urban youth, but in the milieu of the film – as often elsewhere – Hip-hop is an expressive form accessed positively. It could be argued that this goes well beyond the celebration-condemnation mode of exploitation that provides transgressive objects for sale by the culture industry. It is rather an 'outlet' enhanced and extended by an aesthetics of mixing and sampling that booms out from the rooftops and – in one powerful scene – from an upstairs open window that turns an entire estate into an amphitheatre. ADF too would concede their efforts at bringing music technology competence, mixing skills and other media proficiencies to youth is also imbricated in uplift and consciousness raising as a pro-active vocation. A career move with style for otherwise commonsense social work.

This is the format of a curious ragamuffin to riches story, though often the riches are not delivered – 'we want to get paid' as Rakim so often says. Writing and research on music resonates here since Hip-hop does often have a claim to be the soundtrack of the streets. Again the track is another road metaphor, but this time with connotations of getting 'off the beaten track' and curiously of hunting, as well as, of course, music. But by now it is obvious that Hip-hop is also *the* vehicle of expression for suburban youth creativity, and it might be said, their gener-alised, lumpenised, alienation.

ADF play within a tradition of minstrels in politics. They want the reworked audio for the film to provoke discussion. They screen it for new audiences and it is debated in detail on the interactive activist/fan website that is part of ADFED, itself styled as an activist-oriented youth politics forum. Workshops organised by ADFED included one by Sonia Mehta in 2003 involving Ash Sharma on the development of ADFED as a music technology training provider working with visual media and exploring the politics of sound. Discussion within ADFED and on the ADF chat site is not uncritical. For example, the politics of screening action cinema as entertainment is measured against questions about the best ways to organise, and politicise, the music industry, organisations like Rich Mix arts centre and anti-racist campaigns. Concerns about street and police violence are aired and the testosterone-fuelled adventurism of the Paris uprisings are compared with events in the UK that echo those shown in *La Haine*. The film, as ADF intends, also articulates these concerns. This effort of showing films about such topics is almost the only mainstream exposure many youth get to any sort of progressive take on issues of relevance to racism, colonialism and imperialism. This is important, as antidote to the media crusade to present youth as troublemakers, Blacks as thieves or drug dealers and Muslims as either terrorists – court cases, clips from Iraq/Afghanistan bombing runs, Al Jazeera Osama clips – or troublesome 'moderates' that should get 'their own house in order' (Martin Amis, n.d.). In the UK for example, for the majority of the audience of the band, negative images of Muslims as detainees or as suspects on trial in court are countered only by a very few positive images that are paraded on soap operas or very occasionally news media. ADF thereby do useful educa-tional work that would otherwise only be publically available in the increasingly inaccessible and underfunded university course, in obscure magazine or blogposts and perhaps the nether corners of the soon-to-be-closed-down library. Occasionally, maybe, a Saturday newspaper story that might mention something other than murder/death/kill, or sport.

Riff-raff.

It does worry me that some people, scholarly commentators even, can describe events like September 11 2001 or July 7 2005 as obliging 'us' to 'rethink the terms of social theory' (Seidler 2007:xiii). With all due respect to the lives lost on those days, it seems obscene to me that these particular shocking occurrences are the ones to make 'us' think. All over the world, and not only in the suburbs of Paris, another 'we' is subject to a relentless violence, visited by terror, danger, pursuit and threat. Social theory needed rethinking long before – those September and July days – if 'we' on this planet are to wrest control from those who plunder and steal at our expense. Seidler notes that after the bombings 'Life, at least in the West, had become precarious in new ways' (Seidler 2007:xiv). Welcome to a planet of precarity. Are we really obliged to do philosophy here? More recently, Rancière manages in five pages to link the riots of 2005, the poet Mallarmé and the painter Seurat, a black youth from the suburbs, and Deleuze and Guattari in a contemplation that we are all in this together, but separately (Rancière 2008/2009:51-56). I worry that the *racaille* are being used here to do duty for an emblematic 'wretched'; even if 'there is something in common between the prose poem of the refined writer [Mallarmé] and the contemporary form of political art that tries to create new forms of social bond in "bad" neighbourhoods' (Rancière 2008/2009:54). The political art Rancière has in mind are the t-shirt slogans of the group *Campement Urbain*, but if it were not already dated, his reference could easily have been the film *La Haine*, as seen from a faux-chic Boulevard Saint-Germain café.

If we must stoop so low in philosophy as to be forced to pay attention to t-shirt wearing rogues and *racaille* in France, I then want to read what Marx has to say on the precarious position of the lumpen. In *Capital* Marx does briefly mention 'rogues' (1867/1967:898), but the classic theoretical-historical study that must govern any discussion is the brilliant analysis called *The Eighteenth Brumaire of Louis Bonaparte*.

In one part of this rampaging critique, Marx provides a list of those Bonaparte gathered together in the Society of 10 December in order to wrest control of the Empire from competing forces. The list, I cannot help but hear as the inspiration for Derrida's iteration of the gang-bangers:

Under the pretext of incorporating a benevolent association, the Paris lumpenproletariat was organized into secret sections, each led by Bonapartist agent, and the whole headed by a Bonapartist general. From the aristocracy there were the bankrupted roués with dubious means and dubious provenance, from the bourgeoisie there were degenerate wastrels on the take vagabonds, demobbed soldiers, discharged convicts, runaway galley slaves, swindler and cheats, thugs, pickpockets, conjurers, card-sharps, pimps, brothel-keepers, porters, day-labourers, organ grinders, scrap dealers, knife grinders, tinkers and beggars, in short, the whole amorphous, jumbled mass of flotsam and jetsam that the French term bohemian ... dregs, refuse and scum of all classes (Marx 1852/2002:63)

There are too many bomb-torn streets, but my suspicion is that the issue of solidarity with the lumpen car burners in Paris is defining. I take my cue from Mao Zedong. In his early *Report from Hunan*, Mao praises the 'Movement of the Riff Raff' (Mao 1975:29). The 'riff raff' are the 'utterly destitute' lumpen peasantry who we find in China as:

completely dispossessed … People who have neither land nor money, are without any means of livelihood, and are forced to leave home and become mercenaries or hired labourers or wandering beggars (Mao 1975:32)

Mao then provides a detailed report on the achievements of these peasants as revolutionaries able to transform an uprising into Red self-governance. Mao's report is a great example of engaged sociology and it provides a more balanced evaluation of lumpen elements. His amusingly titled section '"It's Terrible" or "It's Fine"' is equally judicious. Mao is praising the ways the peasants had banded together to dominate the landed gentry in Hunan, how their organisation established the basic conditions for a defence of the gains, and the template for the pattern of protracted guerrilla war. His unconditional approval for the 'Movement of the Riff Raff' is unstinting in its praise for the violent suppression of counter-revolutionaries. He does not ever want to say they 'go too far' when they defend the revolution and turn everything upside down (Mao 1975:30).

This evocation of a lumpen Mao is not an obscure historical subject. The problem of organisation and solidarity resonates everywhere today. If not also on the so-called anti-war left with the vexed issue of who to support in Iraq, Libya, Syria – the Islamist opposition supported because it is the objective anti-imperialist force on the ground today, or qualifications of this on grounds that the enemy of the state is not necessarily nor ultimately a friend? Mao learnt this one long ago too. As Dutton points out, the first pages of the *Selected Works Vol 1* asks 'Who are our enemies? Who are our friends?' And declares this to be the question of utmost importance for the revolution – we are talking 1926 here, and betrayals, not least by Chiang Kai Shek were just around the corner.

Again, the question of support and solidarity is important in the expansion of the struggle for the streets in France. Both solidarity and alliance are key to this in France as well, and the comments of Žižek or Badiou are to be considered in perspective as questions of adequate organisation. What is required to win? The comments of Abdellali Hajjat offer a sharp contrast when talking of how 'left-wing sociologists' construct 'dangerous classes' and note:

> the 'vacuum' or the political 'desert' in the popular suburbs, where a majority of the descendants of post-colonial immigration live (either French or foreigners). They claim that France has been the scene of 'jacqueries,' [translators note: 'peasant insurrections'] like in the 19th century, carried out by the 'lumpen of the lower proletariat,' 'without class consciousness.' The implication is supposed to be that if some political force could only organize this rebellion, then all of its subversive potential could be directed in a revolutionary direction. From the comfort of their positions in the media and/or the universities, they do not hesitate to deplore the rioters' 'handicap' (Hajjat 2005).

So in France, as elsewhere. Immanuel Wallerstein is not surprised, and prescient. Anticipating that the French riots will 'soon scorch the world', he writes:

> It amazes me that people are surprised when underclasses rebel. The surprising thing is that they do not do it more often. The combination of the oppressiveness of poverty and racism and the lack of short-term, or even medium-term hope is surely a recipe for rebellion. What keeps rebellion down is fear of repression, which is why repression is usually swift. But the repression never makes the anger go away (Wallerstein 2005)

Žižek of course scoffs at those who try to understand the rabble in France. Could he at any point get to know them? By attributing Lacanian motifs, if not motives, to the actions of these youth, Žižek provides a new mode of obfuscation where any acknowledgement of the intentions, perspectives, organisation or exegesis of the youth themselves, in struggle, as agents, in opposition to state power, is silenced. This is exactly the ruse that Žižek had earlier mocked as 'irony' when 'watching intellectual, sociologists and commentators trying to understand and help' (Žižek 2008:64). A pox on all sides then – do not try to understand or help, but do provide a diagnosis from afar – it is indeed irony for Žižek to attribute impotence in this regard.

Do the youth of the *banlieues* have anything to say? Sadly they do not attend the Summer symposia or the Idea of Communism conference where these issues are debated. In his book *The Parallax View*, Žižek offers corrosive attacks on hypocrisy and liberal illusions which are designed to interrogate the gaps – parallax, dialectical, distort, invert, pervert – in which ideological justification thrives. Here is a gap for sure – but it is not simply solved by talking to the youth, nor by thinking that somehow people like Aki Nawaz from Fun-da-Mental, or John Pandit from ADF, or, in the next chapter, Mathangi Maya Arulpragasam, M.I.A., might have some sort of access code for the lumpenised youth, the word on the street, or even the secret co-ordinates for an anti imperialist anti racist politics for the present. Of course this would be absurd, even if it is the gamble of this book that attention to other players in the pantomime is a useful counter to the authorised state spokespersons whose work does much less to addresses the problems of poetic engagement in the midst of global terror. The lumpen might still be worth consideration, even filtered through performances that point to meaning where others on the Left see silence, impotence and affliction. This would be the message to counter the parallax effect – the bus can be read, a future may still be possible, perhaps art shows the way through the conflagration, signifying in the flames.

Reserve Army.

Who are our enemies? Who are our friends? Žižek is my guide and heads for the slums. To prepare the way, in several sections of the *The Parallax View*, he has discussed Marx's *Eighteenth Brumaire*. He describes the list Marx gives of the Society of 10 December as the 'private army of thugs' that Napoleon recruits to do his dirty deeds and, as I have already done, he recites Marx's alliterative paragraph on 'vagabonds ... tricksters ...[and] gamblers' (Žižek 2006: 335). Žižek's point is that this gang, hired from the residue or 'excess' of all classes is the 'excremental remainder' that, Marx shows, permits Napoleon the third to stand apart from all classes, play class off against class – the gap – and come to be the representative of that class of people who cannot represent themselves, sacking the peasant potatoes.

So far so good, but it seems we may need to distinguish more carefully between the peasantry and the lumpens, and ask just what is at stake in the naming of these fractions. There is something of the pantomime here as well, as when Ranciére writes in *The Flesh of Worlds* that 'The lumpenproletariat is first of all a phantasmagoric name, a stage name, a theatrical embodiment of all the disasters of scholarly speech' (Ranciére 1998/2004:139). Very much along the lines that Žižek will soon follow, Ranciére may have confused this subproletarian category with Marx's comments on the peasant masses in France. In *The Philosopher and his Poor*, Ranciére had warned against something just like this: he calls this 'Marx's hallucinated description' of an 'unnameable and innumerable mass of savage beasts', which according to Ranciére Marx held in scorn because they could 'only increase their numbers like so many potatoes'. This, for Ranciére, has 'nothing evidently to do with any sort of economic, sociological or political analysis'. Indeed, along with the lumpenproletariat, the peasant class is a 'myth': 'The so-called materialist analysis of different social classes is thus a myth manifesting a perpetual flight of identities and the common dereliction of classes' (Ranciére 1983/2004:99) – and we see the lumpen as the class of those that are no longer a class opposed to the peasant class which does not even yet form a class, and comes to be represented by self-appointed masters.

In a footnote on page 417 of *The Parallax View*, Žižek repeats the slur that Marx had a 'barely concealed contempt' for, and dismissed this 'degenerate "refuse" of all classes' as 'lumpenproletariat' which, Žižek adds, extrapolating from Marx's case study, 'when politicized, as a rule serves as the support of proto-Fascist and Fascist regimes' (Žižek 2006:417n26). He says this apropos of a suggestion that contemporary slum-dwellers should also be classified as lumpenproletariat. I sit up and take notice here as it is in volume one of *Capital* that Marx examines the economic and political role of the lumpenproletariat as part of the reserve army of labour: itself diagnosed as floating, latent and stagnant forms of unemployed and under-employed that provide mass support for a brutal wage slavery (Marx 1867/1967:641-3). Cheap labour willing to work, with nothing to sell but labour power, keeps wages low, keeps profits high. The reserve army of labour is an economic category, a component of the unfolding examination of capitalist relations. We must look more closely at the ways, across nearly twenty years of writing, the lumpenproletariat is analytically distinguished from the peasantry who 'cannot represent themselves' etc.

Marx's most famous description of the Society of 10 December is not yet a description of the lumpen as a class, rather it lists those Bonaparte recruited to stand in for them. These pickpockets, tricksters and organ grinders are not the peasants, whom Marx discusses further on:

The small-holding peasants form an immense mass whose members live in similar conditions but without entering into complex relationships with one another. Their mode of production isolates them from one another, instead of bringing them into complex interactions. The isolation is reinforced by the terrible means of communication in France and the poverty of the peasants. Their site of production, the small holding, does not allow any division of labour in its cultivation, no application of science and therefore no diversity in development, no diversification of talent, no wealth of social relationships. Each individual peasant family is almost self-sufficient, producing the greatest part of its consumption directly and getting its means of subsistence more in brutal exchange with nature than in relationships with society. The small holding, the peasant and the family; alongside them another small holding, another peasant and another family. A few score of these make a village, and a few score villages make a department. Thus the great bulk of the French nation is formed by the simple accretion, much as potatoes in a sack form a sack of potatoes. In so far as millions of families get a living under economic conditions of existence that divide their mode of life, their interests, and their culture from those of the other classes and counterpose them as enemies, they form a class. In so far as there is merely a local interconnection among peasant proprietors, the similarity of their interests produces no community, no national linkage and no political organisation, they do not form a class. They are therefore incapable of asserting their class interest in their own name, whether through a parliament or a constitutional convention. They cannot represent themselves, they must be represented. Their representative must also appear as their master, as an authority over them, as an unrestricted governmental power which protects them from other classes and watches over them from on high (Marx 1852/2002:100-1)

An often misunderstood statement, as we will see: 'They cannot represent themselves', Marx writes. This is said of the peasants, the 'potatoes in a sack', not the lumpenproletarians, but this representation of representation (see Spivak 1990:108) must be read in the context of talking about the various social groupings that were the players in a drama, on a stage, where Louis Bonaparte – the Nephew, the rogue – was to strut his stuff. Marx's *Eighteenth Brumaire* is *the* exemplary class analysis. No unsubtle two part class conflict here, rather the dialectical ebb and flow of opportunism and manipulation, of luck and irony, and of cunning, calculating and – Marx grudgingly admits as much – charismatic coincidence in the historical record.

> Through historical tradition it has come to pass that the French peasantry believed in a miracle, that a man of the name Napoleon would bring them back their former glory … But let us be clear about this. The Bonaparte dynasty does not represent the revolutionary peasants, but rather the conservative ones, not the peasant who reaches beyond his social condition of existence, the smallholding, but rather the one who wants to shore it up more firmly, not the country people who want to overthrow the old order under their own steam in conjunction with the towns, but rather the exact opposite, those who are stupidly locked up within the old order and want to see themselves saved and preferred along with their small holdings by means of the ghost of an empire (Marx 1852/2002:101).

What of that phrase – 'they cannot represent themselves' – itself already so theatrical? Is Marx to be condemned for stealing the voice of the downtrodden, condemning them to silence, removing agency? I want to argue no. A dialectical reading has to see that Marx condemns the nephew for taking this voice, for becoming, through sometimes dextrous, sometimes unintentionally successful, manoeuvres and manipulations, the only possible representative figure for a grouping that did not –

because of their atomised and isolated condition, constitute themselves as a class, even as they were a class as such, only not a class for themselves. Alongside this episode, Marx does describe the lumpen in ways that are not explicitly unconditionally supportive – but it is clear that Marx did support such elements later when it came to the communards, even as they were to be wiped out at the hands of a better-organised state power.

And today, what would a contemporary report by, not on, those that Marx called the reserve army look like? What would its composition be? What location? Who would make the analysis? With what methodologies of presentation?

I turn to Žižek discussing 'improvisational modes of social life' in the 'really existing slums'. Following Mike Davis, the example is not Paris or London, but the city of Lagos, in the context of reports that 'now, or soon' the planet will be predominantly urban: more people will live in cities than in the countryside (Davis 2006b). Žižek makes some apposite comments here about the role of fundamental Christianity as the hegemonic ideology prevalent in the slums, and while he warns us to 'resist the temptation to elevate and idealise the slum-dwellers into a new revolutionary class' he does suggest, with Badiou, that we 'should nonetheless … perceive slums as one of the few authentic "evental sites" in today's society' (Žižek 2006:268). The excluded here have nothing to lose but their chains, they are free in a double sense – 'from all substantial ties'; 'from state police regulation' – 'even more than the classic proletariat' (Žižek 2006:268).

This is heady stuff, but I think that despite the denial – the resistance of temptation –idealism has entered without an invite. Does Žižek know the slums? With their highly regulated codes and systems, their significant social and family ties, where pavement space, shanty huts, roadside and underpass locations are substantially organised, regulated, encoded – and not just by the Christian Church. I wonder, because it is when Žižek makes a peculiar *parallel*, and asks a provocative question, when he telegraphs a link between the slums and Harlem, in the process of advocating a new political programme, that I really lose him:

> The slum-dwellers are the counterclass to the other emerging class, the so-called 'symbolic class' (managers, journalists and PR people, academics, artists and so on) which is also uprooted and perceives itself as directly universal (a New York academic has more in common with a Slovene academic than with blacks in Harlem half a mile from his campus). Is this the new axis of class struggle, or is the 'symbolic class' inherently split, so that we can make the emancipatory wager on the coalition between the slum-dwellers and the 'progressive' part of the symbolic class? What we should be looking for are the signs of the new forms of social awareness that will emerge from the slum collectives: they will be the seeds of the future (Žižek 2006:269).

Quite amazing – two classes contend… There is not yet, for Žižek, a connection between New York academic and Harlem – but this does exist – and he does not immediately say that Harlem equals slum – but his grammar implies it in a way that I would hesitate to attribute to conscious intent. Nonetheless, the conflation is there, and covered by an optimism that is quite touching, if naive. What then for the signs he seeks? In a world of urgent problems, why is *urbanisation* continually called in to do duty for bourgeois fears of a 'population explosion' which leads to a threat to 'us' from those who now live amongst 'us'. Perhaps the political project for progressives in the symbolic class will be to go to the slums in some form of a new urban Maoism mission. Žižek prefers Lenin, but his support of Badiou may suggest something else. And his listing of the lumpen is not without significance, naming the terrain of struggle:

We are thus witnessing the rapid growth of a population outside state control, living in conditions half outside the law, in dire need of minimal forms of self-organization. Although this population is composed of marginalized laborers, redundant civil servants, and ex-peasants, they are not simply a redundant surplus: they are incorporated into the global economy in numerous ways, many of them as informal wage-workers or self-employed entrepreneurs, with no adequate health or social security cover (Žižek 2006:268).

I cannot disagree with Žižek except where he suggests Marx was contemptuous of the lumpenproletariat. This list of complaints made on behalf of the lumpenised mobilising slum-dweller itself reminds me of the standard enumerations of symbolic class academic coding. It is a classic Žižek move to say this of course: 'a transgression that consolidates what it transgresses' (Žižek 2005:254). Here it is useful to think of Spivak's rewriting and recoding a constant self-criticism that is fuelled by attentive readings of texts and a patient non-coercive effort to teach in a way that helps rearrange desire – for example, the imperious desire to help with limited experience of understanding (Spivak 2012). I see her work as exemplary contrast, not only because it is symptomatic in Žižek that women are left out or that unexamined 'native informant'-type slum-dwellers do duty for an abstract idealist 'idea' of communism that seems to not quite satisfy criteria of transnational literacy or informed critique. Rather, there is perhaps still much to be learnt from a New York academic who is not so simply blown in from afar, who herself lives in Harlem, who – I find it revealing – does not ever seem to appear in Žižek's reading lists. There is also the question of the ways the financialisation of the globe, neo-liberal oppressions, structural adjustments and even well-meaning do-gooder programmes, with NGO opportunism, have the most severe impact today on South Asia today. And the argument almost inevitably turns again to the Maoists in India...

We should keep in mind that ADF's most successful single was the track 'Naxalite' on the *Culture Move* EP (1998), celebrating the Maoist insurgency that rocked West Bengal and other states from 1967 onwards. There are good reasons to consider what purchase a somewhat exotic revolutionary insurgency has in the texts of the urban commentators, since a strange parallel of interest weighs the balance in favour of the band rather than the theorist. In that earlier footnote on the slum-dweller as Lumpenproletariat, Žižek suggested a 'closer analysis should focus on the changed structural role of these "lumpen" elements in conditions of global capitalism (especially large-scale migrations)' (Žižek 2006: 417n25). To support such moves, a reference to Naxalites appears in Žižek when in *Living in the End Times*, he quotes an 'Indian state official' to make the point that slums, while 'generally perceived as spaces in which gangs and religious sects fight for control', are also spaces for 'radical political organizations, as in the case of India, where the Maoist movement of Naxalites is organising a vast alternative social space' (Žižek 2010xi). Care should be taken not to transpose the Maoist struggle in India from a rural to an urban context – and to be wary of the ways the term Naxalite has been used as a term of convenience for Police 'encounters' with all kinds of miscreants. Žižek's citation, taken from Sudeep Chakravarti's – not 'Sudep' as he has it in the footnote – journalistic account in *Red Sun*, conflates two sides of a conversation about the ungovernability of areas under Moaist control into one quote by a state official. This official is in fact Ajai Sahni of the Institute of Conflict Management, who runs a 'South Asian Terrorism' think tank from the 'heavily guarded residential campus of K.P.S. Gill' in Delhi (Chakravarti 2009:108). Here, looking up the sources reveals how popular journalism does better than informed metropolitan fantasy. For Žižek, the 'slums' remain an undifferentiated 'vast alternative social space', and the Maoists are urbanised and contained as an example of 'inclusive exclusion' (Žižek 2010:ix). That said, by the end of the book Žižek quotes Arundhati Roy's much noticed newspaper report on the Maoists, which explicitly notes that the Maoists involved are rural tribals fighting for their land. She does not call them Naxalites, although the conflation Maoist/Naxals appears in a 2008 Expert Group Planning Commission Report she cites (Roy 2009, Expert Group 2008). Žižek offers an impassioned case for supporting the Maoists against the Indian media which is:

> full of stories about 'red terrorists, replacing stories about 'Islamic terrorism!' No wonder that the Indian state is responding with a major military operation against 'Maoist strongholds' in the jungles of central India. It is true that both sides have resorted to brutal violence, and that the Maoists 'people's justice' is harsh. However, no matter how unpalatable to our liberal tastes this may be, *we have no right to condemn it*. Why? Because the rebels' situation is precisely that of Hegel's rabble: the Naxalite in India are starving tribal people whom the minimum of a dignified life has been denied and who are fighting for their lives (Žižek 2010:395).

Hegel in the jungles. There are problems here of a methodical, conceptual, practical and organisational nature that are rarely discussed in theoretical tracts even when they call for some new emancipatory movement – of signs from the slums, or of a multitude mobilisation. Roy has mainstreamed the story of Indian military repression of tribals in a necessary global news intervention, Žižek refers to Hegel and rabble – the echo in the word is *racille* just as much as it is rebels – and he renders the rural movement not as a Maoism with a programme, but as some sort of Benjaminian 'divine violence' (Žižek 2010:394). While Žižek has reworked the old Maoist reasoning about rural revolts in Hunan – neither 'it's terrible', nor 'it's fine' – nevertheless, where Arundhati Roy can go and talk with the Maoists in Orissa,

Žižek does not. Does he do the same for Paris? For London? Airbrushed into Tottenham? The lumpen youth are made mute. Riff-raffed, from Lagos to Chhattisgarh.

In his 2008 book *In Defense of Lost Causes*, Žižek writes:

> happy are we who live under cynical public opinion manipulators, not under the sincere Muslim fundamentalists [who are] ready to fully engage themselves in their projects (Žižek 2008:160)

To follow the logic of this provocation, those who lament the decline of principles should probably not support cynical politicians but rather should put their faith in the fundamentalists since they really do believe their ideals. I am not so sure this irony is misplaced, but I prefer Les Back's warning of the 'damaging sense of emergency and paranoia that seduces the most principled' and endorse his 'challenge' of 'how to acknowledge these complicities without giving into phobias produced by the so-called war on terror' (Back 2007:138). In Žižek it often seems his critiques of enlightened cynicism supplemented by ideological enjoyment of ethnic nationalism operate via scatological insults and accusations of perversion. Different to Derrida's 'pervertability' of images, mentioned in the introduction (Derrida in Borradori 2003:109), this is played out in Žižek so that other positions from cynical distance through to protestations of support for democratic politics are seen to be supplemented by the perverse or obscene excess of bureaucratic enjoyment. He may have a point here, where liberalism, multiplicities, even 'alliance politics' are the symbolic forms secured through unacknowledged superego support of the obscene. But the protesters are blind and impotent and if efforts to organise the lumpen are perverse, then what is the focus? To write commentaries on these same lumpen, who already well know how their situation is unbearable, seems equally perverted, but now distanced as a voyeuristic anthropological pursuit – a pastime difficult to justify, let alone having to work through the tactical, political, ethical errors of sending ill-prepared cadre to the slums, the suburbs, or the mountains – as in the lessons learnt the hard way in Bengal, not yet learnt in Paris, and not helped by the comic image of 'symbolics', armed with Kant, Deleuze or Žižek, heading out to the shanty towns to compete with Pentacostalists for the souls of the oppressed. Has the time come for progressive symbolics to be better equipped, sent to training camps to brush up on class composition research methods, on questions of Leninist organisation, or the practical rules of engagement for ensuring Maoist party discipline? I want to propose that instead, as indeed Marx suggests, and indeed at the end of his essay *Rogues*, Derrida suggests, it rather seems much more useful to expose the workings of power amongst those that profess to make the commentaries – those that provide a 'political economy', names, designations, interpretations. Such that, if I had a research project that could extend this thinking into a practical project, the focus would be upon the administrative and managerial policy – policing – of the state military machine.

And its cultural wing! Unable to reconstruct my theoretical interests as completely abstract, I remain primarily interested in intellectual, sociological and commentator positions in relation to left organisation and therefore think about the responsibility of analysis vis a vis revolutionary politics and the media. This is possibly quixotic, surreal, and a forlorn desire but it is not as strange as watching old movies dubbed with Hip-hop soundtracks, or videographic renderings of neo-colonial empire dubbed with Paul Weller or Marilyn Manson versionings and updatings of the aforementioned 'Highway to Hell'. I should comment that the twist in the pop video versions that come out of the war zone are not always grizzly jock-strut jingoism of this sort, sometimes the amateur pro-war visual work is complimented by a plaintive aesthetic that owes as much to M*A*S*H (1970, dir. Robert Altman) and anti-war actions of the very best tradition. Add to this a mode of vernacular video art that includes laments for lost colleagues, loneliness and despair at being far from home, and complicated poetics that couple Hendrix at Woodstock ('fucking up the star-spangled banner') with the love-letter anti-war bed-in politics of John and Yoko. The bulk of such offerings on YouTube however, like the apologetic cinema of war mobilised by Hollywood, is hardly an indictment of war, and more often macho and racist posturing of the most virulent kind. I remain concerned, with Žižek, that theories of ethnicity and multiculturalism are too weak as tools for resistance, even if they remain factors to consider. Fast forward: the lumpen today have equally become the manipulated peasants in a sack of the contemporary Bonapartes, the farce of commentary and book sales. Grand theory in the high street stores, cultural product sold with edge, then entrapment and jihadist videos taken to mean little more than the equivalent inverted of the Wikileaks video that got Julian Assange all too much attention. What response is there to the footage that condemns the US as war criminals? A theoretical gymnastics of denial is all. Instead of Lacanian callisthenics or an etymology of the meaning of roads and riots, a more useful orientation might be to map out the development of capital that lumps road construction and suburban alienation closely together – Haussmann's boulevards. This is precisely what the youth on the streets seem to do as the cars burn bright in the night and on screen.

Consider the ironic pose of a wilful but futile anti-capitalist pursing his lips as if ready to kiss the hand that offers a glorious commercialisation of identity and life. There is always something super-camp about an out-of-date revolutionary, but I am tempted to insist that the political economy of the anti-roads movement would move in other directions than that offered by the champions of rebellion from afar – those who call it the French intifada from the safety of their café society, linking political art to poets and painters of the 1880s, and the like. The suburban youth do not even have the bourgeois pleasure of going into those fashion stores and boutiques where Balzac's flirtatious shop attendants await with a view to petty trade.

And so the unemployed youth are the lumpen who are now the object of a fear campaign in the wake of the war *of* terror, even as that term has worn thin, even as branded, ironic, belligerent insistence on a trade mark or remembrance. At the same time, opportunistic military adventurism on the part of the leadership – an adventure going badly in the theatre of war, but not successfully challenged at home – leads to demonisation of specifically Muslim youth and exacerbated racial tensions at the sharp end of economic disenfranchisement. In between, rich war-economy businessmen, both Asian and white, enjoy a profit bonanza on the back of the restitution of imperialism, direct foreign investment in the third world and a service economy at home. Conflict on the estates can only be understood as a particular expression of this wider context.

Do the youth intend their burning cars to send some sort of communiqué? A Message, perhaps even demands? And to whom do they want to communicate: the Police, the Government, Parisians in their boutiques and cafés, or perhaps *only* each other – of course via the media spectacle. The lumpen are what Sarkozy called the *racaille*, and whom Žižek thinks impotent, with no meaning. Derrida lists them as gang-bangers. I think there is something more going on. I think the exploration of the street battles in France suggest a rethink of perspectives and interpretation, the way in which we look – at the towers, at the roads, at the plan. I think the problem of who writes and who is able to speak about whom – and the places where theory scrapes together an alibi for continuing to witter on and on, the elitism of critical thinking and the taint of an 'involved' politics that does not seem to get involved at all. All this seems utopian, and far from the alternate reality conjured by burning cars and falling buildings. The riff raff, the lumpen, the *racaille*, the *voyou*, the 'criminality pure and simple' of the youths of London (Cameron 2011) the *çapulcu* (looters) of Gezi Park, Istanbul (Erdoğan in Harding 2013), the mute, the blind – these are code words for a material and immaterial opposition to the traps of wage slavery, deceits of privatisation and the strictures of race and class supremacism. In the street, in varied ways, across a new set of alliances and composition, there is a hint of something more than muteness or looting. Lack of respect for the law is not lack of respect for oneself or for community, even if it has an appearance form that risks spectacularisation or stereotype in the pantomime theatre of popular opinion, media, theory and governance.

Coda: The Battle of Algiers.

In 2002 ADF initiated concert-screenings of an older film, this time the revolutionary cinematic extravaganza of *The Battle of Algiers*, released in 1966 by Gillo Pontecorvo. This film tells the story of the clandestine resistance movement against the French occupation of Algeria and works well when screened for new audiences with a live ADF soundtrack. Bringing a new audience to an old film, a part of the third cinema movement, quite often overlooked by Drum and Bass fans, carried a powerful allegorical charge at a time when issues of colonial occupation – Afghanistan, Iraq, and Lebanon – were prominent in the media.

As I said at the beginning of this chapter, I am particularly interested in what a British Asian music activist outfit, with a record of anti-racist, anti-imperialist organising, can achieve with the technology of sound and film as a propaganda device. What does this tell us about activism, media, and the intended audience for ADF's experiments at the movies? Some will of course say that the ADF score for *The Battle of Algiers* is no improvement upon Morricone's soundtrack; some will quibble about the sanctity of creative work in the age of digital reproduction; some might suggest that ADF cash in with a radical pose, presenting themselves as advocates of any and every left cause going. It is of course possible to discuss these matters, but I think these are the wrong questions.

It might be interestingly provocative to ask instead after the plausibility of ADF's attempts to get the youth to question; to 'meditate', not in the yogic sense, upon problems of politics, violence, resistance, and on alternate ways of viewing the world. *The Battle of Algiers*, in Pontecorvo's third cinema way, was already a moment of consciousness raising, which ADF now update according to their want. ADF are not sentimental, and they are never in denial about the culture industry as a sapping vortex of commercialisation, but their engagement with the media cannot be described simply as an issue of chains or noise. ADF would want to promote a revolutionary consciousness. I wonder if we can grant them the luxury of thinking so differently?

What ADF have though is not just any kind of politics, nor any greater or lesser disguised evangelical mission, but a purpose and push towards a more fundamental form of thinking; the realisation that a limit to thinking, a narrowing, is a baleful consequence of an unexamined attachment to the silver screen. The jangling soundtrack ADF provides for *La Haine* or *The Battle of Algiers* is intended as alternative to television as mere entertainment, and yet this is the entertainment field. The question of where you organise operates here. ADF member John Pandit is often contemptuous of idle-talk as a substitute for the necessities of organising an alternative to capitalism, imperialism, racism, and in many ways I hear this resonating over and over in ADF's politically motivated use of film, yet he too is a musician in his day job.

The film includes many scenes of significance for the question of organising, and of how those involved in an immediate way – in the Kasbah – in struggle are making choices and calculations that deserve close attention. The sequence already examined at the start of this chapter is also discussed by Ella Shohat. Three women pass through the security cordon to place bombs not as a moment of strategic hybridity but as an example where the women 'use their knowledge of European codes to trick [and kill] the Europeans' (Shohat 2003:58). In 'the psychodynamics of oppression, the colonised knows the mind of the oppressor, while the converse is not true' (Shohat 2003:58). The French are taken by surprise. The Algerian women had cut their hair, dressed up as westernised party girls, frocks, make-up, and infiltrated the French quarter in order to plant their bombs. Nikos Papastergiadis describes the scene in detail:

At the precise midpoint of Gillo Pontecorvo's *The Battle of Algiers*, (1966) the ultimate revenge is executed at a cafeteria on Rue Michelet. It is late afternoon and the French colonial middle class has gathered to relax. Couples are having coffee, children enjoying an ice cream and hopeful men hanging at the bar. A young woman in a white dress enters and approaches the bar. A man moves to the side, offers his seat and smiles. She orders a coke, places a bag beneath her feet. She is sexy and cool. Midway through her drink she gets up. 'Leaving?' He inquires. 'Yes.' She replies. 'Pity.' He adds. No sooner has she crossed the road than the bar explodes. Within minutes two other bombs are detonated.

Who can you trust? The enemy could be anyone or anywhere. Prior to the explosions, three women met. They removed their veils and burka. They dyed their hair, dressed like Europeans, assumed an aloof sense of entitlement and subsequently passed every security checkpoint, pausing only to, either take nervous breath, or flirt with the soldiers. The colonizer's greatest fear is not the confrontation of the otherness in the enemy but the unexpected risks in intimacy (Papastergiadis 2003)

We can be perversely fascinated by this intimacy of course – cold and cruel it is. Who are our friends? To get through the security lines the women must pass; to get close to their target – as is the case with the suicide bomber today, getting close to Benazir, getting inside the tube, getting onto the plane – they must know the security protocols and how to slip through. Flirtation helps in this scene, the women are nodded through, they are processed and accepted 'as if' they were like everyone else. That they leave bombs in a café, an airline office, the crowded marketplace, is a consequence of being able to present as the other within. This was calculated, and even if there was some tension – in the film, a lot of tension – and a fear that the checkpoints could not be passed, that alarms would be triggered, meaning defeat, their nerves were the stronger. The tension on display and the tension hidden, and the grotesque inevitability of this form of political warfare, is the impending tragedy and coming chaos, palpable in the film from the start. Watching here, we are alerted by this story to the myriad anxieties of the terror alert, the repetitions of the border control, the security fence, the customs checkpoint – the need to pass, our suspicion of those who try to pass, interrogation, fear. The border becomes a theatrical space of compression. All focus directed there, dissuades us from looking elsewhere, looking at a wider frame. This condensation paradoxically produces a corresponding escalation and the shared threat makes terrorists of us all, the possibility of explosion is everywhere. And the women have barely even spoken. 'Yes' she says.

So perhaps surprisingly, I think we can better understand something about what *The Battle of Algiers*, as a film, achieves by listening to the ADF soundtrack. The event is never simply the cause of bringing about a critical anti-colonialist consciousness in the youth that are attracted to ADF performances. Ostensibly this would be one of the simple planned, even calculated, ends, but no-one would be so stupid as to think there is a one-to-one equivalence between planned intention and effect. Indeed, there is no simple or singular intention possible when an audience, by definition, comes from a wide range of possible contexts. There are plenty of debates about ethics and motivation, even inspiration, in the literature on propaganda, promotion and politics. ADFED itself is a broad constituency, open to many, and ADF have long pointed out their wide 'consciousness raising' orientation.

Unfortunately, this does not mean that film itself, with added live music, is by and by an automatically progressive consciousness raising tool. One particular story drives this point home. In 2002 it was reported that Pontecorvo's film was to be screened – with the original score – at the Pentagon as an instructional text for the generals of the low-intensity warfare operations unit, with the intention of aiding the generals in their thinking about how to win the war in Iraq, and how to deal with a militant insurgency without losing the 'battle for hearts and minds', as the French so clearly did in Algeria. It seems the generals watched less than carefully. The point is not to suggest only that any text – film, event – can be turned to any politics whatsoever – though I am sometimes convinced that all things can be recuperated and co-opted to do service for capital – but that what is required to achieve a radical thinking is something more than the conventions of calculative thought that usually belong to technology, especially technology in the hands of the generals bombing Afghanistan, Iraq, Lebanon, Libya, Mali, Syria…

Not all bombings are the same. Former Labour Foreign Secretary Robin Cook said 'it is an awful fact of life in Iraq that every day brings a comparable toll of violent death … in the ten days following the London bombings [of July 7 2005] there have been no fewer than 30 suicide bombings in Iraq' (in Seidler 2007:108). Recognising that the convenient explanatory line on 'young' 'brainwashed' 'angry' 'misinformed' Islamists – here referring to young British Asian men, but we could substitute the women of the Casbah – Seidler suggests that:

It is not enough to say they have misunderstood Islam. Nor is it not enough to say that this is not Islam. Issues remain about how they can channel their anger into political action within a democratic politics and how they can feel their voices are being understood in all their diversity. We have to recognise and validate their sense of injustice rather than to minimise it through categorically denying that the London bombings have nothing to do with the injustices people feel about Afghanistan and Iraq. We have to recognise and learn to respect the diverse transnational loyalties citizens carry within a cosmopolitan polity (Seidler 2007:109).

Although in parts the wording here is grammatically awkward – he means we should not deny the bombings have *something* to do with Afghanistan and Iraq – the recognition that 'they' includes cosmopolitan Londoners is a step up from other related positions. Similarly, Ken Livingston can acknowledge that 'consistent double-standards about the Middle East [have] created disaffection with youths' (in Seidler 2007:111), and Seidler thinks that 'if this is true about disaffection, it remains open whether people should be taught that suicide bombing against innocent civilians is never morally justified' (Seidler 2007:111). The grammar is stiff here as well, but this leans towards comprehension of the position of those with no obvious way to resist overwhelming military force. This poignant line compares the *The Battle of Algiers* women who pass through the French lines to place bombs in cafes with the French bombardment of Algerian villages: 'give us your bombers [your aircraft] and you can have our baskets' is later quoted from the film (Seidler 2007:187).

Less coherent is the position of someone like Michael Ignatieff in *The Lesser Evil: Politics in an Age of Terror* who seems intent to develop the moral arguments that would justify national defence extended to a global scale on the part of a righteous liberalism.

At best Ignatieff manages to echo JFK as cited in the previous chapter, and perhaps Seidler above, when he writes: 'The way to meet the challenge of terrorism … is to ensure the oppressed always have peaceful political means of redress at their disposal. Where such means are denied, it is inevitable violence will occur' (Ignatieff 2005:x). This paraphrase repetition of Kennedy becomes a common refrain, but in Ignatieff it also comes alongside some rather simplistic assessments of the Russian Revolution – caused by WWI military collapse, not terrorism (Ignatieff 2005:64), as if the Bolshevik Party organisation had nothing to do with it all – and on other examples: Algeria – the FLN did not have support at the beginning (Ignatieff 2005:86), the Palestinians 'were committed to violence from the very beginning' (Ignatieff 2005:103). His position is shaky and often one-sided, he does however set out some criteria:

> Thus while it is possible to justify armed struggle in defense of self-determination, it is possible to do so only under four conditions: the group's just claims have to have been met with violence; the failure to accommodate these claims must be systematic, enduring, and unlikely to change; the claims must be fundamental to the survival of the group; the struggle must observe the laws of war and the rule of civilian immunity (Ignatieff 22005: 103).

The first criteria excludes the September 11 attackers because they did not leave any demands (Ignatieff 2005:99), although their supporters claimed they acted on behalf of Palestine and the 'Holy Lands' – and there are significant archives of video and radio 'messages' in circulation for those who wish to tune in. For Ignatieff the code is legal and he insists that 'when terrorism appropriates justice it is at its most dangerous' (Ignatieff 2005:100). Again this 'no demands' line is set against a continuity of administration. Normal service however is belied by the way the 'rupture in the symbolic' is so often denied (Rancière 2010:104, Žižek 2002:141). That in the days after September 11 all networks on television offered non-stop heavy rotation commentary, only returning to 'normal' programming after several days (Sturken 2007:53) is significant. The other criteria justifying a terrorism that will never be justified are vague, and in the end while Ignatieff does make the 'painful admission that injustice prevails in the Arab states where terrorists find their recruits' he does not and cannot agree that 'violent struggle against such injustice is justified' (Ignatieff 2005:101). The criteria seems to be set up to make the accusation that terrorism is a 'first' rather than 'last resort' of these groups – a point that could also well be charged against States like Israel, the US and Britain, which would be another painful admission. Ignatieff does insist that 'Those who equate the violence inflicted by Israel with that inflicted by Palestinian suicide bombers ignore real differences in institutional accountability', although 'this is not to claim legal oversight is always effective' (Ignatieff 2005:110). His final assessment is that 'the use of terror to secure freedom can poison freedom itself' (Ignatieff 2005:105). Perhaps it has, with the flip-flop of such anxiety repeating the 'no demands' narrative over and over – *so far, so good.*

When he discusses Pontecorvo's film, Ignatieff is more judicious, choosing his exemplary scenes from the film with predictable caution:

While clearly siding with the Algerian revolution, Pontecorvo takes care to avoid any moral caricature of the French, and shows why torture could be seen as a rational and effective way to break up the terrorist cells working in the Algiers Casbah. Nor does the filmmaker conceal the bloody reality of the liberation struggle, showing the full horror of an attack on a café that leaves the street strewn with mangled bodies and traumatized survivors. The film maintains an extraordinary subtle moral balance ... *The Battle of Algiers* thus becomes a testament to the tragedy of terrorist war (Ignatieff 2005:120).

ADF use technology to make us think, not simply consume their sound as entertainment. In this, they are, I feel, an advance insofar as they do more than simply offer a critical note against colonialism, revealing some of the truths about colonial history; rather, revealing plus an activism that militates *for* critical thinking. It is no accident that ADF called an earlier EP *Militant Science*. They explain:

> Whatever anyone says about ADF's so called 'political' lyrics, no one would have taken any notice if it wasn't for ADF's sound and its inherent energy: ragga-jungle propulsion, indo-dub basslines, distorted sitar-like guitars and samples of more 'traditional' Asian sounds (Asian Dub Foundation 2006).

What do these efforts – the disruption of a film with dub bass – when we measure these culture industry efforts against the realities of war, the low-level anxiety that is still the disciplinary control that operates across the urban scene? One end of white supremacy is an inability to connect with affective inequality of discipline – some are sitting in the Festival Hall asked to think, others are dodging drone bombers and hunter-seeker missiles running for their lives. ADF gesture towards this, dressed up as militants, yet cognisant that there is so much more to be done.

It is not the case that the ideas in people's heads are all important, but there is an effort to engage in ADF's Community Music that accesses an anti-racist, anti-imperialism that I do not want to give up. It is not to be dismissed out of hand, despite the pressures of complicity: a culture industry co-option. The mediation here is the appearance form of wider processes and tendencies that help shape ideas and the cultural performance of both belonging and resistance, including staged resistance. The war on terror, the immigration debate, racism and the demonisation of Islam, lumpenisation, cretinisation, all have a brutal economic and imperialist underbelly. Urbanisation, manifest in culture-talk as hybridity, privatisation, manifest in policy-talk as austerity and cuts to benefits and social services, militarism and labour and border control, surveillance as workplace, and community, discipline; the forms of appearance manifest cultural expressions that must be read as a consequence of, and sometimes creative opposition to, the dynamics of a convoluted system. Analysis cannot read one instance of this convolution as exemplary – as *passages à l'Acte* – if it does not want to risk oversimplification and its own neurotic singular display. Yet a critical choice in favour of cultural expression defective for capitalism, of the appearance of alternatives to the atrocities of our time, is plausible, if not ever the promise of a soft-landing.

Molotov.

'According to Roy Medvedev, Stalin's daughter Svetlana Stalin recalled Molotov and his wife telling her: "Your father was a genius. There's no revolutionary spirit around nowadays, just opportunism everywhere. China is our only hope! Only they have kept alive the revolutionary spirit'" – *so far so good*, Molotov died aged 96 in 1986, China went awry (Citizendia 2009)?

4

Scheherazade's Sister, M.I.A.

Cultural Projects

A 'cultural project' runs alongside the war on terror and impacts upon a diverse range of practices, from the militarisation of public policy, through to entertainment, cinema and the music industry. In a 'nanny state' on the march – where anxiety over 'the ability to make babies' signals white supremacist fear of 'demographic changes' (Bhattacharyya 1998:293, 299; 2008, 92) – there might be reason to revisit the now near impossible role of the storyteller as the site of critique and an alternative to 'Total War'. The storytelling I have in mind has to do with the war at home and with forms of media using humour, jokes and pranks that stress or otherwise reveal this. In this chapter, once again, Walter Benjamin and Theodor Adorno are the bookends that permit some comments on the work of the culture industry performer-curator and musician Mathangi Maya Arulpragasam, also known as M.I.A.

The main focus of this chapter is on M.I.A., and the story-telling is about war and terror in a tangential way. Yet the narrative gets right into the everyday of 'our' lives – and subverts with a kind of dark provocation: one that relies upon a prankster character, who aims to undo the unexamined comforts of power, in ways which need to be analysed. I diagnose a deep anxiety and avoidance in the nexus between war and narrative. While to provide a political economy understanding of the war is possible, for example the obvious global-crisis-inducing expenditures on cowboy versions of imperialism in Afghanistan, Iraq and Libya, there is also just as much a war effort 'at home' and an everyday war economy that is not so clearly 'at war'. The story of the commercial wing of the global war machine is familiar, for example, if we think of companies like Halliburton and Bechtel in Iraq, or British Prime Minister David Cameron heading trade missions to the Middle East to sell weapons, with a photo-op side trip to Cairo if not quite Tahrir Square. A new industrial-imperialism opens up formerly blockaded countries to a wild-west development, but this is presented as glorious democracy, and negotiation with the Taliban. The post-invasion and post-active service camp-follower operation in Afghanistan is to be followed most likely in Syria, Algeria, North Korea – and desta-bilisation as strategy could be documented to good effect. In his 2004 book *Iraq Inc.: A Profitable Occupation*, Pratap Chatterjee looked closely at reconstruction companies, distinguishing oil industry service provision and oilfield reconstruction from weapons and armaments contracts – the latter the bigger of Halliburton's joint interests (Chatterjee 2004:211) – and combining on-the-ground-reports of Iraqi civilian disaffection with examination of the compromises of both the installed Iraqi Governing Council and USAID, State Department, Pentagon/ CIA. Today the military spend of British armaments and aerospace complicity in a militarist policy abroad and a jingoistic nationalism at home is an urgent and appalling tale not to be excused. That democracy might entail a managed policy of abandonment, a destabilisation through chaos and a generally profitable destruction that presents under the label of 'religious civil war' is a hypocrisy that all children should learn.

Gargi Bhattacharyya emphasises over and over that the war on terror is addressed to 'global audiences' (Bhattacharyya 2008:113). It is a war that targets the entire world, not only terri-tories currently under occupation (2008:133) and entails the 'construction of a global public as audience to the war on terror and as a particular relation to … implicate the viewer in the supposedly necessary horrors of counterterrorism' (Bhattacharyya 2008:142). This is a convincing suggestion, since it is clear that the impact of war is cultural and political, as much as theatrical, and indeed I want to extend this argument to say that the theatre of war is universal. Sometimes it is choreographed as a low-intensity conflict 'at home' in the Metropolitan West, where anxiety and paranoia prevail without adequate commentary. Sometimes it is orchestrated, both at home and abroad, as not-quite-innocents locked up and detained, dragged through secret courts and 'control orders', 'Internal Security Acts' and infringements of rights – stripping away ideas of law, justice and due process – with summary detention without trial or drone-strike assassination 'authorised' from on high. It is a deadly dramaturgy, in which pantomime terror creates figures of fear, rumour and distortion – as distraction and cover for a virulent racism, white supremacy and privilege. Also integral to the military-entertainment compact, this is a deeper and longer-lived malaise fully built into the structure of the so-called civil consensus that is the less often told story of the Western war effort. Wherever and whoever 'we' are, we go about our everyday with its effects. The very question of who we are is governed by its co-ordinates. Pranks, oil, death or glory, I want someone to tell that story.

Storyteller *Nights.*

On the eve of the second imperialist World War, the one he did not live through, Walter Benjamin wrote an essay called 'The Storyteller' for the journal *Orient and Occident* (October 1936). In this essay, ostensibly devoted to the works of the writer Nikolai Leskov, but also about fairytales, reading, buying books, magic, Macbeth and Marxism, teaching and tall tales, Benjamin first suggested that the idea of a storyteller seems remote to modern sensibility. The reasons for this are many, but one of them is set out starkly in a way that might give us pause in the context of today's world of terror, fear, hype and lies. With a foreboding of what is to come, Benjamin writes of war stories:

'Every glance at a newspaper shows that it [storytelling] has reached a new low ... our image not only of the external world but also of the moral world has undergone changes overnight, changes which were previously thought impossible. Beginning with the First World War ... wasn't it noticeable that at the end of the war those who returned from the battlefield had grown silent – not richer but poorer in communicable experience' (Benjamin 1936/2002:144).

I think maybe storytelling is the mediation, the mechanism in theory, which processes and gives form to the patina of ideas, the plethora of interpretation that needs to be negotiated in thought. The storyteller asserts and fights for authority, the passive aggressive late-night campfire insistence of 'listen to me, I've a story to tell, a web to spin'. Ideologies of war, children's morality, ghost tales, instruction, newspapers, embedded reporters and the international seeking-telling of ethnographic effort, all participate in this mediation. Not immediacy, but retelling, repetition, recitation.

In 'The Storyteller', Benjamin mentions Scheherazade three times. His point in the essay is to distinguish between memory and mere information, and, following this, I think it worth pursuing the Benjamin-Adorno, Scheherazade, line that the trick is to tell better stories such that despotism might be overcome. We can do this in the interval between ceremonies for yet another anniversary of 9/11, 7/7 or 1/5/11, before the commemoration fatigue sets in, before the public display of the bodies, the photograph of the presidential viewing of the corpses, the interview with the shooter, the collection of the name-tags, the presentation of the flag, the knife-man, the bus, the court case sketches, the sentencing and the revenge ... before the entire predictable and unremarkable electoral apparatus of victory and its hollow negative echo kicks in. We need to think of this interval, and seek there also the formation of a genuine revolutionary people's army that can win, which is of course also a narrative gamble: Scheherazade, you will remember tells her stories as a ruse to buy time from the King who holds her captive.

There are problems with the kind of reading I am risking here, but I can't help the feeling that looking into old texts might help us reimagine new ones. Thinking of Benjamin, I have become more and more interested in the kinds of storytelling possible after war. Or rather, during this present and endless war. Of course, this might also be a way to dress up the facility of provocation, or of the search for provocative metaphors for thought – repetition, recitation, monotony, monography, fable, fantasy, phantasmagoria. I know there is not just one version of Cultural Studies™, and my lists may be tiresome, but for today I'd like to suggest provocative thinking as one of the gambles of storytelling. Telling stories to provoke an outcome different to one that is inevitable if we continue to think, and behave, the way we do now, even if all is not rosy in storytelling land. The examples in this book have to do with those who make music and their persecution. In this chapter, red heads will be discussed, and Wagner. I want to stitch and switch between the contemporary media scene and the ancient narratives of the *Nights* – updated. So to tell a comic-serious next next-story to add to a thousand and one others. I believe it is necessary to – keep on trying to – do this because stereotyping prevails – and is both key to good stories and the most dangerous of games. The point will be to hold comedy and tragedy together, as a diagnosis and intervention in trauma, the provocation as crisis and cure at the end, with no-one rendered mute or blind by *fait accompli*.

To focus upon storytelling is the habit of a literary and anthropological rendering of culture that even when it approaches the media it seeks to do something 'more' than associate culture and tradition with commerce. However, in cinema and television it is storytelling that has found the ideal way to repackage tradition for sale, and avoiding this is voluntary myopia. To develop this argument at a cultural level is to recognise how patterns of melodrama and performance are played out in the ways events come to our attention. The pantomime season at Christmas is now matched with a sinister twin in July that commemorates the bus bombings with an equally ideological storytelling round – teaching kids fear and hate just as much as Christmas teaches them commoditisation. The idea that pantomime is educational, rather than orientalist – Sinbad, Ali Baba, Aladdin – is just as much training in stereotype and profiling as are the melodramatic terror alerts each July and September. These are constructed 'panics', each no doubt grounded in real evidence, solid intelligence, and careful analysis by Special Branch and MI5 – as the tragic deaths of Jean Charles de Menezes and Drummer Lee Rigby could both surely attest. Aki Nawaz as 'suicide rapper' might almost be funny if it were not symptomatic of a wider malaise and complicity in our media reportage – a failure to examine critically and contextually what is offered up to us as unmediated 'news'. What did it say on the side of the bus if not 'Total Film'? We can read all manner of signs here.

As I have said, storytelling is not analysis, but it provides a frame for bringing the flux of isolated instances, experiences and events together. It may also have a critical intent – Scheherazade's storytelling is deceptively, seductively, hostile to the audience she will persuade, change, and in the end love (well, marry) – rearranging dangerous desires through patient narrative towards justice (*pace* Spivak 2008). The gamble of storytelling, at least for Scheherazade, is hedged by way of repetition, but it is not simply the next next next of iteration that succeeds, rather the timing is crucial. With another story always ready and waiting, she must start and end at the appointed hour and does not know in advance if it works.

It turns out that her sister Dinarzade is the keeper of tactical acumen, and so it is again from Spivak that we might learn to look at the forgotten character in an epic for the key. When she tells the king her stories Scheherazade is not alone. Like Bertha Mason in *Jane Eyre*, reconstructed by Jean Rhys in *Wide Sargasso Sea* (Rhys 1965/2000, Spivak 1999), Dinarzade is there for more than incidental reasons. In this case, to keep the timing of the narration – 'sister, if you are not sleepy, please tell us one of your tales to while away the night' – she is not simply the one who listens patiently without interruption or comment. Taught to attend to such calculating silences, we might wonder on just what basis Scheherazade teams up with her sister, so that already in the telling they are more than one, they are many. Dinarzade listens to each of the episodes, elicits them and encourages them. Not just the next-in-line to be sacrificed to the sultan, and more than representative of all those future virgins that would die a thousand deaths if Scheherazade were not a *very* good storyteller. The sister is the unsung facilitator and coach of a desperate last-ditch production. Without her encouragement, without her management of the scene as cultural broker, and even as entre-preneur, there would only be barbarism and death. With the pretence of asking for a story, Dinarzade sets the narrative in motion that eventually undoes the despot. How annoying must have been her demands for these little tales, keeping the King awake till dawn when matters of state will demand he be alert. The constant chatter must have been an irritant, and with no escape or relief, and going to office must have been a getaway route, fleeing the sirens.

Reading political strategy into myth, however, risks the danger of positing a universalism of 'intact literary heritages waiting to be recovered, interpreted and curricularised in … translation' (Spivak 1999:114). We would do well to be careful as to how we recall the sister, even though the role is thankless and too often overlooked. Later I want to suggest that perhaps M.I.A. is also such an enabler. And a sister. But not yet an angel of history in Benjamin's sense, even if he ignores this sisterhood when speaking of the narrative princess, identifying only

Scheherazade as the emblem of epic memory – able to link up stories, to tell one after the next so as to tell a greater history (Benjamin 1936/2002:154). What Dinarzade maybe remembers is also the message or the meaning – at the point of remembering – as part of a wider transformatory program that would insist that things were not always like this; that they need not remain like this; that adversity may be overcome. Scheherazade is not the only one who gambles on storytelling to change the world, to fight the oppressor, to liberate herself and others, including her sister, whose life upon the story too depends.

If there is a danger of rendering the sisters complicit, there is also a problem with storytelling where it becomes allegory. With the *1001 Nights* rendered as fairy tales, the pantomime reduction of significance to entertainment formulas means morality play trades upon stock standard repetitive reactions and stereotype where imagination and critical thinking might have been otherwise less constrained. The reflex-fear reactions of 'he's behind you' and 'so far so good' in Pantomime and such are the work of automated learning. These stories as entertainments and adventure dress-up are both productive as ways to socialise children and to work out moral thinking through narrative and attention. At the same time they are destructive of open creativity, restricting imaginative play, fixing stereotypes in place – pirates riff-raff, bad; heroes, and loyal Viziers, good – setting down story patterns that will be transposed more and more in formulaic ways to eventually manifest as the logical bureau-cratic-admin babble of the administered life and office culture of dull. Then storytelling, around the water-cooler, about TV, itself becomes a kind of advanced pantomime that has forgotten that it is play.

It turns out that the annual Pantomime circuit has itself used the tradition of wry or ironic political analogy to raise questions for school kids about stereotype, terror and racism. There is after all a long pop music involvement in Pantomime in the UK. Cliff

Richard played Aladdin way back in 1962, with the Shadows as Wishee, Washee, Poshee and Noshee. Tommy Steele was also a pantomime favourite, and the Spice Girls not so long ago appeared – it is not a long stretch to see how Keith Richards dressed up in *Pirates of the Caribbean: At World's End* (2007 dir. Verbinski) is in part a nod to the tradition of breaking stereotype with stereotype, where 'political humour allows the audience to laugh at the joke while becoming aware of its own subjectivity and complicity' (Taylor 2007:18)

> Pantomime continues to develop in response to the cultural norms of society with the inclusion of topical and political references, references to the media and the inclusion of contemporary music and dance (Taylor 2007:69-70)

No surprise then that pantomime is a site where we might find the 'aftermath' of the war on terror. You may have 9/-11 fatigue, but what about the kids? Get 'em while they're young. There is reference to Saddam Hussain in *Snow White* – he was found hiding in a cave (Taylor 2007:137). *Dick Whittington* offers endless opportunity for jokes about the London Mayoral elections, Red Ken or Bombshell Boris each giving the guy dressed up as a cat a run for his money. The *Dick Whittington* story involves a merchant being accused of minor theft and having to leave London only to turn back – the bells tell him to – and he makes his fortune in the orient. Wittington in Morocco, gleaning his wealth as if by magic from a Sultan and returning to electoral success in the city, and still greater banking fortune, is a tale easily tuned to the financial crisis and austerity Britain. To point out that pantomime is ideological, and repeat the Old Bard line that 'all the world's a stage', is still a ruse by any other name. Humour playing with power.

Yet does my plan to nominate M.I.A. as latter-day Scheherazade not also deserve an orientalist critique of the kind say Rustom Bharucha levels against Peter Brook for universalizing the Indian epic Mahabharata? Aren't I somehow setting myself up as Scheherazade too, wanting to tell stories to undo power and casting Aki Nawaz as Sinbad? Yes, probably this too is the orientalist move – to ransack the cultural repertoire of the past for conveniently elegantly edifying narrative. Improbably, in the era of white mythology, a necessary displacement of exoticism against its keepers might also be part of the project that would undo tyranny – we must all tell such tales, and have kings dethroned.

The pantomime take-up of stories from the *Nights* pays little heed to the traditional narrative. Sinbad updated, Ali Baba 2.0. Playing fast and loose with the text, contemporary pantomime is something more akin to an interpretation machine, parsing contemporary events through clown-like characters, and caricatures, for kids. Deeply racist at times, the pantomime characterisations are more reminiscent somehow of the childhood game Chinese Whispers than translation, even allowing for idiom. On *Chinese* Whispers, I am keen to rename the game White House whispers or Gitmo spin, considering the source of the information upon which the war on terror is run, confession gained from torture, intentionally doctored 'dossiers', distorted facts and the pornographic scenes in the situation room in 2012 when Hillary and Barack watched the snuff film of Osama's slaughter (more below). Remember Scheherazade being interrogated each day in Guantánamo and the fibs she rightly tells to get the guards off her back. The *Nights* themselves are more verifiable than much of the source code upon which the Pentagon relies. Scheherazade confined in Gitmo far from her sister is still talking to save her life, and cure the King of his hatred for women and his terrible vengeance; at the same time, children are being taught morality tales; an ideological instruction handbook that, rendered as fairytale, if not just for kids, reinforces the idea of the Arab world as infantile and barbaric.

The *Nights*, in its bastardised pantomime form, is a perfect vehicle for the opportunist and sensationalist storyteller. Here, episodic narration is all that scans; the joke, the skit, the punch-line and the lead item in an election campaign we call the nightly news is remembered – Uday and Ousay Hussein were shot and horrendously displayed, thankfully not in front of their *1001* frescos (mentioned in chapter 2). Gaddafi was effectively lynched, almost live on terrorvision – with Hilary Clinton filmed saying 'wow' to her blackberry on getting the news. In our contemporary ur-story of morality, political vision and sustained ethical action are less readily retained, though in the long run this is what prevails. Scheherazade is interrogated for information, the fact of her incarceration left aside by the press who are more concerned with which orange jumpsuit she wore, by which designer. The activist Left, unable to transmute recurrent episodes of outrage into the sustained proletarian anger that would found a movement and organisation capable of overthrowing the old powers, also puts such figures on a pedestal. This is a burden too far for a mere entertainer. The storyteller is for the campfire in the breaks between battle – a sustaining function, not the main fight.

Repetition is also the key to the *1001 Nights*, as it is the fulcrum of stereotyping. Without the reiteration of caricature there is no caricature – the paradox is that more exposure of this characterisation does not necessarily disarm. The knowing stereotype is the ideal scapegoat. In the *Nights* there are stories inside stories. Telling them in order is Scheherazade's greatest skill, with Dinarzade's help, to weave ever more elaborate tales upon tales, tales that lead to other tales that always lead to yet another tale pending. This might however be grounds for thinking there might be trouble, even as the next next format inspires the works of many oppositional currents, say the Surrealists with their admiration for the experimental writing of Raymond Roussel, or Oulipo group word games or especially the multiple starts in Italo Calvino's *If on a Winter's Night a Traveller*. There are any number of similar examples, most of them less elaborate, so this strategy can be analysed as repetitive trinketisation under a careful control. A patient weaving of narrative towards a greater purpose keeps sight of the whole. We could see this today as a parable of just-in-time machinic production, but it is also a feudal structure, of oral history, storytelling and kinship systems etc. In a comment that will seem still more relevant later, Theodor Adorno quips of Richard Wagner: 'repetition poses as development' (Adorno 1952/2005:31). Repetition can be brilliance, and here also necessity, and even though the stories are of one night, or in most cases an episode of a story cycle in each night that make up, over several nights, the adventures of, for example, the interloper Sinbad, perhaps the entire cycle must be recognised as a triumph, and for any appreciation of oral traditions both valuable and amazing, as an undoing of despotic power, an allegory of strength. And yet...

The influence of the *Nights* extends everywhere, as should any good story epic cycle told over hundreds of hours and housing a political diagnostic, strategic place-marker and complicity with power. Here, in a long quote from the brilliant *Minima Moralia* Adorno finds a convergence with Marx and one of his most famous themes on art. It is art that both expresses the sublime and destroys it, like an express train that hurtles across a landscape is both a miracle of travel and yet too quick for appreciation of travel's grandeur. This is an analytic point that bears as much on the place of art after terror as it does on the possibility of an alternative to terror. Towards the end of this rather long quote the possibility of living without the terror is broached. Or at least an inkling of this possibility is attested to in art. An echo of sorts, like the trace of a story told as you fall into sleep perhaps.

Modern practical luxury is a contradiction in terms... The child reading the *Arabian Nights*, intoxicated by the rubies and emeralds, wondered why possession of the stones should cause such ecstasy, when they are described, after all, not as a means of exchange, but as a hoard. In this question is involved the whole dialectic of enlightenment. It is as reasonable as it is unreasonable: reasonable in recognizing idolization; unreasonable in turning against its own goal, which is present only where it need be justified to no authority, indeed to no intention: no happiness without fetishism. Gradually, however, the child's sceptical question has spread to every kind of luxury, and even naked sensual pleasure is not proof against it. To the aesthetic eye, which sides with the useless against utility, the aesthetic, when severed violently from purpose, becomes anti-aesthetic, because it expresses violence: luxury becomes brutality. Finally it is swallowed up in drudgery or conserved in caricature. What beauty still flourishes under terror is mockery and ugliness to itself. Yet its fleeting shape attests to the avoidability of terror. Something of this paradox is fundamental to all art; today it appears in the fact that art still exists at all. The captive idea of beauty strives at once to reject happiness and to assert it (Adorno 1951/1974:20-1)

Let us look at the steps of this short meditation – the child adduces an analysis, of hoarding that is not far from the first steps of Marx's *Capital* where the miser's love of gold is examined and found as a precursor to, but not actually yet, capital. The capitalist must not hoard, but rather must set capital to work – or rather, set workers to work with capital so as to expropriate still more value, and capital. Not a means of exchange – not a use-value – means this hoard is a mere idolatry, or so we could reason. Yet, 'No happiness without fetishism' – the dialectic in play here shows that the miser's luxuriant miserliness is in contradiction, indeed captive in a system that 'presupposes privilege, economic inequality' (Adorno 1951/1978:120). If the baubles are not denied as baubles and made to do duty at the market, they partake of no value – here value is 'severed from its purpose' – it is cut out from the market only through violence, through the violent property claims of those who would appropriate luxury to themselves. This beauty is, not just for the child, only a story, a fiction that staves off, inconsequentially, the terror. Then, next dialectical step, even as it caricatures and displaces luxury into terror or terror into luxury, the beauty glimpsed but unattainable in the fetish object at least shows that terror might, perhaps, be overcome. The paradox suggests what Adorno elsewhere calls, 'a secret omnipresence of resistance' in art (Adorno 1991:67). Here art is captive and endures a double dilemma – the word is *'festge-haltene'* (Adorno 1951:157), which may have the meaning of detain, but is usually 'held onto'. It holds out a promise, that it cannot achieve – this, we will see, is the nuanced meaning of the injunction that there can be no art after Auschwitz.

M.I.A.

And yet I still hope stories can be told in the storyteller-challenged world. In the theatre which so often retells those twisted tales, almost any fiction is plausible – so long as, following pantomime tradition, the villain comes from the left and the hero is a girl. I nominate Mathangi Maya Arulpragasam, aka M.I.A., as the new Scheherazade. Her sonic concoctions are parables that illustrate our predicament, and speak truth, in their way, to power.

This section examines the video provocation of M.I.A., in collaboration with Romain Gavras, and I investigate the way stereotypes that are knocked down seem to threaten to just get right back up again. I consider the efforts and difficulties that have occupied certain musicians, writers, filmmakers and commentators in the context of a murderous and violent repetition that has to be called, without too much hyperbole, 'Total War'. I take M.I.A.'s video *Born Free* as exemplary for a survey of the absurd and often worrying scrapes British South

Asian musicians have gotten themselves into under the new civil (un)liberties environment of the contemporary city and argue that if we can agree that the co-constitution of the war 'over here' and 'over there' should be recognised differently, then our responses may also need to be different. We could surely not be comforted by my characterisation of the war 'here' in the secure metropolitan 'green zones' as low-level anxiety in a state of civil liberty erosion, creeping authoritarianism and disguised militarism – in costume and design – but that is the condition of war. That there is a discourse, architecture and fashion of low-intensity warfare seems as evident as it is subject to the most desultory disregard. The point would be not so much to complain that this pseudo-war goes on, but that an absent-minded full-scale mobilisation is recognised inversely as paralysing, at best, or at worst, leads people to a capricious denial. Blood on our hands but not even an attempt to wash it off; after its initial artic-ulations, the slogan 'Not in My Name' was barely legible in the diminishing anti-war movement, itself indicative of responsibil-ities shirked, disavowed and ignored, and thereby deeply damaging. That there is nevertheless a mobilisation and general awareness of the stakes of this war, is evidenced in the expressive production of a large number of the performers that have made some sort of critical comment on the war, in those who listen, watch, purchase and support their music, in those that talk about the issues, in those who demonstrate on the streets, those that join the flotillas to Gaza, those who write to their MPs to express their concern about the denial of civil liberties, deaths in custody, excessive CCTV, repressive immigration laws and procedures, abuse of police powers to stop and search, racism of policy and practice, etc. This is a mobilisation of concern that takes many forms, but at the same time there is sometimes also a general listlessness in the face of the repressive apparatus, in circum-stances where the main violence is, as Ewa Jasiewicz once called it, a kind of 'violence without violence' (personal communication

7 August 2010). A prevailing condition of the 'keep calm and carry on' security that comforts those who are safe 'at home' is that a repressive complicity disables criticism of the pervasive war effect as it appears everywhere, and at best turns anti-war opposition into performance, staged protest and the lyricism of music, song, drum and video. All in all, this is never enough to stop the atrocities of war. As Adorno quite possibly would have argued, an explicit opposition to the holocaust does not guarantee the camp mentality is abandoned, and poetry in such circumstances is barbaric. He was surely thinking of Benjamin when he wrote those famous lines; the point is that every document of civilisation is also a testimony to barbarism; and we now have YouTube and Daily Motion on which to see it.

Stereotypes are nasty. Despite critique of the often-evident simplifications involved, it is easy enough to show how knocking them down can tend to reinforce them. This has been the case with the controversy, somewhat contrived, that surrounds M.I.A.'s Romain Gavras-made video promo for her track 'Born Free', from the album /\/\/\Y/\. Consideration of transliteration and repetitions in music should set the political contexts of the track in relief: from Edgar Varèse's (mis)understanding of Hindu music where he thought ragas could be played backwards with no appreciable loss (Varèse 1936); through Adorno on Wagner and Slavoj Žižek's appreciation of Freudian witticisms, through the work of Zappa, who himself was a big fan of Varèse, and Varèse's favourite instrument, the theremin, itself used in tributes to M.I.A., unusual in Asian Hip-hop, and on and on –. In the video the reference appears to be to immigration crackdowns in the USA; on the album the association is with Sri Lankan army execution of Tamil refugees and the displacement of those seeking shelter from the civil war. But can we think music – musicology, Hip-hop scholarship, pop history – without addressing a wider syncopation?

I also want to insist that M.I.A. and *Born Free* must be understood in a double register. If Bhattacharyya (1998) has made the case that a cultural project runs alongside military projects, now updated with the war on terror (Bhattacharyya 2008), it is my argument that this permanent terror scenario – World War Three – is not fully open to analysis by a culture industry focused Cultural Studies. Market research modes of scholarship – audience studies, facilitation/celebration of identity, diaspora, arts and crafts, ethnomusicology – do not enable a critique of the deployment of culture in war. Instead I think we can both see and hear a critique of this argument in the work of artists who tell truth to power, sometimes as comedy provocation, also very serious, on screen and in song. A privileged example is the Hip-hop, Rap, Drum and Bass, Dub and similar musics of performers such as M.I.A. Recognised by Anamik Saha in the context of an evaluation of work that 'foregrounds the capitalist, industrial context of the politics of representation and recognition that other cultural studies approaches to 'race' and difference tend to ignore' (Saha 2012:739), there is good reason to applaud the ways M.I.A. negotiates a difficult contradiction. It is my contention that M.I.A. attracts because her work is worth discussing as a sustained and popular – indeed, surprisingly mainstream – compromised yet uncompromising engagement and a culturally co-ordinated political agenda that uses provocation and stereo-typing against the grain.

The issues of note M.I.A. references in her music, lyrics and interviews include security paranoia, civil society restrictions, new police powers, surveillance technologies, a massive global information net – CCTV, visa checks, credit check and fraud squads, telephone taps, detention centres, terror alerts and terror alert journalism – all reliant upon a double-play of culture industry gamesmanship. Identity, multiple identities and exotica-exploitation, perhaps even a knowingly self-orientalising and youth culture play are standard. This is more than a some-good, some-bad routine, difference within limits, an 'open' discussion of immigration, citizenship testing, attacks on 'grumblers' and other intellectual types... Are these the cultural forms that enable the commercialisation of fear and the profitability of shallow to thrive or is there something more going on?

Of course there is a dilemma in describing a video in print. The possibility of evoking the metronome rhythm of this clip in prose is limited. The in-your-face cut that accompanies the 'boom' of recognition as it is both heard *and* mouthed by the resonant overweight cop. The scree and clutter of a ragtime avalanche of sounds cascading across random versifying. These sounds and scenes are not easily rendered on the page. The idiom does not translate. Yet it is possible in writing to draw out the significance of the 'allegory' in which uniformed US agents with automatic weapons raid households and bundle figures into buses. The viewer asks what is going on? And will realise soon enough that only certain people are being rounded up for incarceration. At this point the staged pointedness of the video kicks in and we see how all those corralled and herded into the prison bus share a physical singularity – they are all red-heads. This bus is not much different from the iconic school bus of so much middle American suburban cinema and TV. The kids on the bus are not felons, they are – and this is the point – everyone's children. This could be your son, brother, cousin. It could be Jean Charles de Menezes killed by police at Stockwell, London, or a WTC cleaner on the Seventh Avenue express subway – the number 2 train – in New York; it could be the youth of Palestine, or of the London riots.

As the bus moves along a street there is some small-scale resistance – stone throwing – and a hint of an organised opposition, sporting red kaffiyeh scarves and Northern Ireland-style wall murals, but no direct challenge to the dragnet. About twenty red-headed males are taken to a detention facility and forced to run across a minefield at gunpoint. Those that do not are shot, those that do, take their chances with the mines and snipers. The video is graphic and explicit, and designed to provoke. The lyrics compliment a racing soundtrack that offers its own searing and sneering indictment on the part of those forced to live beneath the radar of the state, an aggressive throwing back – of 'this shit' – into the face of power. 'Cause I got something to say' is the refrain, 'I got something to say'.

The red-heads are a simple substitute, all too obvious, for the illegal migrants of the Arizona-Texas border lands. They are also the executed Tamils that M.I.A. had already tweeted about, complaining that no-one else was really shocked. The red-heads are also the Jews, and of course the communists – and it should not be lost on us that it could also be the Jews and the communists that do the rounding up here, not just the US state – Palestine too, Muslims 'at home', as I have said, and the youth of Clichy-sous-Bois, Paris, or Tottenham, Clapham, Birmingham, Manchester, Santiago, Chile, Athens, Greece, Hama, Syria, Sanaa, Yemen, etc., etc. The bus is not London red, but it could be seen as a vehicle of terror. Substitutions and hardly hidden allegories do not make the point more real, but that unreality provokes reaction underlines the point – we rehearse a very real simulacrum of concern, and nothing need be done, in the video the red-heads are really ok, back to work, nothing to see here.

Sensation is fine in the fine arts. M.I.A. works on two levels, mimicry and doubling twinned with repetition. Often described as a curator of a veritable catalogue of other performers' styles and sounds, the forked tongue of eloquence is here deployed to good effect. Such military musterings are all too commonplace atrocities, and all too often ignored. They occur right before the eyes of the world, the detention and deportation round-up, the military police raid – so often a Cold War propaganda story to discredit the Red threat of the Soviets, rarely imagined 'at home' in the civilised tolerant white supremacist West. Nevertheless, the desert-run security agent adventure depicted, as fiction, in *Born Free* is quite possibly very much like the kind of real training exercises 'with actors' that we might imagine are held at the Mojave Desert National Training Centre, US Fort Irwin. It can be assumed that Marines practice running, controlling, chasing, corralling, herding and other cowboy scenarios somewhere. They do this either in the so-called 'terror-town' built in the former New Mexico desert village of Playas, or in the Naval Special Warfare Center in Coronado, California (Wasdin and Templin 2011), which itself was where the test-run rehearsals were held for the Seal Six team raid on the Osama bin Laden compound in Abbottabad in May 2011. There must have been a training run before the actual snuff film was beamed to the White House and watched so avidly by those seen in the notorious 'situation room' publicity photograph. That pantomime scene is a study in the 'segragated American Dream' that Vijay Prashad skewers in his book *Uncle Swami*, diagnosing a:

> structural relationship between ... racism and the imperialism that allows for aerial bombardment and extraordinary rendition, that links the archipelago of prisons that run along the spine of California's interior and the 'black sites' for torture that run along the vein of north Africa and the middle east and upward into eastern Europe (Prashad 2012:183).

Prashad might have also added these US Army training camps and the weapons deal handshakes between neoliberal Western leaders and neocolonial plenipotentiary puppets that rule despotic client states. My point here is that it is no accident that one controversy above all gets the *Born Free* video, and filmmaker Romain Gavras, discussed. And it might not be surprising, given his father had made an exposé of CIA involvement in the counter-revolution in Chile: the film *Missing* (dir. Gavras, C. 1982). The son knows how to shock. It is the young curly red-headed boy, shot point-blank in the head in *Born Free*, that most often upsets the commentators. It is a graphic rendition. But like the killing of Osama, that we did not ourselves watch even though we saw the White House staff stage a viewing, this is only a rehearsal, a citation, and this has a significance we shall see.

Born Free.

Whooo!
Yeah man made powers
Stood like a tower higher and higher hello
And the higher you go you feel lower, oh
I was close to the end staying undercover
Staying undercover
With a nose to the ground I found my sound

Got myself an interview tomorrow
I got myself a jacket for a dolla

And the car doesn't work so I'm stuck here
Yeah I don't wanna live for tomorrow
I push my life today
I throw this in your face when I see ya
I got something to say
I throw this shit in your face when I see ya
Cause I got something to say

I was born free (born free)
I was born free (born free)
bo-bo-born free

You could try to find ways to be happier
You might end up somewhere in Ethiopia
You can think big with your idea
You ain't never gonna find utopia

Take a bite out of life make it snappier yeah
Ordinary gon super trippyer
So I check shit cause I'm lippyer
And split a cheque like Slovakia

Yeah I don't wanna live for tomorrow
I push my life today
I throw this in your face when I see you
I got something to say
I throw this shit in your face when I see you
Cause I got something to say

I was born free (born free)
I was born free (born free)
I was born free (born free)
(bo-bo-born free
Ooooh

I don't wanna talk about money, 'cause I got it
And I don't wanna talk about hoochies, 'cause I been it
And I don't wanna be that fake?, but you can do it
And imitators, yeah, speak it

Oh Lord? whoever you are, yeah come out wherever you are
Oh Lord? whoever you are, yeah come out wherever you are
And tell em!

Songwriters: Maya Arulpragasam; Martin Reverby; Dave
  Taylor; Alan Vega.
© IMAGEM LONDON LTD; WB MUSIC CORP

Fresh from the success of having her tracks 'Paper Planes' and,
with A. R. Rahman, 'O Saya', featured in the Oscar-winning film
Slumdog Millionaire (dir. Boyle, 2009), and having made an

eccentric, but inspired version of the old Jonathan Richman standard 'Roadrunner', previously recorded by the Sex Pistols, in July 2010 M.I.A. released her most defiant video yet. An intended provocation, and some would say coldly calculated use of Gavras's bravura effects and heavy-handed parable. It would be difficult not to have some reaction or opinion. For example, if I might start with the end, what disturbs me a little in the lyrics is that last god-bothering refrain repeated about the Lord. It is of course incongruous to claim to be 'Born Free' and then require some sort of absentee Lord to come out and get the message across – to enlighten people, redeem them from their apathy, re-sensitise them. This special pleading is about as forlorn as hoping that twitter commentary will achieve redistribution of power and wealth adequate to the idea of that 'freedom'. It is as insignificant as a music critic thinking that a pop song ought to have higher ideals and greater efficacy. To be disappointed at this however is misplaced, and what needs to be evaluated is the status of provocations of this sort in relation to movements and mobilisations of viable opposition. Is it plausible to consider M.I.A. in the context of allegories and tropes, pranks and jokes, witticisms and the critique of the fool in the face of power? In *Minima Moralia*, one of Adorno's most telling insights is where he explains that the dialectic is more nuanced than the critics usually manage. Dialectical thinking in a sick world is necessarily paranoid and unreasonable in a way that might also be the fraught condition of poetry: he suggests it is the duty of the dialectician to seem paranoid and that '*dass einzig die Narren der Herrschaft die Wahrheit sagen*' (Adorno 1951:89)/ 'only fools tell their masters the truth' (Adorno 1951/1978:73).

A storm of condemnation welcomed the initial release of the video. As might be imagined, popular and mainstream exposure has not meant M.I.A. is universally admired or understood. Nabeel Zuberi usefully lists a range of responses to her work that revel in their contradictory, exoticist-orientalist perversity:

A cluster of positive and negative types and tropes emerged in countless blog entries and comment threads, major and minor music publications. M.I.A. was a refugee-immigrant done good; a postcolonial pimp and whore; a cultural thief; Arundhati Roy with a drum machine; Mowgli with a spray can; hip-hop punk Situationist; prole art threat and bourgie fetish; terrorist bitch and slumming ragpicker; an average talent with skilled (male) producers pulling the strings. Music journalists also tended to determine her authenticity or lack of it based on signs of middle-class privilege, the veracity of her transnational experience as a Sri Lankan refugee, and whether or not she was an apologist for Tamil terrorism. Much of the commentary was geared to putting M.I.A. 'in her place' (Zuberi 2010:188)

An impressive list and an achievement of sorts. What is curious is the number of responses to the video which have completely missed the point, staging a kind of ponderous shock and outrage, and even sometimes taking the attack upon red-heads themselves as 'real', missing the entire allegorical plotting. There is little to be gained in correcting the most wilful of these misreadings, especially where it is clear they have been maliciously intended.

What is more disturbing, and thereby interesting, are the accusations targeting M.I.A. that claim a form of 'dialectical' and critical insight, insisting that though the progressive intentions of filmmaker and artist may be evident, they shoot themselves in the foot by way of, variously, a didactic schlock-mock horror appeal or a shameless commercialised controversy seeking sensationalism. The modulated tone of such accusing commentaries, for example by Anna Pickard (2010) and Douglas Haddow (2010) in the UK, or by Yaseen Ali (2010) and Stelios Phili (2010) in North America, are shrill in a way that only reasoned and self-regarding ill-informed liberal conservatism can be. Haddow, in a piece called 'The Real Controversy of MIA's Video', especially seeks to impress us with his analytical range, citing Southpark and the IRA as antecedents, and not failing to offer a high-minded diagnosis that takes *Born Free* as symptomatic of a critique that he then claims to extend much further. His mistakes however are compounded when he equates the execution of the red-headed boy in *Born Free* with a famous war atrocity from the Vietnam war. This image was intentionally cited by Gavras, having appeared in several films, including in full in the Monkees' Jack Nicholson and Bob Rafelson film *Head* (dir. Rafelson 1968) and in what is arguably the first extended music video (shot on 2 inch quadruplex video in PAL format and transferred after production to film stock) *200 Motels* (dir. Zappa and Palmer 1971). It was also used as background visuals for the song 'The Story of Isaac' by Leonard Cohen on his 1972 tour – as seen in the long lost and recently reassembled film *Bird on a Wire* (dir. Palmer 2009, see Horowitz 2011) and the still was a backdrop in Woody Allen's *Stardust Memories* (dir. Allen 1980, see Emerson 2011). It is not unknown in music and media circles then, but the details clearly are: Haddow confuses South Vietnamese national Police Chief Nguyễn Ngọc Loan with the victim rather than identifying him as the brutal executioner of communist Nguyễn Văn Lém – the picture taken by Pulitzer prize winner Eddie Adams on 1 February 1968, with film by Vo Suu – original footage discussed by Adams as matter of fact: 'I might have done the same thing' (Adams in Tướng Nguyễn Ngọc Loan: Xử bắn Việt cộng 1968)'.

It is of musicological interest perhaps to note that *Head* also features a Frank Zappa cameo where Frank criticises the Monkees for playing 'pretty white' songs, commends Davy Jones on his dancing, but suggests he spend more time on his music, 'because the youth of America depends on you to show the way' (Zappa in *Head* 1968). The way they show is towards *Easyrider* (dir. Hopper, 1969), which, according to Mike Watt's 'Movie

Outlaw' blog, was funded in part by Monkees profits (Watts 2010). A comprehensive thinking through of the place of music and comedy as serious critique might have more to say about the work of Frank Zappa, and the sort of monkeying around that many would call bonkers. Unfortunately Zappa did not live to give his views on the hypocrisies of the present war, but he was an outspoken critic of the 1991 invasion of Iraq and had spent much of the 30 years of his career lampooning the militaristic tragedy of the US forces. His classic album *Billy the Mountain* (1972) is an indictment of conscription that is funny, surreal and potent in turns. In many ways Zappa is an antecedent.

Does it matter that these connections channel a vortex of cross-reference in the pop culture text? It is part of the pleasure of Cultural Studies that a promiscuous intertextuality prevails. Yet it is just as important to get the participants and references correct – mistaking communists for police chiefs and informed criticism for prejudice are errors of fact even as *Born Free* continues to generate controversy beyond its mild and fictional mannerisms. Haddow goes on to suggest that 'genocide can now be parodied in order to promote a pop record' and calls it a 'dog's breakfast of a subaltern text' which, in his view, does not address the source of the Western viewer's 'desensitization' and 'apathy' in the face of a myriad atrocities. His diagnosis is of 'narrative poverty' (Haddow 2010) apparently infecting much more than merely this music video – his other examples are Spielberg, *The Hurt Locker* (dir. Bigelow, 2008) and *Green Zone* (dir. Greengrass, 2010). Pickard, in her quibbling article, at least recognised a more consistent politics in *Born Free*, despite herself, referring to the view that the execution of the boy contravenes YouTube content policy, she opines:

> And that's not the only reason it's controversial. MIA says that it's not a direct comment on a particular political situation – and since much of her lyrics touch on real situa-

tions of conflict and ethnic cleansing, that's completely plausible. But the fact is that it's coming out at precisely the same time as a law proposed in the state of Arizona that will allow police to detain anyone suspected of being an illegal immigrant. Unsurprisingly, much heat is being generated by news organisations and political blogs that see the video as a direct response (Pickard 2010).

There are far worse fictional scenes in the history of cinema and television, many of them on YouTube – watch almost any war movie in the post-Vietnam era – and it might be worth trying to remember that here Pickard's point in this very paragraph is that the pop song video does not refer to the real, it really is fictional, these are actors, the curly red-haired boy is not Vietnamese – nor for that matter Tamil or Mexican. The point of allegory, of course, is to both allow and suggest a reading that relates different circumstances to the ostensible story being told. It is not a secret or accidental association on the part of M.I.A., who had herself complained on twitter some months earlier at the *New York Times* presentation of Sri Lanka as a tourist paradise while the actual Tamil execution video received only limited attention, and certainly much less attention than *Born Free*.

The critiques offered of M.I.A. by those on the ill-informed 'left' edge of journalism are problematically a part of the low-intensity ideological warfare that runs alongside the deployment of troops, bombs, weapons systems and commercial clean up – Halliburton, Bechtel, USAID (Fogarty 2003). At the same time, M.I.A. has a favoured and important role that extends beyond the apparatus of the music industry that enables her (Saha 2012:739). Her unreasonableness is not credited by many, but M.I.A. is right to rant. In Pickard and Haddow we see however, recourse to a sub-Adorno-esque refrain about M.I.A.'s complicity with the sales department of the culture industry. This should give the warning to any too easy dismissal. Brand visibility is step one –

M.I.A. named as one of the 100 most influential people by *Time* magazine; step two is to do something with that visibility. The question of commercial opportunism is often also raised, for example, by Yaseen Ali in Canadian net paper *Varsity.ca*, where she argues that 'M.I.A. remains an artist who profits on the proliferation of new media. Whether fans download her work, watch her music videos or attend her concerts, there is no way of denying the fact that she has become a brand. She is a product that can be experienced, in the same manner that her politics can be purchased' such that 'M.I.A.'s output becomes something that can be taken up as an affectation – a political idea that can be bought, consumed, and trotted out in the name of "resistance."' (Ali 2010).

Other critics find M.I.A. annoying, her 'babbling is palatable because it's rendered incomprehensible by the jungle beat' (Phili 2010), a 'middling rapper' (TamilNet 2010). My argument is that these are unfair assessments – and I think many of them are simply wrong – spitting too much at a pop video that has at least some merit as a provocation and in any case the issues themselves, whatever the merits of the video or of its critique, remain sharp – people worldwide are subject to arbitrary arrest and detention, by cops very much like the prototype Texan Rangers shown here. So, while there can be continued controversy, commercial sponsors, debates about propriety and taste, there is no question that the withdrawal of the video from YouTube in late July 2010 and the subsequent chatter, have made this a celebrity prank that deserved more nuanced attention.

A July 2010 performance of *Born Free* on NBC evening variety and chatshow 'Dave Letterman', with two dozen all-look-the-same look-a-like M.I.A. clones taking over the stage, is a further prank. One, two, many M.I.A.s? Letterman can only manage a feeble 'Happy Halloween' (in July?) and smirking disapproval in a response reminiscent of Ed Sullivan introducing the Rolling Stones all those years ago. But M.I.A. performing the song separate from the video functions only as an advertisement for controversy. Staged, yet still effective – on Letterman. What the performance offers is a small frisson of non-conformity, but does not further the already known dynamics of prankster opposition. Despite its 'enigmatic quality' (Adorno 1952/2005:33) we are still left with a myopic inconclusive and ambiguous commercial 'rebellion' and the barbarism of art after Auschwitz.

Sell Out, or Tiocfaidh ár lá.

M.I.A. in a way, even when she speaks out, is as silent as sister Dinarzade. And despite the vocal – 'something to say' – this silence quietly orchestrates a strategic narration. It is surely insufficient to denounce music that wants to achieve some effect as some sort of betrayal of its artistic aspect – as if we were sure we knew what art was exactly. Nor is it good to ignore the subordination of music to politics insofar as it may appear as a limitation. What seems best is to hold these critiques together in an attempt, at least, to learn to make or discern more analytic distinctions and the possibility of multiple concurrent determinations. It is my contention that *Born Free* moves beyond representation of identitarian politics by way of exaggeration or obviousness, it explodes the simple emotive pull of complacent documentary realism with hyper schlock effect explosions, of heads, of teens, precisely designed to be so provocative it must be dismissed, tangentially raising the questioning a gear. This is not just news – of actual killings, executions, police violence – but the explosion of a collusion in news realism of state ideology and passivity before the screen. *Born Free* is the pop video no longer complicit with a power that displays the instruments of repression all the more to terrorise. It shows instead how violent reality is by showing a violent fiction, before which passivity is more violent yet. A break with comfortable viewing over dinner, the staged controversy deserves more than a brief pause – it offers a cinema of indigestion.

A wilful bias and misreading of M.I.A., in terms of whether she is a 'sell out', has 'inconsistent' politics, supports terrorist groups or is *merely* a provocateur resonates throughout the discussion. The terrorist charge is alleged, in a particularly pantomime video response to her hit single 'Paper Planes' (2007), by Sri Lankan-American rapper Delon (Delon 2011) – 'an empty ploy for publicity' (Solarsky 2010). Links to the LTTE (Liberation Tigers of Tamil Eelam) are of course contested and characteristically an ideological minefield determined according to when different State's proscribed the organization as 'terrorist' (India in the 1990s, European States after 2001). My interpretation is that on M.I.A.'s 'Paper Planes', the signature gunshot-cash till sonic punctuation – bang bang bang ker-ching – knowingly serves to underline the alienated commercial register; brilliant, but ultimately also a hook ready for recuperation for those who miss the point that pop music is not itself the revolution. If it causes a stink, gets people to talk – about issues – and acts as a support for those who would take politics seriously, then who can complain? On one level, the controversy and the debate is the politics of this form. It would not be inappropriate to suggest that the disconnect between the political narrative of the *Born Free* video and the lack of explicit reference in the song lyrics is the most obvious guarantee that the song is intended politically. But why be obvious? We might consider what it means to repeat the phrase 'I've got something to say' – notwithstanding that *The Guardian* used the very same line twice as headline for a puff piece on the launch day of Tony Blair's so-called 'memoirs' (Kettle 2010). The aphoristic and ironic nature of this assertion of vocal intent in M.I.A.'s hands, as opposed to Blair, is subtle simply because M.I.A. says nothing offensive in comparison to Blair's verbose, dissembling autobiographical cover for his warmongering ways. It is not without reason that a people have been moving Blair's book to the crime or fiction sections of the bookstores – as the sign in the video says, 'our day will come'.

On another level, the search for consistency and depth in pop is also somehow overbearing. Street Fighting Men might end up on sponsored tours that sell automobiles like the 1995 2-door special Rolling Stones edition Golf VW, or Stooges for Capital might end up selling insurance. There have been several Rolling Stones tours sponsored by Volkswagen, for example, The Voodoo Lounge tour of 1995, and we should probably try to forget Iggy Pop's fronting for an insurance company: bizarre, and probably why it works (Dowling 2009). Arulpragasam has married into the well-off Bronfman family and yet can say:

> People reckon that I need a political degree in order to go, 'My school got bombed and I remember it cos I was ten-years-old'. I think if there is an issue of people who, having had first hand experiences, are not being able to recount that – because there is law or government restrictions or censorship or the removal of an individual story in a political situation – then that's what I'll keep saying and sticking up for, cos I think that's the most dangerous thing. I think removing individual voices and not letting Tamil people just go 'This happened to me' is really dangerous. That's what was happening, all the Tamils were being made to look a certain way, and nobody handed them the microphone to say, 'This is happening and I don't like it' (*Clash Magazine* June 28 2010)

Curiously, in the Wikipedia entry citation of this passage the words Tamil and Tamils are edited out and replaced with the more general 'people' when originally uploaded on the site – an exhausting if not exhaustive search of the Wikipedia page history did not reveal who made the edits, but the erasure is not just semantic. There is no question that M.I.A.'s political activism generates discussion, but much of this seems like white noise when not linked to a progressive political group or program. Generalities are susceptible traps even where the question of freedom is raised in *Born Free* in several pressing registers. The difficult question however, is how much weight to place on the possibility of the artist having something to say. 'Born Free' and 'I've got something to say' are lyric lines emphasised and reflected by repetitions in the rhythm, but to an extent perhaps that they are parodic, and so to underline their special pleading, they state their opposite. No longer free, signifying nothing. This might be a harsh diagnosis to offer, even as dialectical speculation, yet it fits the criticisms made of the biographical trajectory of its spokesperson. As Arulpragasam notes herself:

> It was so confusing. From an American media point of view, I should be really happy: 'Paper Planes' is a hit, and you're getting nominated for a Grammy and an Academy Award. But I wasn't paying attention to any of that because it was just the aftermath of a song I'd written two years before. I was having a baby. I was watching thousands of people dying every day on the computer screen [towards the end of the Sri Lankan civil war]. I was going outside the house [in Beverly Hills], having to deal with people protesting calling me a terrorist ... They were calling me a terrorist while I was watching actual terrorism happening on my computer screen (Arulpragasam 2012:119)

Life does matter, and the placing of the music in the hands of such large industry forces, can never be neutral. It is also important to see the lyrics set against the music itself, though final decisions on the significance of opposition counterpoint or complementarity are not easily arbitrated. In the video the themes of liberty from state repression and detention, from the outrages of the military and police's political – ethnic, identitarian – targeting of groups, and the erasure of civil rights are each neatly skewered. Yet the street furniture of this music is false, shop-bought distressed rather than reclaimed or found refuse. A stylised chair designed to look like something salvaged from a car wreck; milk crate coffee tables; mirrors where only the frames are cracked. This is fashion rebellion mass marketed as a poignant reminder that the massive energies of the culture industry would be potent if really politicised, but in this form remain only merchandising. All the problems of how this is art and thereby ineffective, even complicit, are still to work through, but if art could not have political ambitions, even as mere commentary, there would be nothing for *critics*. For the sensibility of *Born Free*, politics is not a specified location or a particular cause, but the possibility of causes no matter who you are, the possibility of bringing awareness and sensitivity to the scenes of injustice and of responsibility to a generalised audience. This sometimes has the danger of becoming preacherly, but there is clearly also the expectation, very often rewarded, that the audiences addressed are fully able to analyse and judge at a level superior to the normative stupification of commerce.

The point is to defend M.I.A. from extant criticisms only to then make a more substantive critique of the form and its trinketisation. There is a dilemma here in disguise: to dress up politics as music may mean both music and politics become pale pantomime imitations of themselves. This is not a problem if it is conceded that no politics or music, as such, can be isolated and that both are invariably intermingled to the extent that they mingle at all. Mimicry itself has a long heritage in social theory – Auerbach (1953), Adorno (1991), Taussig (1993), Bhabha (1994) to name a few. It is Adorno's sense that makes the most sense, where mimicry offers the stamp of identity and renders all things the same even in their 'claim to be irreplaceably unique' (Adorno 1991:68) – a market phenomenon, rendered in the alchemy of the phantasmagoric double life of things, as things and as things in exchange. Think of the endless exchanges that render Marx's coat a commodity, and then see that after more than a ten year run for the war *of* terror, the public, as presented on TV and in shopping malls, are even more inured to this show-boating dressage. We all wear combat fatigues, even our backpacks are designer military issue, little to distinguish the supply lines of the market from the PX. I wear t-shirts from the Old Navy company, desert camo shorts, khaki converse. And the time of this war is endless, always on stage 3 alert, no end to the drone attacks or the mail-shots. M.I.A. wearing a 'Complaints Department'/grenade t-shirt, leaves us with ambiguities as to whether she really has something to say, can readily be heard as an ironic articulation of a vocal impotence, shrill shouting of truths in a vacuum, or a space in which no-one cares if you scream. The prank, and the t-shirt, is the trinketised form of the political movement. The one-off, one-day-a-year event stunt that thrives in the post 68 anti-Leninist style-culture politics of social media. As such, *Born Free* itself masquerades in danger of a reconciliation with the camps as those paid to act like camp guards chase after actors in the fiction of the real. Remember the Osama training sessions at Camp Coronado. So also do our creatives chase the under-assistant west coast promo man as much as the marketing team of Beggars Banquet Records, themselves no stranger to staged controversy, or commercial gain. The entire scenario is ring-fenced by the counting – and interrogation – of sales units. It is forbidden here to even acknowledge the question of profits, even as we nod towards the plight of contemporary detainees we keep an eye on the charts. The barbarity of the commercial holocaust was never more poetic, as we will see. That the *Born Free* video does not itself further the cause of justice for those abused by border-camp machines resolves itself into recognition that without political power, having something to say remains moot. At the same time, it must always be made clear that political power without 'something to say' breeds totalitarianism.

The dilemma, perhaps not so hard to solve for some, in analysis of M.I.A., is that of the close proximity of the provo-cateur-artist and the corporate stager. Married into fortune and industry and at the same time accessing its most maverick radical latitudes, a sister with a business plan alongside the confidence to win by risking all because there is nothing much to lose. It is exactly in this comfortable conjunction that the prankster thrives, kept by the side of the King. Elsewhere I have argued that Orson Welles is the patron saint of pranks – the freedom to experiment is bought by way of a well-funded security, for now, of tenure. This also provokes hostile responses, to which there is no ready comeback. The jester's life is fragile. M.I.A. earns considerable antipathy, in part a consequence of the creative energy and freedom afforded a rogue success, both threatening and jealous-making, and to some extent compromised in a baseless conflation of oppositionality and opportunism. There is an opposition here, but it cannot win on its own terms or while it is complicit in support of what it opposes. This too is the problem of every 'free' radical, never quite free, but looking towards a day of political transformation yet to come.

Within cultural studies, or music criticism, or perhaps even Wikipedia edit wars, the vortextual descent into flame criticism should be tempered with the ambition to make each essay, by way of a writing, storytelling, or theoretical insight, a contribution to political redress. Storytelling as a kind of merchandising of ideas is important, though the extent to which this is promoted cannot override the imperative of political diagnosis and critique. For example, a text on the need for a new media studies must advance a critique and development of thinking on representation. This essay on M.I.A. must then be a theory of pranks like a red head round-up in relation to mobilisation against detention and police power. Perhaps secondarily this writing can contribute in terms of the ways a filmed narrative of consequence is caught up as alibi for that which it ostensibly critiques to the extent that the prank poses the problem and asserts a solution it is not alone capable of delivering. Both Gavras and Arulpragasam as propagandists must be praised and failed in equal measure to the extent that their worthy critique does or does not find a mobilisation or an organisation capable of being more than merely entertained by their provocations. The pranking jester and the fourth army people's theatre both must rely upon those they follow more than opportunistically seek a following.

What then is ripe for examination is the joke.

Witticisms and Wagner.

Alain Badiou has told us that in the face of horror, we should examine comedy more than tragedy. Ridicule can break taboos, puncture pretence – but he does not want to elevate theatrical comedy to a 'polemical' occupation, a salaried cultural service run by professions, a 'grumbling sector of public opinion' (Badiou 1998/2005:75-76).

Polemically, even ridiculously, I have called our present predicament World War Three and I mean it more as horror than witticism. We are, like it or not, in the midst of a global conflagration of a vicious kind, warmer than the Cold War, more extensive than the First, and less morally or ethically clear than the Second. The nightmare visited upon those who attempt to live in the places under siege – Iraq, Afghanistan, Libya, and more – is not the same as the distraction anxiety and perverse joke that is the war economy of the major metropoles, and yet. Consider the imbrication of here and there as co-constituted operative centres of a never-ending battle, sometimes with bombs, sometimes the booms of sound and fury. Compare, for example, the Guantánamo torture music tracklist with the quite similar post-September 11 proscribed radio play list. Was Gitmo the only place to hear Rage Against the Machine? Adorno long ago pointed out that the commodity form that music has become requires it to have no meaning, or rather, its social meaning can be the direct opposite of its 'place and function' in society (Adorno 1978/1999:2). Adorno himself was never adverse to a good jibe about the meaning of music: he wrote the essay 'On

Jazz', or rather, '*Über Jazz*' as Hektor Rottweiler, as a way to avoid the National Socialist censor. We should consider how that essay offers a critique of pseudo-individualism, standardisation, uniformity, the 'myth of pioneer artisanship'. It is of course not just a piece of comedy that a 1936 critique of the Weimar Salon and of the regimented marching music – of the Nazi cultural malaise? – was as much the ostensible topic of *über*-Jazz. The horror was the '*über*'-framework of prevailing fascist thinking. It is important to read between these hectoring lines, insisting, in a kind of contingent writerly dissemblance, on the deployment of artfully provocative statements – elsewhere he will write that montage is passé, poetry after the camps barbaric, the dialectic is antithetical to literary presentation, and much more as we shall see. It is on the authorisation of this trickery that I would have us consider as a 'culture-of-war industry' all the training programs, logistical centres, promotional facilities and media spin that work to maintain the less covert aspects of the war, let alone the many thousands employed in shadier military and surveillance efforts that are the war at home today. It would not be difficult to imagine an appropriate and suggestive research project on the model of Adorno and the Frankfurt School's study of fascist tendencies and personality traits here. Indeed, Adorno himself had made a point of not excluding the possibility of extending the methodology of *The Authoritarian Personality* to 'other patterns of personality and ideology' (Adorno 1950/1975:149). His hostility to studies of mere epiphenomenal cultural forms without context is well documented:

> Sociological research that would prefer to avoid the problems of analyzing production and to confine itself to questions of distribution or consumption remains imprisoned in the mechanisms of the market, even though to investigate this quality should be one of the foremost tasks of a sociology of music (Adorno 1978/1999:6).

In the present book, my subject matter, as has been noted, has to do with media pranks. Pranks and their disconnects. Goodness Gracious. In some sense the cosmic jokes that life plays on us all in this universe of pain. Yet the pranks are chosen here to make a point. Poignancy – and not a little tragedy. Also absurdity. I am not sure their accumulation amounts to an analysis or an indictment, but taken the right way – you have to be able to take a joke – I think the joke, the prank, the feint, even the disguise (Hektor, Rogues, M.I.A.) tells us something about who 'we' may be. Consider these few comments as probes into the identities, and into the current conjuncture, that make up the present swindle called capital – and as a way to give it a decent dressing down. Revealingly, the etymology of *prank* also gives a second meaning of dressing in a showy way. Standing out and performing mischievously, horrendously. Perhaps pranks are a way towards that which seems most difficult – the attempt to unmask the conditions in which we now find ourselves, and by naming them to work the trick – another prank – of transformation.

The great trickster-psychoanalyst Sigmund Freud has much to say about jokes, and it may be anticipated that his work can offer some insight. I am keen to examine this under the sign of the sense of humour of a rehabilitated Adorno. Grumpy Uncle Adorno is often thought of as unfunny and serious, but I beg to differ, and note as initial, and circumstantial, evidence a list of his pet names for himself: Teddy, Hektor Rottweiler, Charles de Kloës, The Great Patchyderm, Weisengrund or just plain W. Despite his love of games and coincidences, it does not really matter that Adorno was born, of all dates, upon September 11th, in 1903, but the anniversary significance of that birthday date will not be overlooked. Rehabilitation of Adorno is underway, for example the 2011 issue of *Telos* points out how Adorno is 'still misrepresented as the pessimistic aesthete, consistently hostile to engaged activism, mass culture, and representational art. Such are the standard stereotypes' (Berman 2011:3) and in *Social and Political Thought* Simon Mussel writes 'Adorno has been often portrayed unsympathetically by many as politically ineffectual, an elitist, a mandarin, an aesthete, and other all-too-familiar caricatures' (Mussell 2010:4). Similar rehabilitation might be due to other figures, Marx hardly needs it just now, with capital in a period of slump and a thousand reading groups convened, but Freud perhaps, having fled continental Europe for England about the same time as Adorno. Add to this Richard Wagner, Adorno's focus in one of his key music studies, also subject to rescue, even by Žižek, who wants to rehabilitate Wagner for all the wrong reasons. While implementing various recovery operations, perhaps we should remember that in present times the left has failed to stem the rightwards reaction, it has not defended the gains of the first period of communist rule, it largely ignores what was required to crush fascism, for example in London the way Mosley's black-shirts were crushed through major mobilisations on the streets, specifically Cable Street, or later the how the National Front were turned back at the Battle of Lewisham, 1977, and, even in terms of its cultural forms, it offers a weak cultural appreciation that still serves up a pantomime Wagner in the same way stereotype is deployed for political gain today. Wagner is denounced as a Nazi before a note has been played. In any case, in the rehabilitation industry we see a veritable cottage industry of theoretical therapy, airbrushing figures back *into* the FB friends list of contemporary philosophy. Recruits to this program of rehabilitations can seem strange allies, in the case of Wagner the often very funny, conflicted punning of Žižek, as well as his more staunchly 'Maoist' colleague and interlocutor, Badiou, and in supporting roles, Rancière and Lacoue-Labarthe, coincide in an effortful reassessment (Adorno 1952/2005, Žižek intro to Adorno 1952/2005, Badiou 2010, with an afterword by Žižek, Rancière 2004/2009, Lacoue-Labarthe 1991/1994). The task is hard, since Badiou in his first paragraph cannot avoid relating Wagner to

WWII, even if staged as a reaction against associating Wagner 'with the horrors of Nazism' (Badiou 2010:ix), the parameters of a debate Wagner did not live to see are continually invoked. Farce. Indeed, with rehab in mind, and with Freud's joke book in hand (*Jokes and their Relation to the Unconcious*, Freud 1905/1960) I recall Žižek introducing 'The Idea of Communism' conference in London in 2009, in the presence of Badiou and Rancière. As Žižek introduced us to his two main scholarly influences, he unconsciously tugged at his shirt above his heart and then wiped his brow each time he said the phrase 'Marx and Freud'. If, as Freud contends, telling jokes is a cover for hostility in which the teller 'strips' the butt of his joke naked, I wonder what this means for Žižek's very funny tic here, and for my latent hostility, and great respect, in pointing it out. Viva Marx and Freud. Subjecting Marx to psychoanalystic gaze has its possibilities, but Marx undressed would of course be another joke – this time to do with that coat he had often occasion to retrieve from the pawn shop so that he might appear presentable enough to enter the reading room of the British Library, so as to continue his economic studies – on Marx's coat see at least about 70 pages of *Capital*, where the coat is made from cotton and yarn, swapped at market for bibles and brandy, exchanged on the table, worn and frayed, resplendent to be seen – consult Stallybrass's comedy of errors thereupon (Stallybrass 1998, red salute Simon Barber).

Marx of course is the proximate trickster – as discussed in the previous chapter, it is in the *Eightenth Brumaire* that he offers his critique of the machinations of Louis Bonaparte. That book starts with memorable lines on repetition in history, first as tragedy, then as farce – Marx makes much of the little Napoleon dressing up as if in the clothes of his great uncle. The peasants left nothing much to wear but a potato sack. Tragedy and farce are the opening lines, but not just jokes, even as Marx suggests Hegel has forgotten to say the repetition was a travesty the second time around. The farcical offers a diagnostic for our time as it did in

Marx's times as well, albeit in different ways. The book *First as Tragedy then as Farce*, by Žižek, is titled in paraphrase of these lines, and Marx is himself quoting a letter from Frederick Engels. The burden of the *Brumaire*, and of Žižek's book, is that politics is not a dress rehearsal, though theatrical metaphors and stage analogies have a particular fitting heritage in relation to our predicament. Žižek offers a critique of violence that positively thrives on a certain bleak theatrical war humour – he quotes with approval Mao Zedong: 'Everything under heaven is utter chaos, the situation is excellent' (Žižek 2009:75 – the translation should perhaps better say 'promising' rather than 'excellent'). This too is not only a joke – the chaotic as diagnosis is cathartic, and everything fragile remains intact, the solid does not melt into air quite yet.

Freud meanwhile would suggest that joking economically offers us coded ways to express social meanings – aggression, hostility, anxiety – without a damaging expenditure of psychic energy and/or avoiding psychic and public censorship. This economy explains our enjoyment of their inappropriate character, and caricature – 'we are compelled to tell our joke to someone else because [we are] unable to laugh at ourselves' (Freud 1905/1960:190). If these conflicted condensations are granted, then the innocuous line 'I was only joking' might be the most hostile phrase we ever hear. The intentional mischief of a joke brings to appearance that which probably would not normally be explicitly named due to the protocols of polite society, formulas of boredom, regulatory uniformity. This however can also be broken, with difficulty. There is a catch of course. Another problem with a prank is that it is a joke that relies upon a close, ironic and dangerous, approximation to something serious. Hence the danger of exposure to those who cannot take a joke – the security forces, the self appointed arbiters of good taste, the war criminals and fat cat capitalists who think sophistication and a civilisational veneer of suits and ties sanitises them from the blood dripping from their hands. Those who staff the departure screening gates are also trigger-happy cops. And for all that I wish a joke could unravel such hypocrisy every time, sometimes I can't take a joke myself, and do not think it all that funny that a man who spills shaving foam on Rupert Murdoch must go to prison while a vicious war perpetrated on the basis of falsified reports about WMDs and 45 minute delivery times does not put a former Prime Minister in the dock.

It is perhaps from the initial moves of Freud that we can understand how these discontented and sullen complaints may indeed seem to be what Rancière identifies as a 'melancholic version of leftism [which] ... feeds off the dual denunciation of the power of the beast and the illusions of those who serve it when they think they are fighting it' (Rancière 2008/2009:35-6). Rancière, without much humour, is critical of a caricature of Debord and a particular French 1960s reading of *Capital*, even where he differs from any too easy formulas by insisting that 'she' can learn from experience. All the time his more elaborate formulas are themselves caught in the bind, and with a possible tendency to see regret and loss where perhaps something else is at stake. Another near contemporary, born the same year as Rancière, the theorist, Lacoue-Labarthe, singles out Adorno's discussion of Shönberg in relation to the 'questioning of Darstellung (art is not essentially [re]presentation)' (Lacoue-Labarthe 1991/1994:124) along similar lines, and notes that Adorno goes beyond Heidegger in relating the problem of *Darstellung* to the difficulty art has today in being anything more than a 'trace', of art having both technical 'fabricated' quality and a spiritual 'great content' (Lacoue-Labarthe 1991/1994:124-5). This is the pressing question of whether creative work in the context of the culture industry organised as if it were industry can nevertheless point towards politics and organisation. In Lacoue-Labarthe's appreciation of the 'well known' effort of Adorno to look forward, to maintain a project of aesthetics that need not appeal to 'nostalgia for a religion …which is to say a community' (Lacoue-Labarthe 1991/1994:125), I see a convergence of Adorno's critique with regard to Wagner's work caught in the first moments of culture industry operations and its latest manifestation in the last lines of *Born Free* by M.I.A. This needs to be explained by way of a triangulation with Žižek, Adorno and Wagner, so as to show how and why a too quick dismissal of Adorno's effort to grasp Wagner in relation to larger economic parameters of 'aestheticized politics' (Lacoue-Labarthe 1991/1994:18), and Lacoue-Labarthe's surprise that Adorno did not instead resort to the Kantian sublime, is part and parcel of a too quick reading.

In Žižek's *Living in the End Times*, we are treated to the spectacle of Žižek using Adorno's critique of Wagner's simple leitmotifs as 'a kind of inner-structural commodification of his music' to then argue that Adorno's various one-liners and dazzling aphorisms are, similarly, at the cost of a deeper theoretical 'substance'. Žižek says, no doubt as po-faced as possible, that 'this unintended self reflexivity is something of which Adorno undoubtedly was not aware, his critique of the Wagnerian leitmotif was an allegorical critique of his own writing' (Žižek 2010:227). It will not be necessary to point out that this 'is an exemplary case of the unconscious reflexivity of thinking' (Žižek 2010:227) which also must ring relevant to readers of Žižek's own trademark style, grinning madly at his own jokes as he writes himself modestly into a trajectory of names that flow: Hegel, Marx, Lenin, Lacan, Žižek – Hutnyk! But jokes aside, the point here is that the suggestion that Adorno's aphoristic style and his critique of Wagner are mutually allegorical misses the significance of Adorno's argument completely. The critique of Wagner is an illustration of the quite substantial theoretical appreciation of how the music replicates the production protocols of industrial capitalism, breaking things into small manageable units, 'the totality is supposed to become controllable, and it must submit to the will of the subject who has liberate himself from all pre-existing forms' (Adorno 1952/ 2005:39). This is presented as a moment in an unfolding dialectical presentation, that will later also show how the commodity character of the music is aestheticised and must purvey illusions, and does so all the more in order to disguise – to 'spirit away' – any trace of its origins in human labour, to emphasize its use value, all the more in thrall to the furthering of 'the cause of exchange value' (Adorno 1952/2005:79). It is not just a quip when Adorno says that in this way Wagner's operas become commodities, 'their tableau wares on display' (Adorno 1952/2005:79) – this is also a substantial critique of the culture industry, of the torn halves of a promised cultural freedom that is damaged beyond repair. It is not insignificant that Žižek's introduction to the Verso edition of *In Search of Wagner* studiously avoids any discussion of Adorno beyond a couple of quips to open and then close his preface. That is not to say it isn't impressive that Žižek *presents* Adorno's Wagner book in new times, but it is significant that to some degree Adorno's musical analysis does not move Žižek much. What a shame there is no real mention of the fictions created in these tableaux – the bass instruments mark harmonic progression, light wood winds, diminished forte, affirmation of rhythm and time, all amounting to the creation of an musical fairyland an '*Elfenreich*' through dropping out the bass, use of the 'most archaic' piccolo flute (Adorno 1952/2005:75). Evoking a 'pristine age' (Adorno 1952/2005:76) – itself a strange pantomime-like mistranslation of the spectral '*aestheticized erscheinungsform*' – *erscheinung* should be translated as appearance, but with a sense of apparition and putting in an appearance as if on a stage.

For Adorno, the appearance form of art as *Elfenreich* erases its makings – something bought by way of exclusion of the working class, and the dreams, illusions and popular humour that workers might justifiably need in order to recover or occupy time in reserve. Serious art is withheld from those who might mock seriousness. Why does this matter? At stake is the appearance of scholars handing out life(style) advice to activists and others. Badiou also gets into Wagner, wanting us to decide if Adorno is correct to ask if the suffering and heartbreak in the strings of Wagner is 'irreducible heartbreak, or is it ultimately incorporated into the sentimental effects of the spectacle ... an ambiguous link with religion' (Badiou 2010:62). We know this is the theme, but the resurgence of interest itself might give us cause for reflection on just why what Žižek calls a rehabilitation, of Wagner, should occupy the efforts of so many writers just now. Rehabilitation of Wagner, not Adorno, who Žižek accuses of 'rather vicious' hypotheses in relation to Wagner's difficulties in finding the ending to the *Ring* – this in Žižek's 63-page long afterword to Badiou's book (Žižek in Badiou 2010:193). Still others who have discussed Adorno's Wagner seem to think the *bon mots* are fine but overall miss the substance. For example, when Rancière leaves Adorno adrift, we still do not get the larger modes of production appreciation that also underpins *In Search of Wagner*. Instead: 'The modernist rigour of an Adorno, wanting to expurgate the emancipatory potential of art of any form of compromise with cultural commerce and aestheticized life, becomes the reduction of art to the ethical witnessing of unrepresentable catastrophe' (Rancière 2004/2009:131). This is incompatible with what Adorno has to say about it being an as yet undecided question as to whether art might not yet still hold a 'secret omnipresence of resistance' (Adorno 1991:67) in its kernel of refusal of everything that insists on injunction and dryness. The refusal of the order that 'nothing should be moist' (Adorno 1970/1997:116) is also not just a mischievous, visceral, quip, but a critique of morality and an appeal to life and joy. And the notion that for Adorno simple witnessing of catastrophe might ever make sense is countered so often it is astonishing to still read this criticism. Quoting Adorno on Hegel once more should suffice, Adorno says:

nothing can be understood in isolation, everything is to be understood only in the context of the whole, with the awkward qualification that the whole in turn lives only in the individual moments. In actuality, however, this kind of doubleness of the dialectic eludes literary presentation (Adorno1963/1993:91).

So Adorno's study of Wagner seems richer, far-reaching, and important because it makes the links. The context of the national socialist 'interest' in Wagner hardly needs to be mentioned – Hitler's favourite, used to 're-educate inmates at work camps etc. – but Adorno consistently points to a wider limitation in thinking the social mediation that frames the music. We might also see a similar mediation of terror in the present, and so to readdress Wagner is important not so much for Wagner, but as a wager – Scheherazade's gamble – that would oppose the white supremacist exceptionalism that co-ordinates detention programmes, restricted immigration, machine production, militarization, authoritarianism with appeals to fantasy. In this way, 'culture' in general, and music in particular, disguises the true face of the total war economy and fails to engage within a culturalist project that threatens 'us' all. On music, Adorno quotes Nietzsche lamenting the 'fate' of what which threatens our 'ability to transfigure and affirm the world' because we now only have 'decadent music [*Dècadence-Musik*] and no longer the flute of Dionysus' (Adorno 1952/2005:83, 1952/1971:89). It is Lacoue-Labarthe who reminds us, without citation, that Nietzsche thought the decline of Opera, and European music, could be dated from 'the deployment of an enormous machinery of instruments and people to produce the effect of the beyond, and to incite terror' in the overture to *Don Giovanni* (Lacoue-Labarthe 1991/1994:xx). Adorno himself links something like this to the 'anathematizing' of pleasure in Wagner, where 'phantas-magoria is infected at the outset with the seeds of its own destruction' (Adorno 1952/2005:83) – though we should note that the German text says nothing about seeds or infections, and '*ist der Phantasmagorie von Anbeginn das Element ihres eigenen Untergangs beigesellt*' (Adorno 1952/1971:89) might be better rendered as: so the phantasmagoia is joined at the outset with its own characteristic decline. Why is this important? Because Adorno makes a point hugely relevant to the illusion of *Born Free* in that inside the illusion dwells disillusion, and that Wagner's model is *Don Quixote* and he 'puts the hero into the role of the man who fights against windmills' in an effort to re-establish the old feudal immediacy, as opposed to the bourgeois division of labour enshrined in the guilds and thus 'becomes a potential figure of comedy [*latent komischen Figur*] in the face of bourgeois reality in which the feudal world is transformed into myth' (Adorno 1952/2005:83). The resultant conflict in which Quixote fights the windmill as if to struggle back to the bygone age, and in which the guilds fight one another without comprehending their place in much larger epochal shifts, is 'merely a poor substitute for political action' (Adorno 1952/2005:84). But the windmills are the enemy, icons of the systematic oppression. And the very contradiction of political art, the contradiction that Rancière decries, is identified and transformed into conscious critique by Adorno. It is right here that a song, a dream, a chivalry code that does not compute – each as contradiction played out as illustrative and instructive intervention – can seem particularly relevant as examples of the critical purchase of *Born Free* and of the aphoristic style of Adorno, that both Žižek and Rancière wrongly attribute as a limit. I imagine this as the point at which Adorno does line up, as Rancière points out, with Friedrich Schiller and the 'double bind of aesthetic experience' (Rancière 2004/2009:102). For Rancière, 'Adorno shares the same central preoccupation with Schiller' which is to 'revoke the division of labour implying the separation of labour and enjoyment' (Rancière 2004/2009:102). But this is not a reconciliation, and like Pantomime terror, or a story told to a despot so as to undo despotism, these tales must be brought into critical mediation with a movement and a resistance, at present drowned out in the clamour of the popular.

It should also be noted that at this point in *Wagner* Adorno makes a scathing, one-line, critique of the moment, in the dream and its destruction, where Wagner's effort towards freedom takes on unfreedom with an appeal, in the end, to the Virgin Mary (Adorno 1952/2005:85). Wagner himself is not the problem – saying something new is perhaps more pressing. Adorno contends that in Wagner, the appearance of novelty – *erscheinung* – is resolved and dissolved so that nothing new takes place – (Adorno 1952/2005:31). Reconciled. Even redeemed. Again, the joking appeal to the Virgin Mary is not unlike what happens with the last lyric lines of *Born Free*, the idea of a free world is consigned in a maudlin complaint to a mythical, phantas-magorical ideal that belongs in the outmoded past. The commodity form of the music wears its bourgeois defeat on its sleeve.

And yet! Adorno makes the case for music as a promise and protest that can be renewed. In the last incendiary pages where Wagner is a 'diligent lackey of imperialism and late bourgeois terrorism' he also has his 'commerce' with the 'forces responsible for his own decadence' (Adorno 1952/2005:143). Here, the 'bourgeois nihilist sees through the nihilism of the age that will follow his own' (Adorno 1952/2005:144). Tristan's rebellion is no impotent ascetic's sacrifice, but in *music* a rebellion against the iron laws that rule, in its total determination by those laws, can regain the power of self-determination. And hence, in this music, surprisingly, also the 'promise of a life without fear' (Adorno 1952/2005:145). To snatch this from the surge of Wagner's orchestra is something, to find it in M.I.A.'s *Born Free* is an instantiation of why its important 'to throw this shit in your face when I see ya, cos I got something to say'. A storyteller's conceit that disarms the pantomime of terror, in music, in scholarship, in the press, and in our heads.

Despot Culture.

Adorno offers a defence of Wagner as 'victim of the first manifestation of modern culture industry [his technique] anticipates that of the movies' (Adorno 1959/2003:411). The critique of the culture industry is never far away, though Adorno points out that this 'industry' should not be taken simply as 'industrial', even as it is nevertheless saturated with commercial colours. As such, the music and artistic expression – the storytelling – that 'follows' the working day, and has become ever increasingly its focus, transforms expression. Adorno writes: 'As a branch of leisure-time activity, music comes to resemble the very thing it opposes, even though it only derives its meaning from that opposition' (Adorno 1978/1999:14). Another way of saying this is to simply note the commodified form in which, all day in the stores, on-line, and via all sorts of media, the pop song is given to us as item of exchange. The album – first in vinyl, then as plastic CD – as well as the promotional video – first on MTV, then via YouTube, Daily Motion or iTunes – are surely the most brilliant forms yet devised for the mass commodification of cultural arts. Everything on TV, everything turned into an item, readily available at affordable market-set prices in bite-sized chunks, culture comes in stackable squares – even when round – and variety, as well as all manner of cultural commentary from politics and sex to sex and politics, can be yours for keeps, in colour, 24x7.

If, as Adorno suggests early on, each musical production must compete in the marketplace so as to redeem its exchange value as commodity or be ignored – perhaps as wasted, or unpaid, labour – then it is worth considering the unfolding of capital further as a diagnostic of musical production. The audience brought together by technical means, or in the festival circuit, or in the nightclub, seem not so different to the co-operative forms of labour managed by instruments and factory conditions. In this not just allegorical reading, shall we question how music is redeemed at piece rates, and the place of the reserve army of listeners, maintaining aesthetic skills while not employed, thus disciplining proper recompense for those officially endorsed as paid musicians, producing a total sonic regime of alienated production? The sound of this is a cacophony of popular styles, reduced to five inch disks and three minute video clips, and the true alienation here is the political evacuation of expression and aesthetics, where not even awareness of the commodification of music through and through can disrupt the staging of its sound-track for deeply conservative ends. It is just this sort of grim recognition that has got Adorno a bad reputation, but we could be more careful, as I have shown above, in jumping to conclusions. Adorno suggests that it remains an unanswered question whether in the inauguration of great art there might still be something that resists the culture industry – a 'secret omnipresence' (Adorno 1991:67). Julia Kristeva is another theorist who insists we should not ignore 'decorative' literary or aesthetic work, even when she acknowledges that oftentimes such work can be co-opted and complicity with commerce. In discussion of Dada and Surrealism and the early work of Louis Aragon she does not demand we immediately 'pass on to social revolt' (Kristeva 2002:80). Certainly the resistance can be betrayed, but there is something in revolt – what she calls 'psychic revolt, analytic revolt, artistic revolt' – that 'refers to a state of permanent questioning, or transformation, an endless probing of appearances' (Kristeva 2002:120). Following Hegel, but surely echoing Adorno, she says 'without negativity, there is no longer freedom or thinking' (Kristeva 2002:114). It is Marx that informs here. In his letter to Ruge he takes as credo 'the ruthless criticism of everything that exists' (Marx 1843). The point is to change it...

Suicide Bomber. This then is the place to acknowledge the date of writing, and the art of revolt, storytelling under curfew in World War Three. Lessons from Adorno and Kristeva would insist that we neither take 'artistic revolt' in isolation from social and political questions, nor think that a quick 'dialectical' denunciation of the apolitical, commercial or opportunistic character of mediate expression be sufficient. There are many examples where artistic expression has run afoul of the wider context, and become absurd or darkly comic. I have written of this as pantomime terror in relation to Aki Nawaz from the group Funda-Mental in chapter one. I think the cases of ADF's *Gaddafi* opera and the limp controversies around M.I.A. belong also to a wider syncopated and hysterical complex. Smokescreens and other deceptions prevail.

Hijinx not Hijack. The press of course loves to talk about flawed teenagers, much maligned family members. This case would be funny if it were not also a trial and ordeal, for the person concerned, and for her family, who were shamed and disappointed. 23 year old Samina Malik of Southall was the self-styled 'lyrical terrorist', convicted in November 2007 under section 58 of the Terrorism Act (2000). Found guilty of possessing downloaded 'terrorist manuals' she was confined for five months after coming to attention when an email excahnge was found on the computer of the 'convicted terrorist' Sohail Qureshi. Searches of her home and workplace found a 'cache' of terror materials and evidence that she had posted several 'Jihadist' poems on a website, and written lyrics on the reverse side of till receipt paper at her job in a WH Smith newspaper shop at Heathrow – specifically the phrase 'The desire within me increases every day to go for martyrdom'. Eventually sentenced to nine months prison, suspended because of the five months served under house arrest, her conviction was overturned by the court of appeal in 2008. Nevertheless, that a jury could, in the worlds of Lord Chief Justice Phillips, 'become confused' (*Guardian* 17 June 2008) particularly highlights the extent to which youthful pranks no longer raise a smile. Hijinks not a hijack was the order of the day and the unfortunate rhymes of Ms Malik highlight this – her threat was minimal, but escalated in the interest of a good story – Scotland Yard's Counter Terrorism Command looking for conviction and journalists looking for a print credit. That Malik worked at Heathrow airport was considered part of the evidence associating her with terror, but it need hardly be pointed out that a great many people who live in Southall work at the airport. Her downloaded documents – *Al-Qaeda Training Manual*, 'Terrorism Handbook', Mujahideen Poisons folder – were continually described as 'a library of terror' (Times 2007). The 'library' amounted to merely 24 documents – some only poems – which were not considered to be of significant practical support to active terrorists on appeal. In email contacts with Sohail Qureshi, she is said to have reported to him that security check levels at Heathrow remained high – something that you or I might also have told any prospective visitor, possibly adding the advice that one should arrive a little earlier because of the tedious queues. Quereshi seems to have been something a braggart, it is not clear that his claimed trips to Afghanistan to attend and to even lead training camps were anything more than exaggeration. Malik's contact with him was only through on-line chat (BBC News 2008). It is not clear if she shared her 'poetry'.

Mistaken Identity. Kenan Malik (no relation) points out that Samina was a fantasist whose only 'crimes' were writing bad 'doggerel ... ditties' about beheading and downloading freely available 'inflammatory material' from websites (Malik 2009:187). Self-styled Islamic 'terrorists' are incompetent and amateur and no threat, suggests Malik. For Malik such terrorists are a social malaise, with a mindset akin to the 'poisonous' inanities of the BNP (Malik 2009:180) but nothing more. The bigger problem is the failure of the left – and right – to recognise that its own opportunism has allowed these poisons to thrive. I disagree with this assessment because the portrayal of Samina

Malik as lumpen-terrorist in the press feeds a recurrent pattern, in which corporate, police and press efforts display such figures as a kind of alibi for several other motives. It is not accidental that every year around July there is some sort of incident that, with more or less comic and tragic consequences, keeps up the pantomime dress show of 'terror alerts', and the Police force employed to contain them, in the public eye. The killing of Jean Charles de Menezes in Stockwell is a well-known case of 'mistaken identity' in which officers who executed a Brazilian man who looked a little too much like a 'bearded terrorist' wearing an oversize jacket in summer. Funnily enough, despite an inquest, there was no prosecution of the murderous police, nor responsible higher up officers, despite the curious disappearance of the on-board CCTV footage and of the oversize coat and backpack.

Youth Terror. There are of course a great many examples of the absurd. A rather obscene competition has been taking place to identify the world's youngest terrorist – previously a 14 year old arrested in England, in 2010 the prize was awarded to an 8 year old American Cub Scout from New Jersey whose name appeared on a 'no fly list' when he and his mother tried to board a plane in Florida. Another peculiar case of mistaken identity, he was put on a terrorism watch list by Homeland Security because he shared his name with another suspect. When he was two years old he was patted down at Newark according to the New York Post (*Associated Press* 14 January 2010). Not all such cases are so clearly comic. In July 2006 in Forest Gate, Mohamed Abdulkuhar was shot in the shoulder when 250 police raided the home he shared with his brother. An inquiry found the shooting was accidental and there was no 'intent' on the part of the police – a difficult calculation given it took 250 officers to storm the house of the brothers, who after a number of days in detention, were found to be 'clean' – almost a year after the murder of Jean Charles de Menezes.

Photocopy Terror. Two more UK items, not quite mistaken identity, but the over-reaction is clearly a consequence of a frayed civil liberties fabric: In 2008, on the 14th of May, postgraduate student Rizwaan Sabir and administrative manager, Hicham Yezza from the University of Nottingham were arrested and detained for six days under the Terrorism Act 2000, for being in possession of an edited version of the *Al-Qaeda Training Manual.* Rizwaan Sabir had sent the training manual that he had downloaded from the United States Department of Justice website for printing to Hicham Yezza, who was assisting him in writing his PhD proposal. Both were cleared of terrorism-related offences, but Hicham Yezza was immediately re-arrested for visa irregularities. In response to this incident, a protest 'prank' involved many academics and activists visiting the same Department of Justice website and downloading the same manual, printing it out and bringing it to demonstrations in support of Yezza. Eventually imprisoned for an immigration offense – deception – although he was working under his own name at Nottingham, Yezza spent five months in jail, and was released in August 2009. In the same year, on the 14th of September, Oxford graduate Stephen Clarke was arrested after someone thought they saw him taking a photograph of a sealed man-hole cover outside the central public library in Manchester. He was detained under section 41 of the Terrorism Act 2000, held for 36 hours while his house and computer were searched, and then released without charge.

Shoes and Underpants. That is why perhaps we see the fool's madness in the recurrent airline panics. Even where the 'incident' was not a mistaken identity but a failed terrorist with identity problems, and – excuse me making fun of this – a person with a media image problem, there is a comic as well as a tragic element. The so-called 'Underpants Bomber', Umar Farouk Abdulmutallab, on Flight 253 in December 2009, was always going to be a difficult public relations sell in the celebrity fashion world of today. More pitiful than the equally media unfriendly face of the failed 2002 'Shoe Bomber' Richard Reid – whose hot foot lighting antics evoke the Marx Brothers more than Jihad, just as the Underpants Bomber was the butt of many comedian jibes. My guess is that the foolish thinking on display here was not far from the flawed logic of the Danish cartoon controversy after offensive line-drawing portrayals of the Prophet Mohammed were published in the newspaper *Jyllands-Posten* in 2009. And just to be sure there are pranks in this collection from all sides, I would like to know the provenance of the reports, in the US in 2010 and in England in 2011, at the start of July of course, which revealed to the world that Al Queda were developing 'Breast bombs' by implanting explosives in women's breasts, and bellies, as well as men's buttocks, so that when the operation scars had healed, these cosmetically enhanced suicide bombers could pass through security undetected and then inject their breasts, bums or bellies, with a detonator, causing untold destruction (Burke 2010, and Rushe 2011).

I am laughing incredulously, except that I see all these examples on the spectrum of low-intensity anxiety in a global war. A pantomime propaganda that offers psychological warfare as 'sensory overload' (Goodman 2009:33) and this appears in examples where a comic theatre plays out third global war. It may be that this absurd nexus of culture industry and military-entertainment makes it possible to suppress recognition of the contradiction between cultural expression and commodification. Play, trick, prank and transgression then appear as the necessary and complicated diminutive modality of that which is really serious because we cannot but laugh, or else we'd cry. With cartoons contained and containing dangerous wit, we can only draw traces and diagrams around the stark impossible truth. Recognizing no illusions in chivalry, feudalism, or even bourgeois democracy, let us play out this or that interpretive schema as a gesture towards moving beyond that ideal communion where only the fool Don Quixote speaks truth to power when he attacks windmills thinking they are monsters – which of course today they are, but they are also much more. We can ask if it helps us to mock the ways escalating terror threats prepare the ground for significant terror-effects? Those cowering in their mental bunkers while they carry on with everyday life are perhaps less well served by lampooning which increases the tension with an oblique recognition – a perfect deflection of what is going on within the thereby acknowledged but unacknowledged box of the cartoon or conceit of stand-up theatre. But a prank is also an example of refusal, a vote against conformity and against compliance with politeness. If we are to understand anything at all about Samina Malik's lyricism, we should understand the attraction and the pleasure –indeed the right and the necessity – of her saying such offensive things. And we should form organisations to defend such rights.

Osama bin Laden snuff film. The photogenic scene of May 1st 2011 showing Hilary Clinton and President Obama watching the televised – remote closed circuit – Seal Team 6 raid on bin Laden's Pakistan compound is a snuff film scene. In the cramped comfort of the White House situation room, with a large group of advisors and aides, they seem to express both astonishment and concern. However, we do not see the TV. We do not hear the TV. We do not even see this *as* TV – the picture is a still, and mute: silence, not even static, no radio-cam, no shouting, no pop pop pop shots. Later even the 'shooter' will be ignored.

Gaddafi. ADF's Gaddafi opera anticipated his fall – or rather NATOs protracted execution by proxy, after every Western leader of note had shaken his hand, Blair, Sarkosy, Obama. Contact. What we do not see as much are the widespread lynchings of black African workers in 'liberated' Libya (ProtectSouthOssetia 2011, Human Rights Investigations 2011).

Total War Against Islam. A training officer in the USA was dismissed for teaching a course that modeled a total war against

Islam scenario for the better instruction of the army intelligence officer core. Closed down by the Pentagon after objections, the course leader suggested that the USA 'might ultimately have to obliterate the Islamic holy cities of Mecca and Medina without regard for civilian deaths, following second world war precedents of the nuclear attack on Hiroshima' (Associated Press 2012).

It could be said that these are examples of spectral as well as real forces, which both appear in the world in distorted form, apparitions of a possibility we cannot yet quite properly glimpse except through the prism of horror. The Woolwich murder of Lee Rigby also allowed a widespread screening, and publication, of gratuitous horror pictures. Numb, and mute perhaps, the performance of these horrors amount to a grotesquerie. They abide in the fairytale – a *kinderfabel* in Marx – that gives us the form of something that signifies something else, even when we cannot quite name that something else, our deepest fears and darkest secrets, that of course we know are raging underneath a never quite calm – *so far so good* – appearance. These are snapshots from a pantomime, and the culture industry thrives on the visible contradiction, enabling spin. Can we counter this? Is there something to learn from an autonomy of art that comments also on politics, but only in reified form? There should be no doubt that M.I.A. milks the culture industry opportunistically, even when it comes back to bite her for radical content on display. The challenge this leaves in place for political groups is to make something of art in the service of revolutionary politics, and also to defend against such attacks, as a supplement to political organization. This is an ongoing story, even if *Born Free*, or for that matter *Cookbook DIY* or ADF's versioning of *La Haine* are now dated as disruptions, and carefully archived in the annals of socio-cultural commentary such that Žižek or Badiou must move their arguments forward to other examples, only the names changed. It was ever thus, but there is something to learn from

ADF's lyrical demand for the release of framed-up race attack victim Satpal Ram, or M.I.A.'s critique of human rights abuse in Sri Lanka or the USA.

Scheherazade in Guantánamo.

If our storytelling hero Scheherazade were subject to arrest, special rendition, torture and detention, I imagine her as M.I.A., defiantly shouting out home truths to the interrogators and sending flamboyant secret mix tapes out through the underground tunnels. Scheherazade as a covert-beam MTV VJ, taking seriously the time that low-level military on rotation to Iraq or Afghanistan need to upload their Humvee patrol and night vision helmet-cam footage onto YouTube with heavy metal soundtracks, death metal CNN clips and feeds from drone planes and smart bombs to thumping rhythm. Cue the Hanging Channel, with kaleidoscopic explosion videos from Bikini Atoll to the Hindu Kush, the snuff cinema of the Whitehouse Situation Room and the wall to wall coverage of the Woolwich killers in London, which then barely registered the hundreds of anti-Islam incidents in the days after, including arson and the torching of a mosque and a faith school. The Hanging Channel is MTV for WWIII, with all tracks on a geo-synchronic global satellite-grid platform delivering a 1001-day playlist for an alienated and distracted despotic regime.

If M.I.A. is a contemporary Scheherazade we will have to twist the ur-story just a little to accommodate the music industry, internets, MySpace, YouTube, fan cultures, press controversies and shock-jock radio talkback, let alone music press and academic musicology. These are also the despotic, which rule through commodity power. M.I.A. does not want to redeem women in the face of the King, but rather to avenge a more systematic betrayal. Yes, she sleeps with the enemy, but it is public apathy in front of atrocity that must be combated with better stories. What can a poor girl do, but sing in a rock and roll band? Sleepy London Town wakes up and riots, but only to a media kerfuffle; the staged controversy of provocation in *Born Free* has a wider more subtle point. Yet, it troubles me that few see that the cultural power of the prank is as gesture and – only – part one of a political program that would be capable of undoing the vast punitive and class biased legal-military-commercial apparatus. This means secret courts and police that condemn and kill while bonus-rich bankers, expense-account scheming politicians and eavesdropping shop-your-mother-for-a-story journalists seem exempt from prosecution. The increasing privilege of the super-wealthy contrasts with cuts to services, decline of community support facilities and racism as the default position to defend the white supremacist social structure of advantage. As mentioned before, following Bhattacharyya (2008), a cultural project accompanies war, and in the last ten years this takes the form of a scorched earth policy that transforms the social compact into a paranoid 'big society' conflict, transforms the daily life of every city in the world, every airport, every institution, major sporting event, transport system and significant building. Citizens everywhere are subject to an array of Matrix checks and civil liberty restrictions manifest as tedium – security lines, surveillance, extended queues, generalised paranoia. Alongside this, a forced inattention, slightly amused, amounting to a passive anxiety that never lifts, and can never be lifted, and which also entails an absent-minded acclimatisation to racism and Islamophobia – some years ago that which would have attracted significant opprobrium, racial profiling, now passes unremarked, or rarely remarked, and hardly challenged in the mainstream press or the apparatus of administrative power. We are all subject to suspicion, some more than others, and terrorist cells are identified in all manner of association, triggering house searches which turn up documents that amount to 'terror libraries'.

Why these comic-tragic, absurd with consequences, kind of

events? They prevail alongside a virulent anti-Muslim sentiment that escapes popular attention despite its prominence – a dirty public secret – and a system-wide low level anxiety manipulated for short term economic gain – military contracts, electoral advantage, media visibility... But is Cultural Studies today able to examine, and to perhaps redress, current iniquities when its brief as cultural industry adjunct is dressed in the new cloth of research council operationalism and obsession with impacts? A buttoned up discipline engaged in a polite negotiated democracy of civil society and social commerce is the central conceit of a Cultural Studies tending towards facilitation of culture as industry. Is calling the current predicament absurd anything more than a debased gibberish on the part of someone who also does not know what is going on? Scholarship is not – even when critical – a separate and insulated domain. However inconsequential the interpretations and declarations of the learned professors, however little impact can be measured, storytellers of the lesser rank still amount to a badly dressed cheer squad for various avatars of identity, ethnicity, meaning and culture that further the war effort. Those who will insist that music studies, or popular culture commentary, stick only to a discussion of music or culture and complain of the propensity to find resistance and politics in subcultural consumption miss the point. There is a danger of complicity, even when it is 'only' storytelling: a futile game unless organised, as Scheherazade's sister well knew.

To cope, some of us dress in designer fatigues just to endure. I have argued that uniform-chic is in, stereotypes breeding the extension of role-play to the soundbite scenarios of news as entertainment are now complete. Any critique or questioning is caricatured or pigeon-holed as misanthropic or a relic – at best critical voices appear between glossy covers marketed by Verso or pod-cast lectures by Žižek at the ICA. Tate Modern sells the critical books in its souvenir shop beneath a successful bistro with a few art rooms attached. The play area that is the Unilever sponsored project space is a great bourgeois family recreation zone. Or perhaps the relevant picture is more like an over-developed and re-imagined version of the 1950s. The scenario in which we find ourselves is Cold War plus: to the strategic ensemble of that détente and its paranoid other-fear add the actuality of both endless unwinnable occupation-wars in other lands re-designed as architectural-commercial training zones, with professional NGO and consultant sinecure, with a constant threat, and occasional actual-tragic blasts – the events of September 11 2001 in New York, 12 October 2002 in Bali, 11 March 2004 Madrid, July 7 2005 in London, Mumbai in November 2008 etc., are not merely 'incidents' – plus a secret police-like internal security regime, perhaps not as systematic and coherently worked out as that under National Socialism, or even under the terror of the 1930s Soviet Union, but nevertheless a system-wide internal attack, replete with fifth column hysteria and arbitrary arrests, detentions and torture.

Certainly we recognise antecedents in several earlier scenarios. September 11th as significant date is so often refer-enced as a kind of Year Zero of the new World War that it is easy to forget that corporate and military expeditionism had already set out a new world order in Iraq in 1991, had already made enemies of Islam in the guise of the Ayatollah in 1977, had brought the world to the brink of catastrophe with the Cuban missile crisis of 1961, had introduced the scorched earth landscaping program to Vietnam, Cambodia and Korea, after already making the world a temporary home with the hitherto unimaginable destruction of Hiroshima and Nagasaki in August 1945. Pearl Harbour is the moment when American isolationism was finally fully reversed – since then economic, military and cultural interventionism governs US State policy. The Marshall Plan post-war, a sustained military effort and codename Hollywood has transformed the world to make the idea that

September 11th changed everything both comic, yet serious. It is the latest but was not the last in a long saga of adventurisms, code name Geronimo.

What may have been of more significance about World War Two was not the immense military deployment – *blitzkrieg*, naval battles, air power, nukes – nor the ideological-symbolic – Hitler and Churchill's speeches, code-breaking, Yalta – but the social war. Unlike World War One, which for England and Germany happened in France, away from view, WWII visited destruction at home, and upon home life. The war economy was a social economy and its impact extended to all areas, all social relations – family, workplace, community, nation – and in many ways this has shaped responses to future wars. The social, psychic and technological character of the present war pervades and subsumes the everyday, everywhere. Whether it is resignation and denial or fear and prejudice, the impact of total war has been normalised. Railway station and international airport security and willing compliance with total surveillance – body scans – substitute for critical comprehension of what is going on. Suspicions are rife, and of course even when we know the people in charge are not to be trusted, this does not encourage any organised movement. Security fears and silence under the terror are borne of looking out for oneself, a competitive spirit forged in commerce, honed in fire, consequence: the endless war. Hobbes be damned.

M.I.A.'s work *is* poetry after Auschwitz in the spirit of that dialectical thinking that Adorno intended when he recognised that aesthetic production that did not balk in the face of industrialised terror was complicit with that terror, hence barbaric. M.I.A.'s next venture with Gavras was the video for 'Bad Girls' – a cheeky update on the magic carpet fantasy where tricked out automobiles become flying sedans, their riders djinns defying gravity (Gavras 2012). Critical of chauvinist parenting and policing preventing women from driving in Saudi, the video was made in Morocco and does not declare explicit political intent even as it offers a sly comment on the so-called Arab Spring and the aspirations of the children of wealthy middle class Arabs. It also garners over 30 million hits by the end of 2012, compared to only 3 million total viewings for *Born Free*. The latter count skewed of course because initially the video was pulled from the You Tube site for its explicit cross-border politics and its portrayal of violence and the camps. It is not hard to assume the two-play of critique *and* cars can be generalised to other atrocities of advanced capitalist culture, irredeemably part and parcel of a perverted gift economy of our present. Who would insist on a blanket criticism of this music, as music or as politics, if it were not a way of smothering dissent? A waterboard is as subtle, choking off critical thinking just where it struggles for breath and an asphyxiated cultural milieu. To ask for more demands a complete and coherent politics that music alone can never alone achieve. In this context, it might seem fraught to try to write poetry in the face of atrocity, but if we expand the phrase in question just a little we find that the words 'to write poetry after Auschwitz is barbaric' are just one pole of a dialectic faced by cultural critique. The other pole is that this 'also eats away at the understanding that tells us why it became impossible to write poems today' (Adorno 1967/1981:34 [translation modified, the English puts 'corrodes' for the more primal *'frißt…an'*, Adorno 1977/2003:30]). Here we are setting out the contours of an impasse: on one side an injunction, on the other the decay of our reason for that injunction. This is dialectics.

We can expand the quote some more. The next sentence is instructive: 'So long as the critical spirit remains cocooned in self-satisfied contemplation, it is not up to the task of confronting the absolute reification' (Adorno 1967/1981:34). In *Minima Moralia*, Adorno had said 'Anything that is not reified, cannot be counted or measured, ceases to exist' (Adorno 1951/1974:47) – the care with which we should read Adorno can be demonstrated if we consider the ways even this sentence can be misconstrued. There is a danger in thinking that grumpy old Adorno sees the whole world at risk of being reduced to calculus. The sentence might also be taken to mean that Adorno would have us defend all that cannot be measured – love, art, great music – but Adorno is not such a romantic. We should read the sentence as an assertion within an unfolding dialectical exploration, an attempt to think through the movement of contradiction and to rail – yes, to have a position – against resignation to both instrumentalism and romanticism. There is some mockery there too in the sentence about poetry after Auschwitz – would it in any case be so barbaric as to write poems about a death camp – yes, I know, Robert Benigni made a comedy about one (*Life is Beautiful* 1997), and so M.I.A. and Gavras have made a video. But of course Adorno is critical of this 'ready-made' opportunism in the culture industry that would remember the past only to 'consign it to oblivion' (Adorno 1951/1974:47). If we expand the 'Auschwitz' quote even further, we see that the cynical 'hucksters' are the ones who will take advantage of such efforts, and grin' while treating the remembered past as so much neutralised 'trash'. Even the place of humour here is exposed as complicit, so that with a smirk, critique is also reduced to 'idle chatter' [*Geschwätz*] (Adorno 1967/1981:34, 1977/2003:30). This itself sets up the voice that will speak the words about barbarism – and it is not Adorno's voice, but a staged voicing of one side of the dialectical exposé

> ...dragged into the abyss by its object. The Materialistic transparency of culture has not made it more honest, only more vulgar. By relinquishing its own particularity, culture has also relinquished the salt of truth, which once consisted in its opposition to other particularities. To call it to account before a responsibility which it denies is only to confirm cultural pomposity. Neutralized and ready-made, traditional culture

has become worthless today. Through an irrevocable process its heritage, hypocritically reclaimed by the Russians, has become expendable to the highest degree, superfluous, trash. And the hucksters of mass culture can point to it with a grin, for they treat it as such. The more total society becomes, the greater the reification of the mind and the more paradoxical its effort to escape reification on its own. Even the most extreme consciousness of doom threatens to degenerate into idle chatter. Cultural criticism finds itself faced with the final stage of the dialectic of culture and barbarism. To write poetry after Auschwitz is barbaric. And this eats away at [translation modified] even the knowledge of why it has become impossible to write poetry today. Absolute reification, which presupposed intellectual progress as one of its elements, is now preparing to absorb the mind entirely. Critical intelligence cannot be equal to this challenge as long as it confines itself to self-satisfied contemplation (Adorno 1967/1981, 34).

Indifference to the fate of others means complicity with totalitarianism, but it can also take the form of self-declared anti-totalitarianism projected and reversed – a self-aggrandizing interventionism, bombing villages to save them from themselves. This barbarity requires storytelling to undo power, but we have turned the storyteller into a detainee under duress who sits beside us, mute. How can I describe this absent-minded anxiety that produces simultaneously a never-say-die stoicism and an unexamined access-all-areas racism, capitulating to corporate greed and extreme police power, from DNA swab to remote drone assassinations if not by calling this despotism? 'Silence under the terror' impoverishes us all, and it is unseemly violent to laugh over this, but necessary. It is no joke that the extension of the convoluted components of previous wars and previous abject politics means this situation can only be described as an attack upon everyone. The red-heads in *Born Free* are more than an allegorical everyone: in that image there is a warning that we are all running into the minefields, headlong and without end. Shall we become accustomed to it? For how many nights and under what phantasmagoric house arrest?

What we must continually ask is whether Auschwitz will be repeated? Or indeed, if its next iteration is already being prepared, only this time for other Jews, communists, gays. These others might be red-heads, or Muslims, or musicians, *or you*. That some poetry continues to 'quiver' with 'utmost horror' (Adorno 1969/2005:48) is only art if there remain those who can respond and try to halt the reaction, not simply self-congratulate in egotistical theoretical grandeur.

References

Adorno, Theodore (1947/2003) 'Wagner, Nietzsche, and Hitler', *Musikalishe Schriften VI*, Frankfurt am Maim: Surkamp, pp404-412.

Adorno, Theodor (1950/1975) 'Studies in the Authoritarian Personality', in *Soziologische Schriften 11.1: Gesammelte Schriften 13*, Frankfurt am Maim: Surkamp pp143-508

Adorno, Theodor (1951) *Minima Moralia: Reflexionen aus dem beschädigten Leben*. Frankfurt: Suhrkamp.

Adorno, Theodor (1951/1974) *Minima Moralia: Reflections on a Damaged life*. London: Verso.

Adorno, Theodor (1952/1971) *Die musikalischen Monographein: Gesammelte Schriften 9.1*, Frankfurt am Maim: Surkamp

Adorno, Theodor (1952/2005) *In Search of Wagner* London: Verso.

Adorno, Theodor (1963/1993) *Hegel: Three Studies*, Cambridge, Massachusetts: MIT Press.

Adorno, Theodor (1966/1973) *Negative Dialectics*, London: Routledge and Kegan Paul.

Adorno, Theodor (1967/1981) *Prisms*, Cambridge, Massachussetts: MIT Press.

Adorno, Theodor (1969/2005) *Critical Models: Interventions and Catchwords* New York: Columbia University Press.

Adorno, Theodor (1970/1997) *Aesthetic Theory* Minneapolis: University of Minnesota Press.

Adorno, Theodor (1971) 'Die Freudsche Theorie und die Struktur der faschistischen Propaganda' in *Kritik. Kleine Schriften zur Gesellschaft*, Frankfurt: Suhrkamp, pp 34–66.

Adorno, Theodor (1977/2003) *Kulturekritik und Gesellschaft 1: Prismen, Ohne Leitbild*, Frankfurt: Suhrkamp.

Adorno, Theodor (1978/1999) *Sound Figures*, Stanford: Stanford University Press.

Adorno, Theodor (1991) *The Culture Industry: Selected Essays in*

Mass Culture, London: Routledge.

Adorno, Theodor, Benjamin, Walter, Bloch, Ernst, Brecht, Bertholt, Lukacs, Georg (1977) *Aesthetics and Politics: The Key Texts of the Classic Debate Within German Marxism*, London: New Left Books.

Ali, Nasreen, Virinder S Kalra, Salman Sayyid (2006) *A Postcolonial People: South Asians in Britain* London, Hurst.

Ali, Suki, (2003) *Mixed Race, Post Race*, Oxford: Berg.

Ali, Yaseen. (2010). *The commodification of resistance* [online], The Varsity, 6 July 2010, Available from http://thevarsity.ca/articles/31433 (accessed 10 June 2011)

Amis, Martin n.d. *Why give the man air? His self-regarding publicity is sufficient.*

Apocalypse Now (Film, 1978) Directed by Francis Ford Coppola, USA: American Zoetrope

Arulpragasam, Mathangi Maya (2012) *MIA*, New York: Rizzoli.

Asad, Talal (2007) *On Suicide Bombing*, New York: Columbia University Press.

Asian Dub Foundation (1998) *Culture Move* [LP] London: London Records.

Asian Dub Foundation (2006) *About Asian Dub Foundation* [online] discussion board, available at http://www.asiandub-foundation.com/adf_home_fs.htm (accessed 11 December 2006).

Associated Press (2012) *US military course taught officers 'Islam is the enemy'* [online] The Guardian, May 11, 2012, available at http://www.guardian.co.uk/world/2012/may/11/us-military-course-islam-enemy (accessed 12 December 12, 2012).

Auerbach, Erich. (1953). *Mimesis: The Representation of Reality in Western Literature*. Princeton: Princeton University Press.

Back, Les (1995) *New Ethnicities, Multiple Racisms: Race and Nation in the Lives of Young People*, London: UCL Press

Back, Les (2007) *The Art of Listening*, Oxford: Berg.

Badiou, Alain (1998/2005) *Handbook of Inaesthetics*, Stanford:

Stanford University Press.

Badiou, Alain (2005) *Infinite Thought: Truth and the Return of Philosophy*, London: Continuum.

Badiou, Alain (2006) *Polemics* London: Verso.

Badiou, Alain (2010) *Five Lessons on Wagner* London: Verso.

Badiou, Alain (2011/2012) *The Rebirth of History: Times of Riots and Uprisings*, London: Verso.

Bailey, Frederik. G. (1969) *Strategems and Spoils*. Oxford: Basil Blackwell

Bald, Vivek (2007) 'Lost in the City: Spaces and stories of South Asian New York, 1917–1965' in *South Asian Popular Culture*, 5(1):59-76.

Balibar Étienne and Immanuel Wallerstein (1991) *Race, Nation, Class: ambiguous identities*, London: Verso

Balibar, Etienne (1991) 'Is there Neo-Racism?' in Balibar, Etienne and Immanuel Wallerstein *Race, Nation, Class: Ambiguous Identities*, New York: Verso.

Bataille, Georges (1985) *Literature and Evil*, London: Calder and Boyars

Battle of Algiers (Film, 1966) Directed by Gillo Pontecorvo

BBC Comedy (2005) *Sanjeev Bhaskar*, BBC [online] available from http://www.bbc.co.uk/comedy/profiles/sanjeev_bhaskar.shtml (accessed 10 April 2008)

BBC News (2003) *Sesame street breaks Iraq POWs*, [online] BBC News 20 May 2003, available at http://news.bbc.co.uk/2/hi/middle_east/3042907.stm (accessed 12 March 2007).

BBC News (2008) *Man jailed over terrorism charges*, [online] BBC News 8 January 2008, available at http://news.bbc.co.uk/1/hi/7176832.stm (accessed 13 August 2012).

Beller, Jonathao (2006) *The Cinematic Mode of Production: Attention Economy and the Society of the Spectacle*, Honover: Dartmouth College Press.

Bend it Like Beckham (Film, 2002) Directed by Gurinder Chadha, UK: British Sky Broadcasting.

Life is Beautiful. (Film, 1997) Directed by Robert Benigni, Italy: Cecchi Gori Distribuzione.

Benjamin, Walter (1936/2002) 'The Storyteller: Observations on the Works of Nikolai Leskov' in *Selected Writings Vol 4.* Cambridge, Massachusetts: Belknap Press of Harvard University Press, pp313-355.

Benjamin, Walter (1940/2003) 'On Some Motifs in Baudelaire' in *Selected Writings Vol 3.* Cambridge, Massachusetts: Belknap Press of Harvard University Press, pp143-166

Benjamin, Walter (1982/1999) *The Arcades Project,* Cambridge, Massachusetts: Harvard University Press.

Benjamin, Walter and Theodor Adorno (1999) *The Complete Correspondence 1928-1940* Cambridge: Polity Press.

Berger, John (2008) *Hold Everything Dear: Despatches on Survival and Resistance,* Lodnon: Verso.

Berman, Marshall (2006) *On the Town: One Hundred Years of Spectacle in Times Square,* New York: Random House.

Berman, Russell (2011) 'Introduction' *Telos* 155:3-6.

Bhabha, Homi (1994) *The Location of Culture,* New York: Routledge.

Bharucha, Rustom (1998) *In the name of the Secular: Contemporary Cultural Activism in India,* Delhi: Oxford University Press.

Bhattacharyya, Gargi. (1998). *Tales of Dark-Skinned Women: Race Gender and Global Culture.* London: UCL Press.

Bhattacharyya, Gargi (2008) *Dangerous Brown Men: Exploiting Sex, Violence and Feminism in the War on Terror.* London: Zed books.

Blair, Tony (2005) 'News item' on BBC1, Television 25 July 2005.

Bond, Robert (2006) 'Speculating Histories: Walter Benjamin Ian Sinclair' Historical Materialism 14(2):3-28.

Borradori, Giovanna (2003) *Philosophy in a Time of Terror: Dialogues with Jürgen Habermas and Jacques Derrida,* Chicago: University of Chicago Press.

Boucher, Geoff (2004) 'Antinomies of Slavoj Zizek', *Telos : a quarterly journal of critical thoughts,* no. 129, pp151-172.

Boyle, Danny. (Film, 2008). *Slumdog Millionaire*. UK: Caledor Films/Film 4.

Bradbury, Ray (1953) *Fahrenheit 451*, New York: Ballantine Books

Brar, Harpal (1998) *Bourgeois nationalism or proletarian internationalism*. London: Harpal Brah.

Brennon, Teresa (1999) 'Poetry and polemic', *Race and Class*, 41(1/2):23–34.

Bride and Prejudice (Film, 2004) Directed by Gurinder Chadha

Bromley, Carl (2000) 'The last Uprising' *The Nation* 31 January.

Bronte, Charlotte (1847/2003) *Jane Eyre* (originally published under the pseudonym Currer Bell), New York: Barnes and Noble.

Brown, Mark and Luc Torres (2006) *G-had and suicide bombers: the rapper who likens Bin Laden to Che Guevara* [online], The Guardian, June 28, 2006, Available at http://arts.guardian.co.uk/news/story/0,,1807542,00.html (Accessed 24 March 2008).

Buck-Morss, Susan (2003) *Thinking Past Terror: Islamism and Critical Theory on the Left*, London: Verso.

Bunting, Imogen (2006) *Media Racism* [online] Trinketization, available at http://hutnyk.wordpress.com/2006/07/14/586/ (accessed 25 July 2013).

Bunting, Imogen (2003) 'Rationality, Legitimacy and the "Folk Devils" of May', *Left Curve*, Vol 27, [online]. available at: http://www.leftcurve.org/LC27WebPages/ FolkDevils.html (accessed 29 March 2010).

Burke, Cathy (2010) *Qaeda's surgical strike: Breast and butt bombs* [online] New York Post, 1 February, 2010, availale at http://www.nypost.com/p/news/international/qaeda_surgical_strike _breast_butt_3b7thvAVUmH8N2Lxhpx6QO (accessed August 8 2011)

Burton, Richard Francis Sir (1853/1964) *Personal Narrative of a Pilgrimage to Al-Madinah and Meccah*, New York: Dover.

Burton, Richard Francis Sir, trans., (1885/2003) *The Book of the Thousand and One Nights*, Whitefish: Kessinger Publishing

Company.

Burton, Richard Francis Sir, trans., (1885/2007) *The Book of the Thousand and One Nights*, Volume 6, Privately Printed: The Burton Club (collected 2007) 12 Volumes, Milton Keynes: Bibliobazar.

Butler, Judith (2009) *Frames of War: When is Life Grievable?* London: Verso.

Byatt, Antonia Susan, (2001) 'Introduction' to Richard F. Burton ed *The Arabian Nights: Tales from the 1001 Nights*, New York, Random House, ppxxi-xxiv.

Cairns, Stephen (2000) 'Jungles' in Thrift, Nigel and Steve Pile *City A-Z*, New York: Routledge pp125-7.

Calcutta 71 (Film, 1971) Directed by Mrinal Sen.

Cameron, David (2011). *Statement on the UK riots*. [Online] The Guardian 9 August 2011, available at http://www.guardian.co.uk/uk/2011/aug/09/david-cameron-full-statement-uk-riots (accessed 9 August 2011).

Chakravarty, Sudeep, 2009 *Red Sun: Travels in Naxalite Country*, New Delhi: Penguin.

Chapman, Michelle (2007) *Movie analysis: The representation of the banlieue in La Haine*, [online], Helium, available from http://www.helium.com/items/404050-movie-analysis-the-representation-of-the-banlieue-in-la-haine (accessed 20 June 2007).

Chatterjee, Pratap 2004 *Iraq: A Profitable Occupation*, New York: Seven Stories Press.

Chow, Rey (2002) *The Protestant Ethnic and the Spirit of Capitalism*, *New York, NY*: Columbia University Press

Cinema Paradiso (Film, 1988) Directed by Giuseppe Tornatore

Citizendia (2009) *Vyacheslav Mikhaylovich Molotov* [online], available from http://www.citizendia.org/Vyacheslav_Molotov (accessed 2 December 2009)

Clash Music (2010) 'Agent Provocateur M.I.A. interview' June 28, available from http://www.clashmusic.com/feature/agent-provocateur-mia-interview (accessed 12 July 2010)

Cleaver, Eldridge (1972) 'On Lumpen Ideology' reprinted from *The Black Scholar*, Nov-Dec, 1972 [online], available at http://www.anarco-nyc.net/anarchistpanther/otherwriting8.html (accessed 27 November 2006).

Community Music (2011) *About CM* [online], available from http://www.cmsounds.com/about (accessed 10 January 2011).

Cookbook DIY (Film, 2006) Fun-da-mental, Directed by Kashan W Butt, Nation Films.

Cusick, Suzanne G. 2006 'Music as Torture/Music as Weapon' in *Revista Transcultural de Música/Transcultural Music Review* 10:1697-0101 [online], available at http://www.sibetrans.com/trans/trans10/cusick_eng.htm (accessed 12 March 2007).

Davis, Mike (2006a) *Buddha's Wagon*, London: Verso.

Davis, Mike (2006b) *Planet of Slums*, London: Verso.

Debord, Guy (1967/1995) *Society of the Spectacle*, New York: Zone books.

Debord, Guy (1988/1998) *Comments on the Society of the Spectacle*, London: Verso.

Delon (2011) *MIA paper planes remix (the terrorist suporter)* [online] YouTube video, available at http://youtu.be/y_VvOCDQK48 (accessed 12 September 2012).

Denselow, Robin (2006) 'I wanted to know what was behind the archetype' *Guardian* 1 September, 2006 [online] available from http://www.guardian.co.uk/music/2006/sep/01/classicalmusicandopera (accessed 1 September 2006)

Derrida, Jacques (1967/1974) *Of Grammatology*, translated with an introduction by Gayatri Chakravorty Spivak, Baltimore: Johns Hopkins University Press.

Derrida, Jacques (2001/2005) *Paper Machine* Stanford: Stanford University Press

Derrida, Jacques (2003/2005) *Rogues: Two Essays on Reason* Stanford: Stanford University Press.

Dissanayake, Wimal (2003) 'Rethinking Indian Popular Cinema:

Towards Newer Forms of Understanding' in Guneratne, Anthony and Dissanayake, Wimal *Rethinking Third Cinema*, London: Routledge pp202-225

Dobie, Madeleine (2008) 'Translation in the Contact Zone: Antoine Galland's *Mille et une nuits: contes arabes*' in Medeski, Saree and Felicity Nussbaum, *The Arabian Nights in Historical Context: Between East and West*, Oxford: Oxford University Press, pp25-49.

Dowling, Stephen (2009) *The science of selling out*, [online], BBC News Magazine. 20 February, available from http://news.bbc.co.uk/1/hi/magazine/7901003.stm (accessed 2 February 2010).

Duneier, Mitchell (1999) *Sidewalk*, New York: Farrar, Strauss and Giroux.

Dutton, Michael (1999) *Streetlife China*, Cambridge: Cambridge University Press.

Eco, Umberto (1983) *The Name of the Rose*, London: Harcourt

Ek Din Pratadin (Film, 1979) Directed by Mrinal Sen

Emerson, Jim (2007) *Blood rights* [online], Scanners, 11 October, available at http://blogs.suntimes.com/scanners/2007/10/blood_rights.html (last accessed 6 August 2011).

Expert Group (2008) *Development Challenges in Extremist Affected Areas: Report of an Expert Group to Planning Commission* New Delhi: Government of India.

Fogarty Thomas A. (2003) *Companies bid on rebuilding Iraq: Halliburton, Bechtel benefit from experience and political ties*, [online] USA Today, 26 March 2003, available from http://usatoday30.usatoday.com/educate/college/business/articles/20030330.htm (accessed 2 June 2012).

Freud, Sigmund (1905/1960). *Jokes and their Relation to the Unconcious*. New York: Norton.

Fried, Richard (1990) *Nightmare in red: the McCarthy era in perspective*, Oxford: Oxford University Press.

Frow, Gerald (1985) *"Oh Yes It Is!": A History of Pantomime*, London: BBC.

Fukuyama, Francis (2004) *New York Times* 25 July 2004, available at: http://www.nytimes.com/2004/07/25/books/an-antidote-to-empire.html (accessed 10 February 2013).

Fulford, Tome (2008) 'Coleridge and the oriental Tale' in Medeski, Saree and Felicity Nussbaum, *The Arabian Nights in Historical Context: Between East and West* Oxford: Oxford University Press.

Fun-da-Mental (1999) *America Will Go to Hell*, [EP] London: Nation Records.

Fun-da-Mental (2006) *All is War*, [LP] London: Nation Records.

Fun-da-Mental (Film, 2006) *Cookbook DIY*, Directed by Kashan W Butt, Nation Films.

Furedi, Frank (2007) *Invitation to Terror: The Expanding Empire of the Unknown*, London: Continuum.

Gajjala, Rahdika and Venkataramana Gajjala, eds., (2008) *South Asian Technospaces* New York: Peter Lang Publishers.

Guardian Editorial (2008) *Through a glass darkly* [online] The Guardian August 21, 2008, available at http://www.guardian.co.uk/commentisfree/2008/aug/21/terrorism.terrorism (accessed 21 August 2008).

Gavras, Costas (Film, 1982). *Missing*. USA: Polygram Film Entertainment.

Gavras, Romain. (Film, 2010) *Born Free*. UK: El Nino. Retrieved from http://www.dailymotion.com/video/xd2w3j_m-i-a-born-free-video-official-real_music.

Gavras, Romain (Film, 2012) *Bad Girls* [online] YouTube video available at http://youtu.be/2uYs0gJD-LE (accessed 3 January 2012).

Giroux, Henry A. (2006) *Beyond the Spectacle of Terrorism: Global Uncertainty and the Challenge of New media*, Boulder: Paradigm Publishers.

Goodman, Steve (2009) *Sonic Warfare: Sound, Affect and the Ecology of Fear*, Cambridge, Mass: MIT Press.

Goodness Gracious Me (TV programme, 1998-2001) BBC2

Gopinath, Gayatri (2005) *Impossible Desires: Queer Diasporas and South Asian Public Cultures*, Durham: Duke University Press.

Guardian (2008) *Through a Glass Darkly* [online] The Guardian 20 August 2008, available at http://www.guardian.co.uk/commentisfree/2008/aug/21/terrorism.terrorism (accessed 12 July 2013)

Guneratne, Anthony and Dissanayake, Wimal (2003) *Rethinking Third Cinema*, London: Routledge.

Gung-Ho: Rewi Alley of China, (Television documentary, 1980) Directed by Geoff Steven [online] available at http://www.nzonscreen.com/title/gung-ho—-rewi-alley-of-china-1979 (accessed 8 August 2013).

Gung Ho (Film 1986) Directed by Ron Howard. Paramount Pictures.

Haddawy, Husain, trans., (1995) *The Arabian Nights: based on the fourteenth century manuscript edited by Muhsin Madhi*, New York: Norton and co.

Haddow, Douglas. (2010) *The real controversy of MIA's video*, [online], The Guardian 1 May, available from http://www.guardian.co.uk/commentisfree/2010/may/01/mia-video-real-controversy (accessed 12 May 2010).

Hajjat, Abdellali (2005) *France's Popular Neighbourhoods Are Not A "Political Desert"* [online] Sketchy Thoughts, available at http://sketchythoughts.blogspot.com/2005/12/frances-popular-neighbourhoods-are-not.html#jumpto translated and reprinted via Kersplebedeb: http://www.kersplebedeb.com/2005riots/hajjat.html (accessed 2 December 2005).

Harding, Luke 2013 *Turkish protesters embrace Erdoğan insult and start 'capuling' craze*, [Online] The Guardian 10 June 2013, available from http://www.guardian.co.uk/world/2013/jun/10/turkish-protesters-capuling-erdogan (accessed 9 July 2013).

Hardt, Michael and Antonio Negri, (2004) *Multitude: War and Democracy in the Age of Empire*, New York: The Penguin Press.

Harvey, David (2003) *Paris: Capital of Modernity* New York: Routledge

Haughton, Gerald (2007) *Review of La Haine,* [online] *The Edge* available at http://www.theedge.abelgratis.co.uk/filmsgl/lahaine.htm (accessed 12 January 2007).

Head (Film, 1968) director Rafelson.

Heidegger, Martin (1955/1977) *The Question Concerning Technology, and other essays,* New York: Harper Torchbooks, pp3-35.

Henri, Tom and John Hutnyk, (2013) 'Contexts for Distraction' *Journal for Cultural Research* 17(2):198-215.

Henriques, Julian (2011) *Sonic Bodies: Reggae sound systems, performance techniques and ways of knowing,* New York: Continuum.

Higbee, Will (2006) *Mathieu Kassowitz,* Manchester: Manchester University Press.

Highway of Death (2007) YouTube documentary video [online] available from http://www.youtube.com/watch?feature=related&v=1ljXnV4Ibpk (last accessed 20 June 2013)

Highway to Hell (2006) YouTube video [online] remix with AC/DC track, available from http://www.youtube.com/watch?v=FX05dWBoeUs (accessed April 7 2008)

Horowitz, Dave (2011) *Watching Leonard Cohen's "Bird On A Wire" 38 years after it was supposed to come out,* [online], Jewcy Music, 7 April 2007, available at http://www.jewcy.com/arts-and-culture/music/leonard-cohen-bird-on-a-wire (accessed 30 July 2011).

Human Rights Investigations (2011) *Libyan rebel ethnic cleansing and lynching of black people,* [online] available at http://human-rightsinvestigations.org/2011/07/07/libya-ethnic-cleansing/ (accessed 7 December 2011).

Hutnyk, John. (1996) 'Media, Research, Politics, Culture' *Critique of Anthropology,* 16(4), 417–28.

Hutnyk, John (2000) *Critique of Exotica: Music, Politics and the Culture Industry,* London: Pluto Press.

Hutnyk, John (2005) 'The Dialectic of Here and There: Anthropology 'at Home' and British Asian Communism', *Social Identities* 11(4), pp345–361

Ignatieff, Michael (2005) *The Lesser Evil: Political Ethics in an Age of Terror* Edinburgh: Edinburgh University Press.

Injustice (Film, 2001) Directed by Ken Fero and Tariq Mehmood, UK: Migrant Media.

Iraq – Highway to Hell (2006) YouTube video US Army/Marilyn Manson [online] available at http://www.youtube.com/watch?v=bOWmTyrz1RA (accessed 9 April 2008).

Jameson, Frederic (2011) *A New Reading of Capital* [online] *Mediations* Vol 25, available at http://www.mediation-sjournal.org/articles/a-new-reading-of-capital (accessed 27 March 2011).

Jacobs, Jane (1961/2002) *The Death and Life of Great American Cities*, New York: Random House.

Kalra Virinder and John Hutnyk, eds., (2000) 'Music and Politics' special section of *Postcolonial Studies* Vol. 1(3).

Kalra, Virinder (2000a) *From textile mills to taxi ranks*. Aldershot: Ashgate.

Kalra, Virinder (2000b) *Vilayeti* rhythms: Beyond Bhangra's emblematic status to a translation of lyrical texts. *Theory, Culture and Society*, 17(3): 83-105..

Kaur, Raminder and Ajay J Sinha (2005) *Bollyworld: Popular Cinema Through a Transnational Lens*, New Delhi: Sage

Kaur, Raminder and Virinder S. Kalra (1996) 'New Paths for South Asian Identity and Musical Creativity' in Sharma, Sanjay, John Hutnyk and Ash Sharma (eds) *Dis-Orienting Rhythms: the Politics of the New Asian Dance Music* London, Zed books, pp217-231.

Kavkazcentre.com (2006) *Brits skeptical about 'war on terror'*, [online] Kavkazcentre.com, http://kavkazcenter.com/eng/content/2006/08/22/5362.shtml (accessed 23 September 2006).

Keith Michael (2005) *After the cosmopolitan? Multicultural cities and the future of racism*, New York, NY: Routledge,

Kettle, Martin (2010). *I've got something to say* [online], The Guardian, 1 September 2010, available from http://www. guardian.co.uk/politics/2010/sep/01/tony-blair-a-journey-interview (accessed 1 September 2010).

King, Martin Luther (1967) 'Beyond Vietnam: A Time to Break Silence', Speech at the Riverside Church, Harlem, [online], circulated by *Information Clearing House* 4 April 2007, available from http://www.informationclearinghouse.info/article2564. htm, (accessed 28 February 2008).

Kollerstrom, Nick (2011) *Terror on the Tube: Behind the Veil of 7/7* Palm Desert: Progressive Press; 3rd Revised edition.

Koshy, Ninan (2003) *The War on terror: Reordering the World*, New Delhi: Leftword.

Kracauer, Sigfried (1937/1972) *Orpheus in Paris: Offenbach and the Paris of His Time*, New York: Vienna House.

Kristeva, Julia (2002) *Revolt, She Said.* New York: Semiotext(e).

Kumar, Amitava (2000) *Passport Photos*, Berkeley: University of California Press

Kumar, Amitava (2002) *Bombay London New York*, New York: Routledge

Kumar, Amitava (2010) *A Foreigner Carrying in the Crook of His Arm a Tiny Bomb*, Durham: Duke University Press.

Kundnani, Arun (2007) *The End of Tolerance*, London: Pluto Press.

Kureshi, Hanif (1998) *My Son the Fanatic*, London: Faber and Faber.

La Chinoise (Film 1967) Directed by Jean Luc Godard, Athos Films.

Lacan, Jacques (1966/2006) *Ecrits*, New York: Norton.

Lacoue-Labarthe, Philippe (1991/1994) *Musica Ficta: Figures of Wagner*, Stanford: Stanford University Press.

Landry, Donna (2008) 'William Beckford's Vathek and the Uses of Oriental Reenactment' in Medeski, Saree and Felicity Nussbaum, *The Arabian Nights in Historical Context: Between East and West*, Oxford: Oxford University Press, pp167-194

Lathan, Peter (1984) *Its Behind You: The story of Panto* London: New Holland Publishers.

Makdisi, Saree and Felicity Nussbaum, eds., (2008) *The Arabian nights in historical context between East and West*, Oxford: Oxford University Press.

Malik, Kenan (2009) *From Fatwa to Jihad: The Rushdie Affair and Its Legacy*, London: Atlantic Books

Mankekar, Purnima (1993) 'Television Tales and a Woman's Rage: A nationalist Recasting of Draupadi's "Dis-robing"' *Public Culture* 5(3):469-92.

The Descent (Film 2005) dir Neil Marshall.

Mao, Zedong (1975) *Selected Works of Mao Zedong*, Volume one, Beijing: Foreign Languages press.

Marx, Karl (1843) *Letter to Arnold Ruge* [online] Marxists Internet Archive , or, from the Deutsch-Französische Jahrbücher, September 1843, available at http://www.marxists.org/archive/marx/works/1843/letters/43_09.htm (accessed 8 August 2011).

Marx, Karl (1852/2002) 'The Eighteenth Brumaire of Louis Boneparte' in Mark Cowling and James Martin 2002 *Marx's Eighteenth Brumaire*, London: Pluto Press

Marx, Karl (1867/1967) *Capital: A critique of political economy, Vol. 1: The process of capitalist production*, New York: International Publishers.

Mathew, Biju (2005) *Taxi! Cabs and Capitalism in New York City*, New York, NY: New Press.

Mavens (1998) *Word of the day: gung-ho* [online] Words@Random, available from http://www.randomhouse.com/wotd/index.pperl?date=19980126 (accessed 12 January 2012).

McGregor, Andrew S., (2010) *The last minutes of Hasib Hussein*, [online] Terror on the Tube: The London 7/7 bombings: A murder Investigation, guest post on Nick Kollerstom's blog, 8 November, 2010, available at: http://terroronthetube.co.uk/inquest-articles/the-last-minutes-of-hasib-hussein/ (accessed 12 January 2012).

Miller James L. (1978) 'Review of Roman Pantomime: Practice and Politics by Frank W. D. Reis in *Dance Research Journal*, Vol. 11, No. 1/2 pp. 52-54.

Mitchell, W.J.T., (2011) *Cloning Terror: The War of Images, 9/11 to the present*, Chicago: University of Chicago Press

Mitra, Royana (2011) *Akram Khan: Performing the Third Space* PhD thesis, Dept of Drama and Theatre, Royal Holloway, University of London.

Mitropoulos, Angela (2001) 'Movements against the enclosures— virtual is preamble'. [online] available at http://www. antimedia.net/xborder/ (accessed 12 December 2010).

Moore, Henrietta and David Held, eds. (2008) *Cultural politics in a global age*. Oxford: One World.

Moore, Rachel 2000 *Savage Theory: Cinema as Modern Magic*, Durham: Duke University Press.

Mortimer, Gavin (2010) *France's 'generation of scum' can expect a hostile reception after a 'shameful' World Cup* [online] The Week, available from http://www.theweek.co.uk/football/13787/ france-exit-south-africa-beaten-and-humiliated (accessed 25 June 2010).

Müller-Doohm, Stefan (2003/2005) *Adorno: A Biography* Cambridge: Polity.

Mussell, Simon (2010) 'SPT Conference on Theodor W. Adorno: 40 Years On, Conference Report' *Social and Political Thought* 17:4-11.

Newton, Huey (1972) *To Die for the People: The Writings of Huey Newton* New York: Random House

Obachike, Daniel (2007) *The Fourth Bomb* London: Floran Publishing.

Orr, Bridget (2008) 'Galland, Georgian Theatre, and the Creation of Popular Orientalism' in Medeski, Saree and Felicity Nussbaum, *The Arabian Nights in Historical Context: Between East and West*, Oxford: Oxford University Press, pp103-130.

Ozaki, Ruth (2013) *A Tale for the Time Being*, New York: Viking.

Paglin, Trevor (2006) *Torture Taxi: On the Trail of the CIA's Rendition Flights* Brooklyn: Melville House.

Papastergiadis, Nikos (2003) "Ambient Fears" in *Metaphoricity and the Politics of Mobility*, eds. Maria Maragoin & Effi Yiannopoulou, Rodopi, Amsterdam, 2006, pp119-140.

Phili, Stelios (2010) *M.I.A. distracts from music with nonsensical message* [online], Washington Square News, 12 July 2010 available from http://nyunews.com/arts/2010/06/27/28mia/ (accessed 28 July 2010)

Pickard, Anna (2010) *Does MIA's Born Free video overstep the mark?* [online], The Guardian 28 April 2010, available from http://www.guardian.co.uk/music/2010/apr/28/mia-born-free (accessed 28 July 2010).

Pirates of the Caribbean: At World's End (Film 2007) director Gore Verbinski, Buena Vista.

Prashad, Vijay (2000) *The Karma of Brown Folk*, Minneapolis: University of Minnesota Press.

Prashad, Vijay (2001) *Everybody Was Kung Fu Fighting: Afro-Asian Connections and the Myth of Cultural Purity*, Boston: Beacon Press.

Prashad, Vijay (2007) *The Darker Nations: a people's history of the third world*, New York: New Press.

Prashad, Vijay (2013) *Uncle Swami: South Asians in America today*, New York: The New Press.

ProtectSouthOssetia (2011) *Obama's Massacre in Libya*, [online] available at http://youtu.be/r4oOAjCbXUg (accessed 7 December, 2011).

Puwar, Nirmal (2004) *Space Invaders: Race, Gender and Bodies Out of Place*, Oxford: Berg.

Rafelson, Bob. (1968) *Head,*. USA: Raybert Productions.

Rancière, Jacques (1983/2004) *The philosopher and his Poor*, Durham: Duke university Press.

Rancière, Jacques (1992/2007) *On the Shores of Politics*, London: Verso.

Rancière, Jacques (1998/2004) *The Flesh of Worlds*, Stanford: Stanford University Press.

Rancière, Jacques (2001/2006) *Film Fables*, Oxford: Berg.

Rancière, Jacques (2003/2007) *The Future of the Image*, London:Verso.

Rancière, Jacques (2004/2009) *Aesthetics and its Discontents*, Cambridge: Polity Press.

Rancière, Jacques (2005/2006) *Hatred of Democracy*, London: Verso.

Rancière, Jacques (2008/2009) *The Emancipated Spectator*, London: Verso.

Rancière, Jacques (2010) *Dissensus: On Politics and Aesthetics*, London: Continuum.

Ray, Satyajit (1993) *Ray in the looking Glass*, Calcutta: Badwip.

Rhys, Jean (1965/2000) *Wide Sargasso Sea*, Harmondsworth: Penguin.

Rollings, Grant (2006) *Fury at Suicide Bomb Rap*, [online] The Sun, 30 July 2007 available at http://www.thesun.co.uk/sol/home page/news/53959/Fury-at-suicide-bomb-rap.html (accessed 2 August 2007)

Roy, Arundhati 2009 *Mr Chidambaram's War* [online] Outlook India.com 9 November 2009, available at http://www. outlookindia.com/article.aspx?262519 (accessed 3 July 2010).

Rudin, Mike (2009) *Unmasking the mysterious 7/7 conspiracy theorist*, [online] BBC News, available from: http://news. bbc.co.uk/1/hi/magazine/8124687.stm (accessed 30 June 2009).

Rushdie, Salman (1998/2006) *The Satanic Verses*, London: Verso

Rushdie, Salman (2009) 'A Response' in Herwitz, Daniel and Ashutosh, Varshney (2009) *Midnight's Diaspora*, Delhi: Penguin, pp136–140.

Rushe, Dominic (2011) *Al-Qaida could use hidden 'belly bombs' to attack passenger planes, US warns* [online] The Guardian, 6 July 2011 available at http://www.guardian.co.uk/world/2011/jul/ 06/al-qaida-belly-bombs-planes-warns (accessed 8 August 2011).

Saha, Anamik 2012 'Locating MIA: 'Race', commodification and the politics of production', *European Journal of Cultural Studies* 15(6):736-752.

Said, Edward (1978) *Orientalism.* London: Routledge and Kegan Paul.

Said, Edward (1981) *Covering Islam: How the Media and the Experts Determine How We See the Rest of the World.* New York: Pantheon Books.

Said, Edward (1986). *After the Last Sky: Palestinian Lives.* New York: Pantheon Books.

Sammy and Rosie Get Laid (Film, 1987) Directed by Stephen Frears

Sanguinetti (1979) *On Terrorism and the State, The Theory and Practice of Terrorism Divulged for the First Time,* Michigan: University of Michigan Press.

Schivelbusch, Wolfgang (1988) *Disenchanted Night* Berkeley: University of California Press.

Scott, Stafford (2013) 'All Tottenham Needs Justice' *The Guardian,* Thursday 25 July:p.28.

Seidler, Victor Jeleniewski (2007) *Urban Fears and Global Terrors,* London: Routledge.

Sharma, Sanjay (2003) 'The sounds of Alterity', in M. Bull, & L. Back (eds) *The Auditory Culture Reader,* Oxford: Berg. pp409-18.

Sharma, Sanjay (2006) *Multicultural Encounters,* London, Palgrave Macmillan.

Sharma, Sanjay, Hutnyk, John and Sharma, Ash (1996) *Dis-Orienting Rhythms: the Politics of the New Asian Dance Music,* London: Zed books.

Sharma, Sanjay and John Hutnyk eds., (2000) 'Music and Politics' special issue of *Theory Culture and Society* Vol., 17(3).

Sharma, Sanjay and Sharma, Ash (2000) 'So far so good, so far so good: *La Haine* and the Poetics of the Everyday' *Theory Culture and Society,* 17(3):103-116

Shohat, Ella (2003) 'Post-Third-Worldist Culture; Gender, Nation and the Cinema' in Guneratne and Dissanayke pp51-78.

Slate (2008) *The Sandbox* [online] Doonsbury site available at http://gocomics.typepad.com/the_sandbox/2008/03/5-years-1-year.html (accessed 27 March 2008)

Solarsky, Mathew (2008) *M.I.A. Responds to pro-terrorism accusations* [online], Pitschfork. 6 August 2008, available from http://pitchfork.com/news/29930-mia-responds-to-pro-terrorism-accusations/(accessed 12 August 2008).

Southall Rights (1980) *23 April 1979.* London: Crest.

Spivak, Gayatri Chakravorty (1988) 'Can the Subaltern Speak?' *Marxism and the Interpretation of Culture,* Ed. Cary Nelson and Lawrence Grossberg. Urbana: University of Illinois Press. pp271–313.

Spivak, Gayatri Chakravorty (1990) *The Post-Colonial Critic,* New York: Routledge.

Spivak, Gayatri Chakravorty (1993) *Outside in the teaching machine.* London: Routledge.

Spivak, Gayatri Chakravorty (1999) *A Critique of Postcolonial Reason: Toward a History of the Vanishing Present.* Cambridge: Harvard University Press.

Spivak, Gayatri Chakravorty (2004) 'Terror: A Speech After 9-11' *Boundary 2,* summer 80-111.

Spivak, Gayatri Chakravorty (2008) *Other Asias,* Oxford: Blackwell Publishing.

Spivak, Gayatri Chakravorty (2012) *An Aesthetic Education in the Era of Globalization* Cambridge, Mass: Harvard University Press.

Stallybrass, Peter (1998) 'Marx's Coat', in Patricia Spyer ed. *Border Fetishisms: Material Objects in Unstable Spaces,* London: Routledge, pp183-207.

Stardust Memories (Film, 1980). Directed by Woody Allen, USA: Rollins-Joffe.

Swedenburg, Ted (2009) 'Fun^Da^Mental Islamophobic Fears: Britain's "Suicide Bomb Rappers"' *vis-à-vis: Explorations in*

Anthropology, Vol. 9, No. 1, pp123-132.

Taussig, Michael (1993) *Mimesis and Alterity: A Particular History of the Senses*, New York: Routledge.

Tamilnet 2010 *NYT corrects journalistic "error" on MIA article* [online], Tamilnet, 4 June 2010, available at http://tamilnet. com/art.html?catid=13&artid=31895 (last accessed 2 August 2010).

The 7/7 Ripple Effect (Film 2007) Muad'Dib, available at http:// ww6.jforjustice.co.uk/ (accessed 12 January 2009).

The Arabian Nights (Film, 1974) Directed by Pier Paolo Pasolini, United Artists.

The Green Zone (Film, 2010) Directed by Paul Greengrass, StudioCanal.

The Hurt Locker (Film, 2008) Directed by Kathryn Bigelow, Universal Studios.

The Kumars at Number 42 (TV programme, 2005) BBC2.

The Last Bolshevik (Film 1992) Directed by Chris Marker, Icarus Films.

The Razor's Edge (Film, 1984) Directed by John Byrum, Columbia Pictures.

The Scotsman (2006) *I feared they were going to kill us all, says man shot by police*, [online], The Scotsman, June 14 2006, available from: //www.scotsman.com/news/uk/i-feared-they-were-going-to-kill-us-all-says-man-shot-by-police-1-1121791 (accessed 6 May 2008.)

Times (2007) *Poetic Shop Assistant Guilty of Building Library of Terror*, [online] Times Online, available at http://www. timesonline.co.uk/tol/news/uk/crime/article2836243.ece (accessed 5 January 2012).

Tướng Nguyễn Ngọc Loan: Xử bắn Việt cộng (1968) YouTube video [online] available at http://youtu.be/LD4zRszg5cQ (accessed 20 June 2013).

Varèse, Edgard 1936 *The Liberation of Sound*, [online], lecture at Sante Fe, available at http://www.zakros.com/mica/soundart/

s04/varese_text.html (accessed 2 August 2010)

Gajjala, Rahdika and Venkataramana Gajjala, eds., 2008 *South Asian Technospaces* New York: Peter Lang Publishers.

Viswanathan, Gauri. (1989) *Masks of Conquest: Literary Study and British Rule In India*. New York: Columbia UP.

Wallerstein, Immanuel (2005) *The inequalities that blazed in France will soon scorch the world* [online], The Guardian December 3, 2005 available from http://www.guardian.co.uk/france/story/0,11882,1656922,00.html (accessed 3 December 2005).

Warner, Marina (2011) *Stranger Magic: Charmed States and the Arabian Nights*, London: Chatto and Windus.

Wasdin Howard E. and Stephen Templin (2011) *A veteran of Seal Team 6 describes his training*, [online], Vanity Fair, 4 May 2011, available at http://www.vanityfair.com/politics/features/2011/05/navy-seal-team-six-excerpt-201105 (accessed 7 August 2011).

Waters, Hazel (2004) 'Editorial: The Politics of Fear: Civil Society and the Security State' *Race and Class*, 46(1):1-2.

Watts, Mike (2010) *Movie Outlaw* [online], available at http://movieoutlaw.blogspot.com/2010/06/head-1968.html (accessed 2 August 2011).

Wild West (Film, 1992) Directed by David Attwood.

Wilson, Amrit (1978) *Finding a Voicevoice: Asian Womenwomen in Britain*, London: Vintage.

Wilson, Amrit (2006) *Dreams, Questions, Struggles: South Asian Women in Britain*, London: Pluto.

Wit, Michael (2000) 'Montage, My Beautiful Care, or Histories of the Cinematograph' in *The Cinema Alone*, M.Temple, J.S. Williams (Eds) Amsterdam: Amsterdam University Press pp33-50

Zappa, Frank and the Mothers of Invention. (1972). 'Billy the Mountain' from *Just Another Band from L.A.* USA: Bizarre.

Zappa, Frank and Tony Palmer (Film, 1971). *200 Motels*. USA: Bizarre Productions.

Žižek, Slavoj, (2002) *Welcome to the Desert of the Real*, London: Verso.

Žižek, Slavoj (2004a) *Iraq: The Borrowed Kettle*, London: Verso.

Žižek, Slavoj (2004b) 'Ethical Socialism? No Thanks: Reply to Boucher' *Telos*, December: 173-193.

Žižek, Slavoj (2006) *The Parallax View*, Cambridge, MA: MIT Press.

Žižek, Slavoj (2008) *Violence*, London: Profile Books.

Žižek, Slavoj (2010) *Living in the End Times*, London: Verso.

Zuberi, Nabeel. (2008). 'Sampling South Asian Music' in Gajjala, Radhika and Venkataramana Gajjali. (eds) *South Asian Technospaces*. New York: Peter Lang Publishers, pp49-70.

Zuberi, Nabeel, (2010) 'Worries in the Dance: Post-Millennial' in Andy Bennett and Jon Stratton eds. *Britpop and the English Music Tradition*, London: Ashgate pp179-192

Zulaika, Joseba and William A Douglas (1996) *Terror and Taboo: the Follies, Fables and Faces of Terrorism*, New York: Routledge.

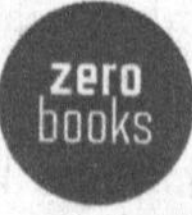

Contemporary culture has eliminated both the concept of the public and the figure of the intellectual. Former public spaces – both physical and cultural – are now either derelict or colonized by advertising. A cretinous anti-intellectualism presides, cheerled by expensively educated hacks in the pay of multinational corporations who reassure their bored readers that there is no need to rouse themselves from their interpassive stupor. The informal censorship internalized and propagated by the cultural workers of late capitalism generates a banal conformity that the propaganda chiefs of Stalinism could only ever have dreamt of imposing. Zer0 Books knows that another kind of discourse – intellectual without being academic, popular without being populist – is not only possible: it is already flourishing, in the regions beyond the striplit malls of so-called mass media and the neurotically bureaucratic halls of the academy. Zer0 is committed to the idea of publishing as a making public of the intellectual. It is convinced that in the unthinking, blandly consensual culture in which we live, critical and engaged theoretical reflection is more important than ever before.

www.ingramcontent.com/pod-product-compliance
Lightning Source LLC
Chambersburg PA
CBHW012253240726
48655CB00009B/3289